# ROUSSEAU
# AND ROMANTIC
# AUTOBIOGRAPHY

HUNTINGTON WILLIAMS

OXFORD UNIVERSITY PRESS
1983

Oxford University Press, Walton Street, Oxford OX2 6DP
London Glasgow New York Toronto
Delhi Bombay Calcutta Madras Karachi
Kuala Lumpur Singapore Hong Kong Tokyo
Nairobi Dar es Salaam Cape Town
Melbourne Auckland
and associates in
Beirut Berlin Ibadan Mexico City Nicosia

Oxford is a trade mark of Oxford University Press

Published in the United States by
Oxford University Press, New York

British Library Cataloguing in Publication Data.
Williams, Huntington
Rousseau and romantic autobiography. – (Oxford
modern languages and literature monographs)
1. Rousseau, Jean-Jacques–Criticism and
interpretation
I. Title
843.'5  PQ2043
ISBN 0–19–815538–7

Library of Congress Cataloging in Publication Data
Williams, Huntington, 1953–
Rousseau and romantic autobiography.

(Oxford modern languages and literature)
Bibliography: p.
Includes index.
1. Rousseau, Jean Jacques, 1712–1778.
2. Autobiography. 3. Romanticism. I. Title.
II. Series.
PQ2043.W5 1983   848'.509   82–14538
ISBN 0–19–815538–7

Typeset by Thames Typesetting, Abingdon
and printed in Great Britain
by Hazell Watson & Viney Ltd, Aylesbury, Bucks.

*To*
*my Mother*
*and Father*

# ACKNOWLEDGEMENTS

I wish to thank here the several societies and many individuals who offered encouragement and financial support for this book. The Marshall Aid Commemoration Commission, administered by Geraldine Cully, made possible three years of study in England, during which time the book was conceived and largely written. The Camargo Foundation, directed by Russell Young, provided aid in Cassis, France during three months of revision. At Balliol College, Oxford, I benefited from the guidance of Carol Clark, Alan Montefiore, Ray Ockenden, and Mary Tiles, and from the College's friendly yet scholarly environment. The Reverend Tom Comber, Mary White, and Shay and Barbara Gee made me most welcome at St. Margarets-at-the-Well and in Binsey, my home away from home.

To acknowledge intellectual indebtedness is a less straightforward task. Among the few major critics who combine an interest in Rousseau and autobiography, Starobinski and DeMan are definite influences. The work of Philippe Lejeune spurred my initial research, and he later offered direct encouragement. Among other readers and friends, Peter Brooks first introduced me to Rousseau's work in a Yale College seminar, Martin Joughin offered cogent advice on how to conclude, and Tamar Jacoby and Walter Mead gave editorial comments that helped turn thesis into book.

To my thesis supervisor, Professor I. D. McFarlane, I express a special gratitude. He accepted me as a student when this book was a very unformed project, and taught me to state and find my thoughts for myself.

# CONTENTS

# NOTE ON REFERENCES

Quotations from Rousseau are drawn mainly from the *Oeuvres complètes* as published by Gallimard in the Bibliothèque de la Pléiade. A Roman numeral followed by Arabic numbering – for example, (I: 163) – indicates the volume and page reference, respectively.

If the work from which the passage is drawn is also important to my argument and not clear from the context, I indicate its title – for example (*Émile*, IV: 256). Spelling, accent, and punctuation in the Pléiade edition conform to Rousseau's original usage; this differs in minor ways from modern French, and may change occasionally from one passage to another. Rousseau was idiosyncratic in this respect.

In anticipation of the fifth volume of the Pléiade edition, I refer to different editions of Rousseau in two other instances. Quotations from the *Essai sur l'origine des langues* are taken from the Kremer-Marietti edition of that work – for example (*Essai*, p. 104). The quotations from the *Dictionnaire de musique*, in Chapter I, refer to Volumes VI and VII of the 1865 Hachette edition of the *Oeuvres complètes* – for example (*O.C.* VI: 254). Quotations from Rousseau's letters refer to the *Correspondance complète*, edited by R. A. Leigh – for example (*C.C.* VII: 279).

# INTRODUCTION

Autobiography has attracted much attention recently, both in book-shops and in learned journals.[1] The life story, told by the person living the life, enjoys a public currency that once belonged almost exclusively to the novel and, in an earlier age, to devotional literature. Readers are fascinated by real models. As the celebrity and the literary critic take the places of saint and scholastic in a cycle of devotion and analysis, the work of a major autobiographer, Jean-Jacques Rousseau, deserves re-examination.

Every autobiographer asks, 'What has given meaning to my life?' Why this question should arise, why one should write to answer it, are thorny problems in themselves. The autobiographer usually disregards them. Writing, he remakes the past, and confers moral sense on his experience. I aim to investigate this process of conferring value in Rousseau's autobiography, and to show how it involves a type of discourse not normally associated with 'true' stories; that is, fiction.

Fiction is not easy to define. The disclaimer that often introduces moderns films and novels – 'Any similarity or resemblance to any person or persons living or dead is purely coincidental' – is a starting-point. Fiction is discourse that has no reference to the actual world. It may be coherent, possess a design. It may amuse, bore, or delight. But fiction refers ultimately to itself alone; it is no cause for libel.

Rousseau takes this definition a step further. In the *Discours sur l'inégalité,* his important theoretical work published early in 1755, he describes a State of Nature. This prototypical fiction is 'un Etat qui n'existe plus, qui n'a peut-être point existé, qui probablement n'existera jamais, et dont il est pourtant nécessaire d'avoir des Notions justes pour bien juger de nôtre état présent' (III: 123). Rousseau, conceding that his portrayal of natural man has no actual reference, goes on to claim that it has value as a guide for judgement. Carrying this claim into his autobiographical activity makes him the first modern autobiographer.

Rousseau's procedure here begins with the same 'natural' man he wants to describe. Natural or prehistorical man's conception of reality is interlaced with a network of myth and ritual, through which he orders his world. Because today's man does not participate in the myths, we tend to consider them 'fiction', and prehistorical man 'primitive'. Such a man, even if he could write, would never write autobiography as it is known today. His sense of identity is not personal but social. The hypothetical work he might produce would be, like myth, a collective autobiography.

A personal myth, or an individual relation to fiction — prerequisites for modern autobiography — first emerge in the Christian tradition of confessional literature. Like Rousseau in the Romantic period, Augustine is the outstanding example; he is the first Christian autobiographer, and his project remains unsurpassed in its specific scope and complexity.

Augustine's work is close enough to us still to illustrate a basic premise of my reading of Rousseau: the act of belief transforms fiction into reality for the believer. In the finite terms of a modern, critical perspective, God might be considered the fiction of Augustine's *Confessions*, but one which belief enables him to see as the primary reality. Augustine himself does not indulge this viewpoint. He addresses his autobiography to God; it is a prayer for divine grace and salvation. Through God, he discovers his most profound identity. Through Christian charity, he seeks out his important if secondary interlocutor, the human reader.[2] For Augustine, God is the ultimate source of value, and Scripture the avenue to it. Perhaps the principal feature of his *Confessions* are the biblical quotations sprinkled liberally throughout the text and usually identified by editors in italic print. Through the Word of God, Augustine performs an exegesis of his past. This exchange culminates with the account of conversion — the 'Tolle, lege' passage, in Book VIII — after which personal and scriptural exegesis coincide, and the autobiographical narrative gradually turns into a commentary on the Book of Genesis.

Christian autobiography is an implicit background for Rousseau's work and for what I call more generally Romantic autobiography. Its influence is directly discernible in the title of Rousseau's best-known text, *Les Confessions*. But while his project shares many structural traits with Christian autobiography, it embodies a fundamentally new approach to the question of value. The fiction which Rousseau elaborates, in which he eventually comes to believe, and which, in his autobiography, he attempts to make real, is that of autonomous personal identity.

This emphasis on individuality is hardly confined to Rousseau; it underlies virtually all modern autobiographies. Nor is it particularly straightforward. The emphasis on the individual self is one aspect of a wide-ranging secularization that emerges in the eighteenth century. Brought into focus by Enlightenment and pre-Romantic authors, it is complicated by the support of an aesthetic image of Nature. If God underwrites individual existence for the Christian autobiographer, personal identity in modern autobiography is thought to be 'natural'. This is a major change, and one of its effects, broadly defined, is that personal value and moral sense no longer have their source in a transcendent 'outside', in God or in Scripture. They arise from the interaction between men and their secular fictions, as these are embodied in different texts and at different levels — ideologies at a social level, personal identities in autobiography.

I take Rousseau as exemplary for modern, Romantic autobiography, not just because he occupies a pivotal position historically, but also because he attempts to construct his personal identity primarily in his own writings. Rousseau does not find himself ready-made in the texts of others; the radical internalization which we shall examine is instead one of the major causes of his historical novelty and influence. The current, widespread fascination with autobiography and selfhood, by contrast, is sustained mainly through borrowed images and clichés, through the ghost writing of *Psychology Today, People,* and *Self* magazines, or promotional and advertising copy. Even if the author's name appears on the front cover of a text promoted as autobiography, he or she is not likely to have written it. Personal identity lends itself to imitation, certainly, but the way 'stars' are offered up for public consumption resembles a medieval sale of saints' relics.

Rousseau wrote by hand, not with a word processor, and his autobiographical project, though repetitious and clichéd at times, is honest and more bewildered than those of many authors who come after him. Rousseau's autobiography is a textual exchange with his own pre-autobiographical writings. The *Discours sur l'inégalité, La Nouvelle Héloïse, Émile,* and Rousseau's other theoretical, fictional, and dramatic works are present there, just as Scripture is present in Augustines's *Confessions*. Rousseau constructs an image of himself, literally invents himself in these pre-autobiographical texts. They are sources of certainty and value, important points of reference whereby he interprets his past existence. The autonomous self must write its own scriptures. With ingenuity, it would be possible to demonstrate how in effect

Rousseau quotes himself, to restore the italics to his autobiography, as it were.

Near the end of his writing career (1777–8), Rousseau recounts the following incident. Returning home from an afternoon walk near Paris, he suddenly finds a large dog and fast-moving carriage hurtling directly toward him on the path. He is hurled to the ground. 'Je ne sentis ni le coup, ni la chute, ni rien de ce qui s'ensuivit jusqu'au moment où je revins à moi', Rousseau writes. He then describes the moment of his return to consciousness:

La nuit s'avançoit. J'apperçus le ciel, quelques étoiles, et un peu de verdure. Cette prémiére sensation fut un moment delicieux. Je ne me sentois encor que par là. Je naissois dans cet instant à la vie, et il me sembloit que je remplissois de ma legere existence tous les objets que j'appercevois. Tout entier au moment présent je ne me souvenois de rien; je ne savois ni qui j'étois ni où j'étois; je ne sentois ni mal, ni crainte, ni inquietude. Je voyois couler mon sang comme j'aurois vu couler un ruisseau. Je sentois dans tout mon être un calme ravissant . . .
   On me demanda où je demeurois; il me fut impossible de le dire . . .
Il fallut demander successivement le pays, la ville, et le quartier où je me trouvois. Encor cela ne put-il suffire pour me reconnoitre; il me fallut tout le trajet de là jusqu'au boulevard pour me rappeller ma demeure et mon nom.

*Rêveries du promeneur solitaire* (I: 1004–6)[3]

Rousseau has taken a hard fall, blacked out, and comes to his senses in a disorienting state of shock. His 'prémiére sensation' on returning to consciousness might ordinarily seem dream-like. But Rousseau holds on to the awakening as his link with the real world. The logic of dreams pertains instead to the unmotivated apparition of the dog and carriage. They intrude upon his walk, bowl him over, and vanish.

Rousseau's accident brings to mind an episode recounted in Montaigne's *Essais*, where the author falls while horse-riding.[4] Both writers describe a sense of personal dissolution, a strange yet intimate feeling of calm. The self is unformed and without expression; Rousseau is 'not himself' when he returns to consciousness. All the empirical attributes which give identity to the sensate being – memory, name, flowing blood – have been nullified. In their place emerges an exhilarating, almost impersonal connection to the world. Sartre, recalling an incident in *Les Mots*, describes something similar:

Il y a plus de vingt ans, un soir qu'il traversait la Place d'Italie, Giacometti fut renversé par une auto. Blessé, la jambe tordue, dans l'évanouissement lucide où il était tombé, il ressentit d'abord une espèce de joie.[5]

The centuries are different, the vehicles have changed. But the nature of the accident, and of the detached yet oddly and intimately personal feeling that it induces, remains the same.

An epiphany of this sort does not make a person an autobiographer. But Rousseau's moment in the second 'Promenade', near the end of his career, does correspond in a very interesting way to an episode midway through his life. This is the incident on the road to Vincennes (in 1749), which marks the beginning of his literary vocation. Two descriptions, from different texts, are given:

J'allois voir Diderot alors prisonnier à Vincennes: J'avois dans ma poche un *Mercure de France* que je mis à feuilleter le long du chemin. Je tombe sur la question de l'Academie de Dijon qui a donné lieu à mon premier écrit . . . je sens ma tête prise par un etourdissement semblable à l'ivresse. Une violente palpitation m'oppresse . . . je me laisse tomber sous un des arbres de l'avenuë, et j'y passe une demie heure dans une telle agitation qu'en me relevant j'apperçus tout le devant de ma veste mouillé de mes larmes sans avoir senti que j'en repandois. (I: 1135)

A l'instant de cette lecture je vis un autre univers et je devins un autre homme (I: 351).

Here again an arbitrary event ('je tombe sur la question') provokes a fall to the ground ('je me laisse tomber'). A second black-out ensues. But Rousseau does not seem to mind the physical upheaval he undergoes. More important is his discovery of 'un autre univers', and the unaccountable sense of being completely changed from his earlier self ('je devins un autre homme').

The manner in which Rousseau comes to his senses in the two incidents is difficult to grasp. In the moment of awakening or insight, he exists in a state of pure potentiality. This 'virtual' self is not really personal at all. It corresponds to a notion of Valéry, 'le moi', which Valéry describes in his *Cahiers:* 'L'être profond n'est pas quelqu'un, mais de quoi faire des "quelqu'uns".'[6]

And yet, Rousseau has a name, a body, quirks and traits of character. Some are hereditary, many are acquired. At any given moment in his existence these comprise his 'actual' self; they are what anyone might in fact know of his personal identity.

There can be no airtight division of virtual and actual selves. Actuality *per se* denies possibility and change, and virtuality, catching no foothold in the practice of life, disappears in a wisp of smoke. Whether writing or eating, but in any real event, we are simultaneously a closed set of attributes and an open potential for change. We may become wed to routine or addicted to possibility, but some unexpected upheaval − death, in the final reckoning − will always bring us down to earth, and remind us of our double nature.

When writing, even when writing music, Rousseau makes a steady and willed effort to overcome the dichotomy implicit in his life. This effort is difficult to characterize; it changes during the course of his writing career, particularly as Rousseau shifts from one literary genre to another. The autobiography, a concerted effort from late 1764 onwards, itself involves three very different styles and types of text. The scope of this project distinguishes Rousseau from most other auto-biographers, who generally aim to recount the development of their actual, not virtual selves. It also distinguishes him from memoir-writers, who chronicle their lives from an historical point of view − in a military or political context, for instance − that supersedes their personal history. Rousseau provides this sort of autobiographical account as well as any, but it is secondary in importance to him. He would sooner identify with the principle of personal change, the virtual 'de quoi faire des "quelqu'uns" '.

In considering Rousseau's autobiography along these lines, I discriminate between two senses of the word 'virtual' that bear directly on my thesis. A virtual self is in one sense a potential that can become actual, in the way that the wood in a tree can become a chair or a table. Development or change in personal identity is, in this sense, the virtual self becoming actual, the acquisition or transformation of a personal attribute.

But there is a second sense of 'virtual': something underlies the process of development, a substratum analogous to Aristotle's concept of Substance. This is the sense of the word that interests Rousseau, and this virtuality never 'becomes' actual. From the point of view of the living person, it is absolutely virtual − Valéry terms it 'l'éternel potentiel − ce moi'. To become actual, it has to be invented. Giving meaning to a virtual self in this second sense involves fiction, the production of a discourse in which any reference to any persons living or dead is coincidental and without bearing on factual truth. Yet this fiction is necessary. 'Le moi me contraint à l'inventer', writes Valéry.[7]

My reading of Rousseau's autobiography follows this configuration of concepts in all the works composed between 1749 and 1778. Rousseau's project is an elaboration of the impulse first discovered on the road to Vincennes, and involves two distinct stages. The first, pre-autobiographical stage begins when he takes a cue from God, so to speak, and wills the construction of his own world — his 'autre univers'. Language is the medium of his labour, and through it Rousseau creates a self-referential and self-contained imaginative universe, something I call a world of the text. In the pre-autobiographical works, he gives textual and aesthetic shape to his initial vision, articulates an image of personal identity, and devotes an increasing proportion of his energy to writing.

Rousseau's autobiography begins when he identifies himself within his world of the text and attempts to realize the image of personal identity elaborated there. This is the impossible coincidence of virtual and actual selves — Rousseau tries to move beyond fiction and to write a book that refers to his own life. The autobiography begins with *Les Confessions*, moves painfully through *Rousseau, juge de Jean-Jaques*,[9] and ends with the *Rêveries*. The tensions inherent in Rousseau's project are manifest in this second stage of his career. As if he could engineer his own epiphany, he recreates in writing the heady mixture of intimacy and impersonality we noticed earlier in incidents from his life. We expect a degree of intimacy in autobiography, but the substratum of impersonality that persists even in Rousseau's work surprises him, and he attempts to deny it. As we shall see in Chapter IV, the choice for intimacy makes him an autobiographer, but it requires that he devote half his autobiography to coming to grips with impersonality.[10]

These introductory remarks indicate that the connection between Rousseau's autobiography and his life is not direct. The life is open-ended, the autobiography an attempt at closure; and Rousseau passes from one to the other through fiction, by fabricating a textual world through which he performs an exegesis of his life. The layout of the chapters which follow this introduction is designed to dramatize this thesis in a deliberate examination of the interaction between life and text. Chapter III, 'The Move to Autobiography', is the hinge on which other chapters turn. There I analyse Rousseau's change of focus from life to writing, and interpret his construction of a world of the text.

On either side of this central chapter are life and autobiography, respectively. Chapter I examines reverie as a key to understanding Rousseau's sense of personal identity. Chapter II discusses *amour* and *amitié*, two very different types of relationship with other people. The critical attention directed at Rousseau's life in these early chapters shifts, in later chapters, to the varying structures of his autobiography. In Chapter IV, 'The Writing Self', I examine the three main autobiographical works as successive stages in Rousseau's effort to make his textual world refer to his life. Chapter V reconsiders this same effort from the perspective of the author—reader dialogue in these texts. This last chapter also includes a more general consideration of recent critical arguments about the contractual basis of autobiography.

The five chapters attempt to re-enact a drama of autobiography, not to give a biography of Rousseau. This method of procedure presupposes a fairly specialized working knowledge of the author. To those who do not possess this already, I can only recommend direct acquaintance with the original texts; despite the prevailing Anglo-Saxon allergy to Rousseau's peculiarities, his work offers an astonishing consistency and rigour in its overall direction. My method here also entails an unusual order of presentation. I do not come directly to the autobiography until Chapter IV; and then I interpret it in the light of how Rousseau structures his discourse. Implicit in this presentation is the idea that language is part of the fabric of our world, that an examination of rhetorical structures helps to reveal the real structures of human experience. This assumption concerns the moral import of literature generally. It happens to surface most vividly in the case of autobiography.

# I

## REVERIE IN ROUSSEAU

> When ideas float in our mind without any reflection
> or regard for the understanding, it is that which the
> French call resvery; our language has scarce a name
> for it.                                    (Locke, *Essay*, II, 19)

'Qui rêve s'abandonne', writes the critic Marcel Raymond. 'Il s'agit de
sortir de soi, de son naturel, de s'écarter du chemin tracé.'[1]

Romantic authors share a general interest in reverie, where dreams
and imagination lead outside a particular setting or self. Rousseau, the
major pre-Romantic author, charts a characteristically extreme course.
He makes reverie the 'key' to his personal identity, going against the
rational currents of the mid-eighteenth-century Enlightenment in
France. During the second part of his autobiographical *Dialogues*, for
instance, the character 'Rousseau' remarks to his interlocutor:

Voila, Monsieur, une grande découverte et dont je me suis beaucoup
félicité, car je la regarde comme la cléf des autres singularités de cet
homme. De cette pente aux douces rêveries j'ai vu dériver tous les
gouts, tous les penchans, toutes les habitudes de J. J., ses vices mêmes,
et les vertus qu'il peut voir. (I: 817)

How can one understand this unusual emphasis? Aside from the
specific activity of writing, 'la promenade' and music are the two areas
where Rousseau's 'key' to personal identity is most on display. 'La
promenade' and music show reverie to be a physical, fundamentally
aesthetic process, engaging the senses and the imagination in a temporal
development. Sensation is the starting-point and the personal direction
of sentiment, another key notion, is what emerges. Looking at the
itinerary of the *promeneur*, and at an early musical work, *Le Devin du
village*, we can describe the stages of this transformation directly.

### La Promenade

The word 'reverie' has a revealing history. *Reexvagus* is the basic ancestor, and each etymological element contains a meaning. From *vagare* comes the sense of wandering, vagabondage, or digression; from *ex*, or *extra*, the prepositional sense of being 'outside'; from *re*, the second prefix, a sense of intensity, and of a repeated action. 'Reverie' is a close cousin to 'extravagance'. But the connotations of outlandish or haphazard behaviour are also associated with a sense of mental and pastoral ambulation.

For Rousseau, being 'outside' refers first of all to walking in the open air, and *Les Confessions* include numerous descriptions of reverie during 'la promenade'. One, in Book IV, recalls his return voyage to Chambéry and to Mme de Warens after a first, adolescent visit to Paris. 'La chose que je regrette le plus dans les détails de ma vie dont j'ai perdu la mémoire', he begins,

est de n'avoir pas fait des journaux de mes voyages. Jamais je n'ai tant pensé, tant existé, tant vécu, tant été moi, si j'ose ainsi dire, que dans ceux que j'ai faits seuls et à pied. (I: 162)

The phrase 'jamais je n'ai ... tant été moi', supports the link between reverie and personal identity, although Rousseau also mentions his loss of memory and his desire for written journals. Without them, the passage continues in the generality of the present tense. The author works in the writing of Book IV to re-enact the past:

La marche a quelque chose qui anime et avive mes idées: je ne puis presque penser quand je reste en place; il faut que mon corps soit en branle pour y mettre mon esprit. La vue de la campagne, la succession des aspects agéables, le grand air, la bonne santé que je gagne en marchant, la liberté du cabaret, l'éloignement de tout ce qui me fait sentir ma dépendance, de tout ce qui me rappelle à ma situation, tout cela me dégage mon ame, me donne une plus grande audace à penser, me jette en quelque sorte dans l'immensité des êtres pour les combiner, les choisir, me les approprier à mon gré sans gêne et sans crainte. Je dispose en maître de la nature entière; mon cœur errant d'objet en objet s'unit, s'identifie à ceux qui le flatent, s'entoure d'images charmantes, s'enivre de sentimens délicieux. (I: 162)

Reverie begins when Rousseau places one foot in front of the other, as the repetitive physical movement of walking sets off the mental *déplacement* of thought. He says in Book IX: 'je ne puis méditer qu'en marchant; sitôt que je m'arrête je ne pense plus, et ma tête ne va qu'avec mes pieds' (I: 410). But the meditations of the *promeneur* have little in common with rational cogitation. Walking brings the imagination into play, an active, affective faculty based in the body and the senses. 'Chez nous c'est le corps qui marche, chez les orientaux c'est l'imagination', Rousseau writes in an admiring vein elsewhere (I: 816, note 1). Much as he enjoys walking for its own sake, its role here is preliminary, as a trigger in the process of reverie.

If we look closely at this passage, two different stages of reverie are reflected within Rousseau's writing style. No sooner does he state the link between walking and thinking than his syntax begins to resemble what he describes. A series of nominal clauses corresponds to the 'succession des aspects agréables' while the walker is moving through the countryside. The nominal clauses begin to coalesce around the idea of separation and distance. 'L'éloignement de tout ... de tout', Rousseau repeats, as though removing himself from any hindrances which might keep him 'inside', in a fixed place. But the voidance and gradual fading at one level occasion an upsurge of energy at another; and as Rousseau rids himself of obstacles, the syntactic reiteration of his text mounts in a rhetorical crescendo.

Between the noun 'situation' and 'tout cela dégage mon ame', the extended sentence shifts register. Abruptly, the nominal clauses issue in a main verb, *dégager*. This verb refers primarily to Rousseau's feeling of freedom. In a literal sense, he has undone the chains ('gages') which, in his opinion, restrict his everyday actions. Striding through the countryside, he discovers an individual space, and a momentary independence from social convention. Reverie thus implies a personal release, an unshackling of identity.

But 'dégager' also points to another sort of release. As the first in a set of verbal constructions, in the second part of the passage, it leads the way from the opening series of nominal clauses – a syntactic transition. This is not a simple matter, but the centre of the reverie description. For all their rhythmic repetition, the nominal clauses do not succeed in bringing Rousseau *into* anything. They consistently lead him away from his immediate context, into 'éloignement' and absence. And the nominal reiteration is, in principle at least, infinitely extendable. Only when it breaks into a verbal pattern does the passage unbind the succession of nouns, marching feet, and mental images, to form a new, still undetermined structure. At a stylistic level, the use of the word 'dégager' reinforces the impression of a change from one order of experience to another.

Rousseau's reiteration of verbal clauses is the truly dynamic portion of the description. In them, he effectively enters time. The sudden elevation of 'jeter' leads to 'combiner . . . choisir . . . approprier'; until, at the culmination of 'je dispose en maître de la nature entiére', Rousseau sees in nature only that which is readily identifiable as his own, and deploys an infinite power over all that surrounds him. Despite an apparent disorder, the *rêveur* therefore experiences a comforting feeling of control. His 'cœur errant' goes astray, but in the direction of a greater sense of unity and identity. It is significant that the passage offers no specific instances of natural surroundings at this juncture. When the walker dominates 'la nature entiére', nature loses its natural-ness, and objective details are transformed into humanized 'images' or affective 'sentimens'. But however 'dégagé' Rousseau may feel, he gives one indication of a new, emerging pattern, and it is quite different from the 'succession' which preceded it. 'Mon cœur . . . s'entoure', he states. This verb is the first hint of a circular, non-successive configur-ation.

What, more exactly, is the transition from noun to verb above the centre of the reverie experience? How does it occur, and why? Rousseau sets out in the urgency of *déplacement*, enacted in walking, in imagining, and re-enacted in the syntax of his writing. But he arrives at a sense of being eminently *in* place, in step and time with a world which is no more than an extension of himself. Seen in spatial terms, it could be that the various levels of *déplacement* somehow coincide, so that Rousseau's feeling of being out of step vanishes entirely. This moment of coincidence occurs, in the passage above, at the break between the strings of nominal and verbal clauses. But the shift from one to the other is curious, since it takes place *between* the reiterations, and involves no textual elements whatsoever. The transition itself is a gap, introducing a discontinuity into the flow of the sentence. In rhetorical terms, it could be described as a caesura.

We are now in a position to appreciate the unobtrusive 'tout cela' which is the actual subject of the main sentence. 'Tout cela' is some-thing of a stylistic tic in Rousseau. Like the opposition of 'tout' and 'rien', it surfaces frequently and without apparent purpose throughout his writings. As such, it introduces a degree of unconscious continuity in the passage above, and balances the discontinuity of the break in nominal clauses. One might assume at first glance that 'tout cela' simply resumes the first reiteration. I would suggest, however, that the shift from noun to verb marks a qualitative change as well as a quantita-tive resumption. 'Tout cela' refers to the entirety of the series, not just to any one of its elements, nor even to those which the author specifies in this section of Book IV.

It is not surprising, after his rhetorical *tour de force*, that Rousseau should dismiss his earlier regret at not having kept a journal. The passage goes on:

On a, dit-on, trouvé de tout cela dans mes ouvrages, quoiqu'écris vers le declin de mes ans. O si l'on eut vû ceux de ma prémiére jeunesse, ceux que j'ai faits durant mes voyages, ceux que j'ai composés et que je n'ai jamais écrits ... pourquoi, direz-vous, ne les pas écrire? et pourquoi les écrire, vous repondrai-je: Pourquoi m'ôter le charme actuel de la jouissance pour dire à d'autres que j'avois joui? Que m'importoient des lecteurs, un public, et toute la terre, tandis que je plânois dans le Ciel? (I: 162)

Once the activity of writing has elevated Rousseau to the same exalted state described in the narrative, he spurns the idea of writing altogether. Here a small element of retrospective illusion is discernible. In reverie, Rousseau is certainly free to dispense with the thought of a reader or of any person besides himself. The experience is utterly private and self-sufficient. And he may also dispense with the need to consult journals from the past, since the present act of writing creates this past anew. Rousseau fairly invents the past which he records so ecstatically. There is nothing amiss in this, as far as *Les Confessions* are concerned – the invention of a past which the author assumes to be true could be an essential part of autobiographical writing. But one wonders how much Rousseau derives his assurance from the act of writing or from other elaborations, such as music.

In Book III of *Les Confessions*, a second passage describes a 'promenade' that dates from Rousseau's initial visit to Mme de Warens. This walk gives rise to the following reverie:

Je ne sentois toute la force de mon attachment pour elle que quand je ne la voyois pas ... Je me souviendrai toujours qu'un jour de grande fête, tandis qu'elle étoit à vêpres, j'allai me promener hors de la ville, le cœur plein de son image et du desir ardent de passer mes jours auprés d'elle. J'avois assez de sens pour voir que quand à présent cela n'étoit pas possible, et qu'un bonheur que je goûtois si bien seroit court. Cela donnoit à ma rêverie une tristesse qui n'avoit pourtant rien de sombre et qu'un esprit flateur tempéroit. Le son des cloches qui m'a toujours singulierement affecté, le chant des oiseaux, la beauté du jour, la douceur du paysage, les maisons éparses et champêtres dans lesquelles je plaçois en idée notre commune demeure; tout cela me frappoit d'une impression vive, tendre, triste et touchante, que je me vis comme en extase transporté dans cet heureux tems et dans cet heureux séjour, où mon cœur possédant toute la félicité qui pouvoit lui plaire la goutoit dans des ravissemens inexprimables, sans songer même à la volupté des sens. Je ne me souviens pas de m'être elancé jamais dans l'avenir avec plus de force et d'illusion que je fis alors. (I: 107–8)

In many respects this second passage resembles what we have just seen in Book IV. Writing in the past tense, Rousseau begins by taking his distance, first from Mme de Warens – who is the object of his imaginings here – and then from the social environment of 'la ville'. Separation from the company of others, and a form of absence from himself seem to be preconditions of the reverie experience. A series of nominal clauses again enacts his departure. By the last of the clauses – 'les maisons éparses et champêtres dans lesquelles je plaçois en idée notre commune demeure' – he is so far removed from town and from anything but his own desire that the reader cannot be sure of its reference. Are the scattered houses those through which he is walking, or those which he and Mme de Warens will inhabit at some future date? A coincidence between present and future occurs at this moment, in a caesura. The enumerative order of the nominal sequence dissolves into 'tout cela'; and Rousseau then rejoins the passage in a verbal clause – 'je me vis comme en extase transporté'. As *passé simple*, it contrasts with the rest of the description, and indicates the instantaneous nature of his release.[2]

Rousseau later describes his intuition as a 'vision prophétique'. At the moment of 'extase', the present and the future are identical. The *rêveur* suddenly escapes time. Everything he desires for the future is visually fulfilled in the promise of the present, and, if we believe him, actually fulfilled in later circumstances. 'Et ce qui m'a frappé le plus dans le souvenir de cette rêverie quand elle s'est réalisée', the passage continues,

c'est d'avoir retrouvé des objets tels exactement que je les avoit imaginés. Si jamais rêve d'un homme éveillé eut l'air d'une vision prophétique ce fut assurément celui-là. Je n'ai été deçu que dans sa durée imaginaire; car les jours et les ans et la vie entiére s'y passoient dans une inaltérable tranquillité, au lieu qu'en effet tout cela n'a duré qu'un moment. Helas! mon plus constant bonheur fut en songe. Son accomplissement fut presque à l'instant suivi du réveil. (I: 108)

Rousseau will describe his 'bonheur' in Book VI, in the account of 'les Charmettes' – a second version of the fullness of time, which I discuss in Chapter III. Revelation and fulfilment in the current prophecy are thus textual acts as well as episodes from his past. At either level, however, the passage involves two different orders of time: one successive, in which the future follows on the present; the other instantaneous and non-successive, or not really temporal at all, since present and future are identical. Though prophecies can be tested and proved only in successive time, they can be made only if the future can be read in the present.

The hint of a circular structure to the 'extase' of reverie becomes significant in this regard. If the successive order of physical time resembles Rousseau's sequence of nominal clauses and moves in a single, irreversible direction from past to future, the circular order of his 'sentimens' and 'images charmantes' offers different possibilities. As the *rêveur* is 'transported' outside time, time becomes reversible. Prepositional oppositions – forward and backward, inside and outside – begin to break down. This temporal reversibility reconciles a superficial discrepancy in the two 'promenades' we have examined. 'Jamais je n'ai si bien senti tout cela que dans le retour dent j'ai parlé', the author has remarked in Book IV. There he was returning from Paris to Chambéry, and from the present of his narration to a forgotten episode in the narrated past. Yet the passage from Book III mingles present and future with equal assurance and exhilaration. It would seem that reverie enables Rousseau both to penetrate the restrictions of a closed past, and to determine the direction of an open future. For past and future belong only to the successive ordering which is transformed at the instant of caesura and 'extase'. The circle, by contrast, will eventually become a privileged image for Rousseau, designating his escape from an irreversible, objective temporal order, into one in which time has been made affective and reversible.

Several preliminary conclusions about reverie might now be drawn. First, the transition in Rousseau's experience of 'la promenade' leads him to an 'outside' which is very different from the open countryside. When he imagines himself larger than any of the particular elements of personal identity, the *rêveur* stands outside himself, and sees his life as a whole. The ecstasy of this intuition frees him momentarily from all constraint, and primarily from the constraints of time. For Rousseau, to be 'in time' means to experience the entirety of time from an atemporal perspective. At this level of distance from the social world, and of discontinuity from his everyday self, he paradoxically discovers himself in proximity to a fundamental unity, which he takes to be personal identity. A consciousness of enormous power accompanies this discovery. 'Je' and 'tout cela' form a sort of apposition, and it is disturbingly difficult to distinguish self and world, inner and outer, what is Rousseau and what is Nature.

## Time and the Imagination

Rousseau emphasizes two impressions of time in the reveries we have seen thus far. One is his feeling of absolute continuity — 'car les jours et les ans et la vie entiére s'y passoient dans une inaltérable tranquillité', he remarks. But this continuity is also described as a 'durée imaginaire', and in fact lasts no more than an instant. 'En effet', he goes on, comparing the time of the prophetic reverie to its actual fulfilment at 'les Charmettes', 'tout cela n'a duré qu'un moment'. What is the relation between these two aspects of time, continuity and instantaneousness? Are they compatible?

An instant is discrete and discontinuous with other instants; continuity implies a fused, ongoing process. Rousseau's reveries, however, do not permit this distinction. The passages from Books III and IV describe the continuity of an ongoing process, and manifest it both in the activity of walking and in the parallel rhythms of the author's prose. But the phrase, 'en effet tout cela n'a duré qu'un moment', underlines the instantaneity of the non-verbal caesura, and makes Rousseau's 'bonheur' discontinuous with the 'réveil' of everyday experience.

The sense of continuity that Rousseau desires may be possible only when time has been abolished, as in the ecstatic experiences he describes above. Yet these comprise only an instant if measured in actual time. When the conflicting temporal frameworks are held together, we encounter a paradox — the idea of a continuous instant, or of Rousseau finding the 'clef' to his identity in what is fundamentally an intuition of transition.

We shall come back to the instant. Its inherently dual structure tends to encourage the ambiguity touched upon here. Rousseau's phrase, 'durée imaginaire', indicates in any event that his practical resolution of the problem of time takes place in the imagination, at a fictional level. Even if 'tout cela n'a duré qu'un moment', within that moment *all* of time seems to be contained. When Rousseau develops a more extended control over his 'réveil', in the writing activity, this imaginary level may suffice (and even engender its own conceptual system). Making the connection between time and the imagination, he states in *Émile*:

l'imagination . . . réunit en un point des tems qui se doivent succéder, et voit moins les objets comme ils seront que comme elle les désire, parce qu'il dépend d'elle de les choisir. (IV: 418)

One last sentence from the 'promenade' of Book III points to the significance of the imagination in reverie: 'Je ne me souviens pas de m'être elancé jamais dans l'avenir avec plus de force et d'illusion que je fis alors', Rousseau stated there. Taken alone, the word 'illusion' connotes a faulty, merely aesthetic understanding. But the unusual juxtaposition here promotes illusion as an active, positive 'force'. This deserves some attention.

Up to this point, we have noticed mainly the intuitive, passive aspects of reverie. Immersed in the rhythmic, quasi-invocational activities of walking or writing, Rousseau seems simply to receive his 'vision' from a source outside himself. It could be argued that reverie is primarily an involuntary form of experience. The repetition of marching feet in 'la promenade', or Rousseau's related obsession with copying his own texts and others' musical scores, are exercises which point to a mechanical, almost inhuman disposition. These are essential, not just incidental preliminaries to the sudden, uncontrolled 'explosion' of reverie. 'Rousseau', speaking in the *Dialogues* about the passions of 'J. J.', remarks in this connection:

Celles des cœurs ardens et sensibles étant l'ouvrage de la nature se montrent en depit de celui qui les a; leur prémiére explosion purement machinale est indépendante de sa volonté. (I: 861)

But the passive aspect of reverie does not entirely account for its force, and two different stages, or aspects, of the experience seem to be involved. As the active verb, 'm'être élancé', suggests, the *rêveur* also *constructs* his 'vision prophétique'. The powers of illusion, of the imagination, are at play here.

'C'est une chose bien singuliére que mon imagination', Rousseau states at one point in *Les Confessions*. 'Elle ne sauroit embellir, elle veut créer. Les objets reels s'y peignent tout au plus tels qu'ils sont; elle ne sait parer que les objets imaginaires' (I: 171–2). The distinction between 'embellir' and 'créer' effectively separates the imagination from actual objects, and from any basis in perception. For Rousseau, the imagination is essentially elaborative, but it elaborates only what it creates of its own accord. Distance from the actual world, to a large

extent fulfilled by the 'éloignement' of walking, is thus a crucial pre-
condition for an imaginative expansion. Within his reverie, Rousseau
scarcely perceives what in fact surrounds him. He is busy creating his
own 'autre monde' (II: 12).

If imagination and perception denote fundamentally different types
of activity, the attention of the *rêveur* should shift from the actual to
a purely imaginary world. The caesura is a textual indication of this
change of domain, and expresses it as a sheer, uncontrolled state of
possibility. Rousseau does not remain long in this indeterminate state,
however. He immediately begins to structure possibility into a world
of his own design. No longer involuntary, reverie then involves a
profound and controlled exercise of human will, and takes on
Promethean overtones.

The beginning of Book II offers an example of the two different
aspects of the reverie experience. Describing his state of mind just after
he has run away from home in Geneva, at the ripe age of sixteen,
Rousseau states:

je croyois pouvoir tout faire, atteindre à tout: je n'avois qu'à m'élancer
pour m'élever et voler dans les airs . . . en me montrant j'allois occuper
de moi l'univers . . . (I: 45)

But the young man's entry into the big world quickly becomes
subject to the limitations of choice, and a different attitude emerges:

. . . non pas pourtant l'univers tout entier; je l'en dispensois en quelque
sorte, il ne m'en falloit pas tant. Une société charmante me suffisoit
sans m'embarrasser du reste. Ma modération m'inscrivit dans une sphére
étroite mais delicieusement choisie, où j'étois assuré de régner. (I: 45)

The adult author recalls his adolescent discretion with ironic
distance and some humour, but the change of attitude depicted within
the passage is noteworthy. Gagnebin and Raymond have described the
movement from 'l'univers tout entier' to 'une sphére étroite' as a first
and second 'temps' of reverie (I:1254).[3] Following their distinction,
though with modification, we might postulate that it corresponds to
two modes of the imagination. One is an instantaneous intuition of
infinite possibility, received in a brusque and apparently involuntary
divorce from the actual world. It provokes an impersonal, limitless
expansion. The second involves the more extended activity of
transforming the first, indeterminate intuition into a specific expression
of personal desire, as Rousseau circumscribes the imagination in an

elaborative mode, working possibility into an articulate vision of a world which would be *his*. It is difficult to formulate any conclusions about the first stage of this process, since it pertains to a level of experience not directly evident in Rousseau's text. But the second clearly has strong affiliations with his activity as a writer.

The 'other world' of reverie is an aesthetic creation, which Rousseau labels 'le pays des chiméres' (I: 163). Like a work of art, having its end within itself, the elaborative process of the imagination is independent of any external reference. Another description, 'le néant de mes chimeres' (I: 1140), well indicates how the fruits of reverie are *nothing* from the point of view of the actual world. They remind one of the small island in the Lac de Bienne, described in the *Rêveries,* where Rousseau establishes a colony of rabbits. Detached, 'sans nuire à rien', this odd community is meant to enjoy a purposeless life, innocent as the concept of fiction that the author puts forward in his fourth 'Promenade' (I: 1029).

Since the 'autre monde' of reverie has no foothold in actuality, it may seem absolutely useless. For Rousseau, however, the continuity of time and the consistency of sentiment pertain almost entirely to this imaginary space. When he is no longer content to regard it as fictional, when he identifies himself with the fiction, a moral force derives from the illusion. In this sense, to be purposeless and fictional is to be practically purposive, and the aesthetics of Rousseau's reverie become directly associated with the domain of ethics.

The function of the imagination connects here with our introductory distinction between the virtual and actual aspects of the autobiographical self. Rousseau's experience of wholeness in reverie can be characterized as a coincidence of the virtual with the actual, or the moment when the virtual as such becomes actual. In religious terms, this coincidence is one criterion of God (whose Essence is his Existence, and for whom potentiality is a meaningless concept, since he is pure Act). Rousseau assumes a divine prerogative in the human realm, employing that imaginative power to which later Romantic poets and writers will refer as the divine faculty in man. His feeling of omnipotence during reverie should therefore come as no surprise. 'Mais de quoy jouissois-je enfin quand j'étois seul?' he asks in the *Lettres à Malesherbes.*

De moi, de l'univers entier, de tout ce qui est, de tout ce qui peut être, de tout ce qu'a de beau le monde sensible, et d'imaginable le monde intellectuel: je rassemblois autour de moi tout ce qui pouvoit flatter mon cœur, mes desirs etoient la mesure de mes plaisirs. (I: 1138–9)

Rousseau's satisfaction in reverie stems from this equation between desire and fulfilment. The apposition of his 'moi' with 'l'univers entier' is self-delusion as much as it is illusion – what *is* can never coincide with what *can be*. The symbolic, properly human tension between these extremes constitutes the range of the self of reverie and of the written text. But Rousseau's misconception encourages his belief in the autobiography that it is possible for him to write as a self-sufficient author, expressing himself directly, *causa sui*.

Rousseau's imaginative enterprise therefore cut two ways. An involuntary intuition allows him to work possibility into an 'autre monde' of aesthetic and self-sufficient proportions. But it may always return to interrupt this world of reverie. The impersonal force which initially occasions his construction of temporal continuity threatens it also. Even though he is solitary in 'la promenade' (and in the writing activity), the imagination does not serve purely personal ends. Its independence from all forms of actuality includes a disregard for the actual self of the *rêveur*.

One might well speak of depersonalization in this context. Rousseau's taking leave of his everyday self, part of every reverie though most explicit in the account of the second 'Promenade', is implicit both in the mechanically repetitive and in the divine poles of the experience. But such depersonalization in no way undermines its aesthetic mode and force. Consistent with Kant's critique of the topic, personal disinterest is an integral part of aesthetic activity.[4] The act in which Rousseau discovers his identity always involves a distancing from self, and even a self-forgetting.

The temporal ambiguity we left several pages back is thus only one among several paradoxes which stem from contact across heterogeneous domains. Though reverie could be said to be based in discontinuity, as Rousseau absents himself, both from the world surrounding him and from his everyday self, it is also based in the instant of continuity between the actual world and the fictions which he imagines and elaborates. This world and Rousseau's 'autre monde' both are and are not related. They coexist, but can never become the same.

The main paradox of reverie is temporal, however, and evident especially in the instant, which resumes most of the aspects discussed thus far. The instant is the temporal term for transition, or for possibility made actual in change.[5] It both belongs and does not belong to time: though obviously temporal in one sense, it is also without duration, never fully actual, and therefore non-temporal in another sense. Ontologically, the instant presents two faces. It corresponds either to the manifestation of the eternal in time – an epiphany of the divine – or to a sort of non-being, an insinuating, subhuman shadow of man. The intuition of the instant in reverie first gives Rousseau the opening which he elaborates into his personal 'sphére étroite'. But it is also the instant which intervenes to consign this construction to the status of a fiction. He has no choice but to regard it in two lights, as both an occasion and a deterioration.

It follows from these considerations that reverie endures primarily in the form of repetition. The indeterminacy of the experience makes it unfit for representation – an instant can no more be represented than the second world which Rousseau imagines is based on a perception of the actual world, no matter how many similarities his fictions may bear to his life. The difficulty in our own analysis in distinguishing between the experience and the writing of reverie is a major symptom of its repetition. When Rousseau writes, he actively consructs his 'sphére étroite', in the second 'temps' of reverie. But the elaboration obviously involves transformations, and the reveries which the author describes in Books III and IV are not the same as those which he experienced as a young man. The discrepancies between the two pose a problem – the critic risks falling into a vicious circle, if he pretends to explain the experience of reverie by means of a text which may exist as a repetitive effort to 'combler le vide' of the past. But it is impossible to proceed, and to do justice to Rousseau, in any other manner. We have access to his text, not to experience or to the past; and what is important escapes the determination of them all: the exhilaration of presence and absence in the caesura. Rousseau never possesses this instant, though it be fundamentally the same time and again. It possesses him, enough to make him work it in writing. The elaboration of the text, in any event, leads back to the life of the author, through a circuit of which the *Rêveries* will be the final stage. In the description in the second 'Promenade' of an 'herborisation' made just before the surprise of the accident, Rousseau writes:

Enfin après avoir parcouru en détail plusieurs autres plantes que je voyois encore en fleurs, et dont l'aspect et l'énumeration qui m'étoit familiére me donnoit neanmoins toujours du plaisir, je quittai peu à peu ces menues observations pour me livrer à l'impression non moins agréable mais plus touchante que faisoit sur moi l'ensemble de tout cela. (I: 1003–4)

The textual elements of Rousseau's early reveries have taken objective form, with the nominal enumeration becoming a collection of plants and of the sentiments that they evoke. The transition from part to whole, from a series to a totalizing principle outside it, remains constant. But Rousseau organizes and controls the reverie so effectively that the discontinuity of the caesura has disappeared. It might seem that his text *can* coincide with his life – until, shortly after the passage above, life intrudes once more, in the unexpected form of a 'gros chien danois' and a carriage.

### Music

Rousseau's descriptions of the reverie experience in 'la promenade' help to confirm his claim that it is a 'clef' to understanding his identity. But thus far we have seen only him alone: what about reverie in a social setting? Society and his solitary 'extase' seem to be mutually exclusive. The company of Mme de Warens, as described in *Les Confessions*, and Julie's presence, in the communal 'Matinée à l'Anglaise' of *La Nouvelle Héloïse,* induce what could be called social reveries, but the uniqueness of the first relationship and the fictional nature of the second tend to make them exceptions proving the rule. The presence of other individuals normally undermines the imaginative expansion and illusory identification which Rousseau enjoys in reverie.

Music provides the one reverie-like context which is also demonstrably social. Long before and even during his writing career, Rousseau was active in this field. The fond autobiographical recollections of songs sung by 'tante Suson' in childhood, or of the adolescent and disastrous concert given in Lausanne under the name of Vaussore de Villeneuve, are of a piece with his theory of melody and his eventual success with *Le Devin du village*.[6] In fact, Rousseau's musical work constitutes an important bridge between the sort of experience we have seen in 'la promenade' and the activity of writing: it combines the sensuous immediacy of reverie with the constructed, expressive character of a text. Small wonder therefore that the author's development should pass through this intermediary yet intrinsically interesting stage. The story and performance of the *Devin*, and the 'hidden principle' of melody on which it was composed (I: 682), offer a new perspective on reverie, and demonstrate the 'répétition' at play within this and other 'représentations' of his experience.

## Le Devin du village: Story

The story of *Le Devin du village* contains, in relatively primitive form, a plot and character configuration which will recur in Rousseau's more developed and mature prose works. Colette and Colin, two young lovers, have become estranged. Their separation is mirrored by further estrangements within the opera, among rich and poor, and between country and city. Colette appeals for help to the Devin, the main character; and he employs cunning and control to effect the main movement of the piece, a 'retour' to unity (II: 104).

The Devin resembles in many ways the Mentor or Wolmar type of Rousseau's later writing, with the difference that he maintains a magical, rather than rational bearing. Art, not reason, is his gift. But just as Wolmar will speak to Saint-Preux and Julie in *La Nouvelle Héloïse*, the Devin tells Colette in the second scene of the opera, 'Je lis dans votre cœur, et j'ai lu dans le sien' (II: 1100). He remains outside love (the better to restore it), and assumes a lofty, didactic attitude. This position is indirectly gratifying to him. 'A vos sages leçons Colette s'abandonne', the young woman sings; and Rousseau's phrasing is just hesitant enough. Reconciliation depends entirely on the Devin, and Colette abandons herself – a highly erotic gesture. But she abandons herself to his lessons, not directly to him.

The Devin thus occupies an ambivalent position. Manipulating the emotions of Colette and Colin, he deploys a 'pouvoir éclatant' (II: 1110). But he participates in the intimacy of the lovers only by proxy, like a voyeur. The payment they offer him for his help, at the end of the opera, is not so much the specific gifts he collects, 'recevant des deux mains'. Instead, it is the Devin's pleasure at being able to watch the spectacle of their happiness. 'Je suis assés payé si vous êtes heureux', he sings (II: 1109).

Rousseau, speculating in the sixth 'Promenade' about what he would wish if he possessed the ring of Gyges and were invisible and all-powerful, provides the best commentary on the Devin character.

Qu'aurois-je pu desirer avec quelque suite? – Une seule chose: c'eut été de voir tous les cœurs contens . . . peut-être aurois-je eu dans des moments de gaité l'enfantillage d'opérer quelquefois des prodiges. (I: 1058)

The final scene of the opera exemplifies this desire, as the Devin generalizes his magical power of reconciliation. 'Venés, jeunes garçons; venés, aimables filles: Rassemblés-vous, venés les imiter', he commands (II: 1109). The stage fills with village couples for a joyful finale in dance and song. The Devin maintains his distance to the end. 'Si je ne puis sauter ainsi', he sings to them, 'je dirai pour ma part une nouvelle chanson' (II: 1111). Does 'sauter' refer to the dance which the other characters perform on stage, or does it refer to the leap of love, which the Devin effects, like Pandarus, for others, but which he is unable to make himself? One imagines this leading character immobile at the centre of the stage, surrounded by a whirl of dancers and lovers which he puts in motion and directs. They repeat the refrain to his song 'l'Art à l'Amour est favorable'.[7]

## Performance

The libretto of the *Devin* gains in interest when placed alongside the description in *Les Confessions* of its opening night at Fontaine-bleau. The opera's first performance causes Rousseau a great deal of anxiety, like the issue of its authorship (which eventually comes to torment him more than that of any of his prose works). 'Me voici dans un de ces momens critiques de ma vie où il est difficile de ne faire que narrer parce qu'il est impossible que le narration même ne porte empreinte de censure ou d'apologie', he states in Book VIII. Every aspect of the process of public recognition of the *Devin* makes him uncomfortable. Given a choice, he would keep the opera entirely to himself, like a solitary reverie.

J'aurois donné tout au monde pour le voir réprésenter à ma fantaisie, à portes fermées, comme on dit que Lulli fit une fois jouer *Armide* pour lui seul. Comme il ne m'étoit pas possible d'avoir ce plaisir qu'avec le public, il falloit necessairement pour jouir de ma Piéce la faire passer à l'Opera. (I: 375)

The performance turns out to be a rousing success, providing Rousseau with indispensable public recognition – otherwise he would probably not dare to disclose the remarkable fantasy above. The opera even attracts the attention of Louis XV, and an invitation to visit and receive a royal pension – which Rousseau, just as remarkably, spurns. Gratifying as the sort of recognition which he receives on the opening night may be, he accepts it only to the extent that it provides objective assurance of a worth which, once accorded, he feels certain that he already possesses. As soon as the *Devin* meets with acclaim, its author is confident of a superior status greater than any the public can offer him.

Rousseau reconciles the conflicting demands of private pleasure and public recognition of the opera through an attitude which closely resembles that of the Devin. On the opening night, he is at first precariously exposed. Poorly dressed, surrounded by ladies, Rousseau hesitates.

Je ne pouvois douter qu'on ne m'eut mis là précisément pour être en vue. Quand on eut allumé . . . je commençai d'être mal à mon aise: je me demandai si j'étois à ma place . . . (I: 377)

Rousseau chafes under this feeling of social displacement, and would normally pre-empt the situation by actively putting himself out of order. For a moment, the night is in the balance. 'Je me raffermois si bien que j'aurois été intrépide si j'eusse eu besoin de l'être', he remarks (I:378). But the necessity of making a scene is precluded by the theatrical context of the opera performance. Since another stage is set, Rousseau is able to displace his personal uneasiness, and observes himself through the external fate of the work.

The success of the *Devin* projects its author into a powerful reverie. According to *Les Confessions*, the ladies in the audience are especially moved; and Rousseau finds himself in precisely the same position, watching the performance, as the Devin occupies on stage by uniting Colette and Colin. 'Le plaisir de donner de l'émotion à tant d'aimables personnes m'émut moi-même jusqu'aux larmes', he states (I: 379). It is important to realize that he is affected primarily by the effect of his work on the other spectators, not by the performance itself. Like the Devin, Rousseau receives pleasure in the spectacle of their happiness. But his presence has at the same time been absorbed into the activity on stage, and he therefore withholds himself at a distance from the crowd. 'A mesure que la representation s'avançoit l'intérest et l'attention croissoient', he writes in an 'ébauche'.

Enfin au moment de l'entrevue des deux amans, où véritablement la musique a dans sa simplicité je ne sais quoi de touchant qui va au cœur, je sentis tout le spectacle s'unir dans une ivresse à laquelle ma tête ne tint pas. (I: 1164)

At this moment the powers of the Devin on stage and of the composer in the audience coincide, and Rousseau is close to a public version of the solitary 'extase' of reverie. But the social setting ramifies further the paradox of the experience. At one level, the *Devin* occasions a self-revelation on Rousseau's part, and the identity which he manifests through the opera is recognized by the audience in their response to its performance. At another, however, Rousseau shields his identity through the work, and sees only himself in the spectacles on stage and in the audience. Both actors and spectators become accomplices to an author who remains fully off-stage, safe and untouched, yet touched and gratified. His simultaneous presence and absence makes 'se révéler' synonomous with 'se cacher'.[8]

Rousseau wants to have his cake and eat it too: to enjoy success as the actual author of a work, but only from a virtual position of withdrawal, where recognition cannot threaten him. Inside *and* outside the performance of his opera, he feels that he dominates the evening at Fontainebleau. Rousseau makes quick mention of Vaussore de Villeneuve and his musical failure in Lausanne — and then he plunges into an undisturbed reverie. 'Je me livrai bientôt pleinement et sans distractions au plaisir de savourer ma gloire' (I: 379). The extent of his force brings to mind the phrase, 'je dispose en maître de la nature entiére', with nature now explicitly understood as a musical, dramatic, and sentimental order of Rousseau's subjective design.

Reflecting on the audience response, Rousseau employs a tantalizing phrase from Montesquieu to describe his success. 'Dés la prémiére scene', he writes,

j'entendis s'élever dans les loges un murmure de surprise et d'applaudissement ... La fermentation croissante alla bientot au point d'être sensible dans toute l'assemblée, et, pour parler à la Montesquieu, d'augmenter son effet par son effet même. (I: 378)

The idea of an absent cause within a chain of self-propagating effects is one indication of the paradox of Rousseau's reverie here. For *he*, as author of the opera, is the cause of the 'fermentation croissante' in the audience, and he enjoys it as an extension of himself. Consistent with his non-involvement and impersonal distance, however, it also has a life of its own, and rises in a crescendo not unlike the refrain disseminated by the Devin, the succession of marching feet, or the syntactic enumeration of Rousseau's text. The author, moving from part to whole, sees past these partial effects and collects himself at a point beyond them all. The text of *Les Confessions* does not at this point emphasize the disruption of the cause—effect relation. Rousseau is obviously more interested in affect than in effect; that is, in the pleasure the performance gives him. But his desire does involve its own logical structure, of which the phrase, 'd'augmenter son effet par son effet même', is an important indication.

If Rousseau's sense of fulfilment in the *Devin* includes other people only indirectly, as accessories, it is not surprising that he should guard against the possibility of losing control of the opera. Whereas the solitary circumstances of 'la promenade' preclude any such problem, it surfaces immediately for the musical work. The composer promptly swings from a sublime to a mechanical pole of reverie. 'J'ai été à Fontainebleau pour la prémiére représentation', Rousseau writes to his friend Lenieps on 22 October 1752. 'Le lendemain on vouloit me présenter au roi, et je m'en revins copier' (*C.C.* II: 198–9). For him to immerse himself in copying, instead of receiving more accolades, indicates on Rousseau's part a profound mistrust, and a conservative effort to appropriate his moment of public glory in an individual 'jouissance'. Acceptance of the King's offer of a pension, payable in the common, social denominator of money, would be an acknowledgement of the right of others to enjoy the *Devin*. Rousseau will have none of it. He even refuses to incorporate several small changes in the work, suggested by friends, on the grounds that they spoil 'cette unité si peu connüe, qui seroit le chez-d'œuvre de l'art, si l'on pouvoit la conserver sans répétitions et sans Monotonie'; and he reiterates, in an 'Advertisse-ment' written several months after the performance, 'son vrai succès est de me plaire' (II: 1096).

## Theory

'Cette unité', to which Rousseau refers, pertains not only to the *Devin's* libretto and performance, but also to the musical theory on which the opera is based. In the *Dialogues*, he speaks of a 'hidden principle', and in the *Dictionnaire de musique* specifies it under the heading 'unité de mélodie'. 'Lorsque j'eus découvert ce principe', he writes, 'je voulus, avant de le proposer, en essayer l'application par moi-même: cet essai produisit le *Devin*' (*O.C.* VII: 341).

What are some of the fundamentals of this musical theory, and how do they clarify the public reverie we have just observed?

'L'art du musicien', Rousseau explains, 'consiste à substituer à l'image insensible de l'objet celle des mouvements que sa présence excite dans le cœur du contemplateur' (*Essai*, p. 163). The 'objet' of the *Devin* is the 'image insensible' of love and happiness. The Devin restores the movements of love in Colette and Colin; Rousseau introduces them into the crowd at Fontainebleau. But music effects the indirect, magical communication: 'il ne représentera pas directement les choses, mais il excitera dans l'ame les memes sentiments qu'on éprouve en les voyant' (*Essai*, p. 163).

The function of music is thus not representative, since what it conveys is present only to the extent that music provokes its re-enactment in the sentiment of the listener. Music requires listeners for its accomplishment, just as Rousseau uses the audience for the accomplishment of his sentimental project in the opera. To his delight, the spectators in fact participate in its performance. The anthropologist Lévi-Strauss, himself no mean enthusiast of Rousseau, sheds light on this process in a comparison between the functions of music and myth.

Le dessein du compositeur s'actualise, comme celui du mythe, à travers l'auditeur et par lui . . . la musique se vit en moi, je m'écoute à travers elle. Le mythe et l'œuvre musicale apparaissent ainsi comme des chefs d'orchestre dont les auditeurs sont les silencieux exécutants.[9]

To the parallel between the Devin and Rousseau, we should therefore add a third element: the expressive power of music, which allows them to identify with the 'image insensible' of happiness through the movements and response of their 'exécutants' acting on stage and in the audience.

This characterization of music's powers extends well beyond the immediate context of the *Devin*. For Rousseau practically asserts that music is able to express the conditions of its own possibility. According to him, the musician would be able to 'peindre les choses qu'on ne saurait entendre . . . Le sommeil, le calme de la nuit, la solitude et le silence même entrent dans les tableaux de la musique' (*Essai*, p. 162). The examples chosen are significant ones. Silence is not just the opposite of music; it is the undifferentiated background from which any organized sound emerges. To state that music can convey this is equivalent to claiming that painting could render light, or poetry pure sound, while still retaining figure and meaning. Thus music's privileged role for Rousseau's self-expression – the levels of signifying sound and of what is signified are always in coincidence. The actual musical line already contains its virtual meaning.

In little-known corners of his work, Rousseau elaborates this theory. Music is first of all a temporal art: 'le champ de la musique est le temps', he states in the *Essai* (p. 160). The two major aspects of time, simultaneity and succession, are classified musically as harmony and melody: 'La musique n'est qu'un enchaînment de sons qui se font entendre ou tous ensemble, ou successivement' (*O.C.* VI: 254). Harmony is the simultaneous juxtaposition of sounds in a chord; melody the succession of individual notes along a temporal line.

Neither harmony nor melody exists independently of the other, but it is certainly possible to dispute the priority of the two – as shown by the quarrel between Rameau and Rousseau over French and Italian music.[10] Rousseau claimed that melody is more 'natural' than harmony, which he places in a secondary role supporting the central musical effect of a melodic development. The reasons for his preference are not simple; and, given the central instant of coincidence in reverie, it might seem that harmonic simultaneity would suit him better than melodic succession. But Rousseau instead reduces harmony to the single note of unison (which he favours almost as much as melody). 'Naturellement il n'y a point d'autre harmonie que l'unisson', he states. 'Un son porte avec lui tous ses sons concomitants' (*Essai*, p. 153). Superimposing a harmonic to a particular note, in this view, does not add anything to the sound itself, but only redoubles it, weakening its force. The result is a poor musical effect.

Melody, Rousseau argues, is what makes music an *art*, since it imitates a moral world outside the melodic line. 'Il faut que ces suites m'offrent quelque chose qui ne soit ni son ni accord, et qui me vienne émouvoir malgré moi' (*Essai*, p. 158). This 'quelque chose' is not itself musical – it is the 'image insensible' of love, or the Devin, or Rousseau. The imitation of this image, which exists only in the sentiments of a listener, or in the second, aesthetic world of his reverie, is in Rousseau's view the defining characteristic of art. In the *Essai*, as later in the 'Profession de Foi' in *Émile,* he makes the important, difficult distinction between physical sensation and moral sensation, or sentiment. 'Nous donnons trop et trop peu d'empire aux sensations', he remarks. 'Nous ne voyons pas que souvent elles ne nous affectent point comme sensations, mais commes signes ou images, et que leurs effets moraux ont aussi des causes morales' (*Essai*, p. 148). In melody, he continues, sounds are not merely physical sensations, but are already moral in effect. Hence the powerful musical effect of melody:

Les sons, dans la mélodie, n'agissent pas seulement sur nous comme sons, mais comme signes de nos affections, de nos sentiments, c'est ainsi qu'ils excitent en nous les mouvements qu'ils expriment, et dont nous y reconnaissons l'image. (*Essai*, p. 156)

The distinction between physical sensation and moral sensation (sentiment) is important to Rousseau's view of art. It forges a link between aesthetics and ethics in his work. In the context of music, it underlies his more polemical viewpoint about Rameau, the champion of harmony, being a scientist rather than a composer. 'Le seul physique de l'art se réduit à bien peu de choses, et l'harmonie ne passe pas au-delà,' he asserts (*O.C.* VI: 211). Melody, on the other hand, derives its force from a reference to, and expression of, sentiment. Though a 'succession de sons', it possesses a unity which might normally be associated with simultaneity. A melody carries this unity *through* time inasmuch as it conveys a continuous moral idea. For Rousseau, this point cannot be emphasized too strongly: 'tout nous ramène sans cesse aux effets moraux dont j'ai parlé', he reiterates (*Essai*, p. 164).

When we reach the definition of the principle, 'unité de mélodie', it is not surprising to find that it reads like a description of a Rousseau reverie, in which the wholeness of an instant endures through the continuity of a melodic line. He defines it as:

une unité successive ... qui se rapporte au sujet, et par laquelle toutes les parties bien liées composent un seul tout dont on aperçoit l'ensemble et tous les rapports. (*O.C.* VII: 338)

The successive unity of melody is the fundamental reason for Rousseau's attraction to music. For it allows him a particular relation to time — the same as he experiences in reverie — of combining identity and transition in one intuition. The affective effect of this combination in his subjective world is intense; and Lévi-Strauss, comparing music and myth once again, provides the best commentary:

L'une et l'autre (musique et mythe) sont, en effet, des machines à supprimer le temps. Au dessous des sons et des rhythmes, la musique opère sur un terrain brut qui est le temps physiologique de l'auditeur; temps irrémediablement diachronique puisqu'irréversible, et dont elle transmute pourtant le segment qui fut consacré à l'écouter en une totalité synchronique et close sur elle-même. L'audition de l'œuvre musicale, du fait de l'organisation de celle-ci, a donc immobilisé le temps qui passe ... Si bien qu'en écoutant la musique et pendant que nous l'écoutons, nous accédons à une sorte d'immortalité. (*Le Cru et le cuit,* p. 24)

Two entries in the *Dictionnaire de musique* shed direct light from a musical perspective on reverie, although Rousseau's concern has shifted from the experience itself to how to communicate it. The 'tout cela' of reverie has already become the 'tout dire' of *Les Confessions*.

One is the entry *récitatif*, in which he defines the discursive narration linking the arias of an opera. The artist is encouraged to speak rather than sing his words, and to use the vocal accents which once made singing and speaking inseparable in Rousseau's vision of primitive speech. Describing the sub-category of the 'récitatif obligé' Rousseau enthuses that it is:

ce qu'il y a de plus touchant, de plus ravissant, de plus energique dans toute la musique moderne. L'acteur, agité, transporté d'une passion qui ne lui permet pas de tout dire, s'interrompt, s'arrête, fait des réticences, durant lesquelles l'orchestre parle pour lui, et ces silences ainsi remplis affectent infiniment plus l'auditeur que si l'acteur disoit lui-même ce que la musique fait entendre. (*O.C.* VII: 247)

The conformity between this passage and a remark about the *Devin* – 'La partie à laquelle je m'étois le plus attaché et où je m'éloignois le plus de la route commune étoit le Récitatif' (I: 376) – underlines the opera's connection with reverie. When he is 'transporté', the actor interrupts his vocal line in a manner similar to the caesura of Rousseau's text. (Rousseau even provides a theoretical basis for this parallel in his statement, 'la mesure est à peu près à la mélodie ce que le syntaxe est au discours' (*O.C.* VI: 171). This melodic break marks the 'extase' and self-eclipsing distance of the *rêveur,* whose emotion only the orchestra can express. The orchestra then functions as an extension, speaking for the singer – like Nature, the ladies at Fontainebleau, or the dancers surrounding the Devin.

A second entry in the *Dictionnaire* outlines a particular technique for the version of reverie in a *récitatif*. Harmony offers here an unusually useful resource to melody, permitting a refined modulation of the transition in an 'extase'. Under the heading *enharmonique*, Rousseau promotes this expressive tool, the importance of which, he will claim in the *Dialogues*, he alone has comprehended.

'La relation enharmonique' is the musical term for a change of key which remains within one melodic line. Strictly speaking, it is the same note, 'la meme touche sur l'orgue et le clavecin. Mais en rigueur ce n'est pas le même son', because it takes a different value according to the notes and key with which it is combined (*O.C.* VII: 250). Using the *enharmonique*, a singer therefore effects a transition while simultaneously remaining in the narrative line of his *récitatif*. As in reverie, he achieves a paradoxical union of continuity in discontinuity, though now at the level of musical expression rather than in the experience of 'la promenade'. Rousseau warns his fellow composers that the *enharmonique* is 'un passage inattendu dont l'étonnante impression se fait fortement et dure longtemps . . .' (*O.C.* VII: 103–4). And he in fact rejects two of the more startling of these harmonic relations because they are too brusque: 'au milieu de tout cela l'on ne sait plus de tout où l'on est'. But he recommends the use of this volatile tool in its 'vrai lieu . . . le récitatif oblige. C'est dans une scène sublime et pathétique', he states, 'que les transitions enharmoniques sont bien placées' (*O.C.* VII: 104).

Once begun, the parallels between music and reverie in Rousseau multiply rapidly.[11] The major purpose here has been to suggest the depth and consistency of Rousseau's reflection on the topic, which ranges well across the experience of 'la promenade' into musical theory. If his musical works help to clarify the questions of reverie and identity in Rousseau, it is largely because he had the same task in compiling his *Dictionnaire de musique* as he will have in writing *Les Confessions*: how to convey a sense of music which was as new and strange as himself. 'Pour entrer dans ces détails', he states in the preface to the dictionary,

il faudroit, pour ainsi dire, créer un nouveau dictionnaire, inventer à chaque instant des termes pour offrir aux lecteurs français des idées inconnues parmi eux. (*O.C.* VI: 193)

Given the remark in the preface to the autobiography — 'il faudroit pour ce que j'ai à dire inventer un langage aussi nouveau que mon projet' (I: 1153) — it is not too far-fetched to consider Rousseau's autobiographical writing as his 'rêverie seconde', as the extended *récitatif* of an author who would prefer to sing his identity to the world.[12]

## Conclusions

In reverie, Rousseau joins what could be termed the ground of personal identity, in a coincidence of the real and the possible, the virtual and the actual. He recognizes himself at this juncture and wants to be recognized there. But is the basis of personal identity, in the final analysis, really personal in any way? If it is public and common to every and any person, the desire to experience and to appropriate it for oneself alone will cause difficulty.

Reserving this problem for the time when it becomes an issue for Rousseau, we may proceed to formulate a few positive conclusions about reverie. The word has several different meanings, and the experience involves at least two separate stages. Reverie denotes first of all a temporal intuition of possibility, which opens on to a privileged, if indeterminate, form of immediate recognition. One could speak of revelation in this context, of an insight into divine reality. But reverie for Rousseau is primarily a revelation of himself, or of what he might become; and he receives it from the positive force of the imagination, not from God. The presence of the accidental and the gratuitous characterize this first stage of reverie. It allows the possibility of elaborating a vision, but also escapes, undercuts, or intrudes from outside on the vision once it has been elaborated.

The second stage of reverie involves the construction of a personal, aesthetic sphere. Here Rousseau dramatizes his intuition, and works possibility into a determinate, imaginative vision of personal identity. The construction of a work of art is a primary way to give consistency to the vision, although it may be elaborated at the level of experience, in memory. The work of art is reverie in objective form – in Rousseau's case, the form of music or a written text. But he requires special circumstances for the communication of his vision. In *Le Devin du village*, one such public dramatization, Rousseau exercises immediate self-recognition as his own privilege, and communicates it only indirectly and incompletely.

Reverie is the home of sentiment for Rousseau; and one can conclude that the movement from first to second stage is the temporal process whereby sensation is transformed into sentiment, or the arbitrary – accidental non-meaning – into sense and personal direction. In that indeterminate state which his text indicates by a caesura and his music by an *enharmonique*, Rousseau discovers perhaps the most central of his notions, the 'sentiment de l'existence', an individual relation to Being. From the point of view of personal identity, this apprehension involves a necessary moment of fiction, a moment when the illusion of the imagination can be taken as real. It also involves a highly paradoxical temporal structure.

We have in this chapter reached these conclusions primarily through syntactic and thematic aspects of Rousseau's prose, and through the theory and practice of his music. But reverie is perhaps most evident in the overall *style* of his work.

Style is a whole, not so determinate as its various parts, and therefore difficult to pin down. One definition might be proffered, however: style is at once what is most personal about an individual, an index of inalienable singularity, and what makes him a subject of recognition by others, or what is most public about him.[13] Reverie, which Rousseau earlier claimed to be the 'key' to his 'singularités', has clear affinities with his style as an author. The temporality of reverie is taken up in the written text, where the intense lyricism of an instantaneous and ecstatic intuition pervades a worked yet flowing continuity of extensive prose.[14] We recognize Rousseau by this paradoxical style, and understand that it does not simply take him a long time to say what could be stated briefly. For him, the instant opens on to a new and unknown world, or rather to the possibility of creating this world. Rousseau takes and works this possibility to its fullest sense. The gift of style masks much of his effort, the effort to make time stop, or to make it proceeed as personal time. The gift of style makes the text seem natural — as natural as he feels himself to be in reverie.

# II

## 'AMOUR' AND 'AMITIÉ'

Each of us recognises the importance of love and friendship. But the nature of these sentiments is less certain. While 'I love you' and 'he (or she) is a good friend of mine' describe different emotional attitudes, we rarely agree on how and why they are different, or how this affects actual relationships.

Rousseau, who attached great importance to his relationships with others, had definite ideas on these matters. 'J'étois né pour l'amitié', he states. 'Je fus ami si jamais homme le fut' (I:104). This often-repeated remark resounds within a highly developed ethos of eighteenth-century friendship. Pity, a general concept akin to what is now known as sympathy, was considered in Rousseau's time the principal bond uniting men. *Amitié* derived from pity, and the aristocratic ideal required making a show of one's capacity for friendship.

Love belonged to a different order of sentiment. 'Il étoit écrit que je ne devois aimer d'amour qu'une fois en ma vie', Rousseau writes referring to Sophie d'Houdetot, his major love. *Amour* was exclusive and passionate. Its connection with a marriage contract was tangential. Love was momentary and slightly dangerous; the consequences of Rousseau's affair with Sophie, he says, 'le rendront à jamais mémorable et terrible à mon souvenir' (I:439).

Rousseau's reflections on love and friendship give personal expression to these prevailing ideas in mid-eighteenth-century France. They also allow an unusual vantage point on his own life and social behaviour. Although he was not a successful lover of a particularly steady friend, Rousseau did write lucidly about both sentiments, and his thoughts bear indirectly on the autobiography.[1]

### Amitié

Rousseau takes great pleasure in remembering close friends in *Les Confessions*. Some of them are memorable, others less so. The reader quickly recalls Diderot and Grimm, if not 'mon ami Bâcle', the Spaniards Altuna and 'mon ami de Carrio', and many other unsung acquaintances. Rousseau maintains intense, sometimes tempestuous, and usually short-lived contact with such men (I:13; 102; 305; 327).

Readers who get beyond *Les Confessions* find a similar phenomenon, at a different level, in subsequent stages of the autobiography. In the autobiographer's vision of childhood friendship with 'cousin Bernard' one can already discern the outline of 'Rousseau' and 'J.J.' in the *Dialogues,* or of Rousseau reading himself as a 'moins vieux ami' in the *Rêveries* (I:1001). All these instances of friendship are an object of scrutiny in Rousseau's theory of human passions, particularly in *Émile.* The author's own analysis is the best starting point for investigating the significance of *amitié* in his life.

## Origins: the Development of Pity

In Book IV of *Émile*, Rousseau's ideal student undergoes a 'second birth' – the transitional period between boyhood and manhood during which the Mentor must prepare him for entry into society and relations with the opposite sex (IV: 490). *Émile's* change provokes a lengthy reflection on the nature of human passions; and Rousseau, as usual, goes to the basics:

La source de nos passions, l'origine et le principe de toutes les autres, la seule qui nait avec l'homme et ne le quitte jamais tant qu'il vit est l'amour de soi; passion primitive, innée, antérieure à toute autre et dont toutes les autres ne sont en un sens que des modifications. (IV: 491)

In *Émile,* 'amour de soi' is the foundation of human passions. Primarily a principle of individual self-preservation, and to that extent shared by animals and man alike, this 'passion primitive' does not imply self-awareness, a developed emotional state, or any social consciousness. 'Nos passions naturelles sont trés bornées', Rousseau admits (IV: 491). Natural self-love should therefore not be confused with the sentiment of *amour,* nor with any bond to other human beings. It is hardly a sentiment at all, and keeps men in the separation and isolation of the State of Nature. The task of Rousseau's theory, as it shows how such complex sentiments as *amour* and *amitié* derive from this source, thus involves no less than an explanation of the shift from Nature to Culture, from asocial man to the society of humans. Like the immanent notion of Endeavour in Spinoza's *Ethics,* 'amour de soi' may develop into an array of refined passions. But the manner of development is the crucial issue.

The first stage in Rousseau's derivation brings the individual into contact with others, and compensates in a way for his lack of an innate social impulse. 'Amour de soi' is transformed into a different passion, 'la Pitié' (III: 154). 'Natural' man becomes human and social, without any change in his basic nature. That pity should be the first social sentiment is not immediately obvious, but for Rousseau it is the first form of friendship, its prototype. As he says in the second *Discours*: 'Le Bienveillance et l'amitié même sont, à le bien prendre, des productions d'une pitié constante, fixée sur un objet particulier' (III: 155).

The two main elements in this change are the imagination and suffering. 'La pitié, bien que naturelle au cœur de l'homme, resterait éternellement inactive sans l'imagination qui la met en jeu', Rousseau states (*Essai,* p. 121). The prime mover of passions – which itself seems not to be a passion – effects an exchange between two individuals, such that one passes into the identity of the other. Suffering is the second factor. 'En effet', Rousseau continues,

comment nous laissons-nous émouvoir à la pitié, si ce n'est en nous transportant hors de nous et nous identifiant avec l'animal souffrant? en quittant pour ainsi dire notre être pour prendre le sien? Nous ne souffrons qu'autant que nous jugeons qu'il souffre; ce n'est pas dans nous, c'est dans lui que nous souffrons. Ainsi nul ne devient sensible que quand son imagination s'anime et commence à le transporter hors de lui. (IV: 505–6)[2]

If one 'natural' man, whose guiding instinct makes him little more than an 'animal', should encounter another, this asocial instinct of self-preservation would lead him to beat a hasty retreat. But in a situation where one individual cannot threaten the other – such as the example of suffering above – 'amour de soi' is disarmed. Rousseau suggests that in this instance natural man is transformed: he becomes aware of another life by assuming its terms, experiencing his own existence through the 'être' of another. How this change occurs is far from straightforward; Rousseau's own description, 'en nous trans-portant hors de nous et nous identifiant . . .', itself occurs within a question. But it is possible to identify two distinct stages in the process.

First, if a man is able to assume the identity of another person, the individual drive of 'amour de soi' suddenly becomes relative and social.

The particular 'I' and particular 'you' to which it pertains have merged; the first man, no longer just himself, lives also in the second. His instinct of self-preservation takes on a new form at this level. It becomes an impulse toward the preservation of an interpersonal bond. Natural man discovers that he belongs to the more general species of human beings. In Rousseau's account, personal identity — the reappearance of the individual 'I' after this convergence — depends on such a moral and social involvement. 'Tant que sa sensibilité reste bornée à son individu', he says of Émile,

il n'y a rien de moral dans ses actions; ce n'est que quand elle commence à s'étendre hors de lui qu'il prend d'abord les sentimens et ensuite les notions du bien et du mal qui le constituent véritablement homme et partie intégrante de son espéce. C'est donc à ce premier point qu'il faut d'abord fixer nos observations. (IV: 501)

The development of pity also passes through a second stage, however. Absorbed in the other, the pity of the first man is thus far indistinguishable from his 'amour de soi' for himself. In this sense it is a fairly direct extension of self-preservation, taken at an interpersonal level. It becomes pity proper (a sentiment in its own right) when a new, social distance between 'I' and 'you' allows the first man to retain an awareness of his own identity even within his identification with the other. He then knows himself to be exempt from a suffering that he nonetheless feels. Rousseau's remark 'ce n'est pas dans nous, c'est dans lui que nous souffrons', acknowledges this exemption; and he unhesitatingly draws out its benefits. With the advent of pity, 'amour de soi' effectively becomes intentional, directed onto an external entity, and changes from an instinct of self-preservation into a curious state which the author names 'cet état de force qui nous étend au-delà de nous et qui nous fait porter ailleurs l'activité superflue à notre bien-etre' (IV: 514). This excess of sentiment, termed a 'sensibilité surabondante' in *Émile* (IV: 515), is supposedly what the pitier then lends to the suffering individual. In fact, it also arises out of the identification, as we have just seen. The circularity in Rousseau's account poses a problem here, but the self-complacent tone in which it ends is most striking. 'La pitié est douce', he states, 'parce qu'en se mettant à la place de celui qui souffre on sent pourtant le plaisir de ne pas souffrir comme lui' (IV: 504). Or, speaking of Émile, he states also:

Si le premier spectacle qui le frappe est un objet de tristesse, le premier retour sur lui-meme est un sentiment de plaisir . . . Il partage les peines de ses semblables; mais ce partage est volontaire et doux. Il jouit à la fois de la pitié qu'il a pour leurs maux, et du bonheur qui l'en exempte. (IV: 514)

There is an odd discrepancy between the two stages of the identification above. The first moment of transfer into a genuinely social 'être' seems out of step with the smug 'retour' into individual identities, and it is tempting to reject the process as a whole for dislike of Rousseau's particular conclusion to it.

## Assumptions: Imagination and Suffering

Let us return to the two preconditions for the transformation of 'amour de soi' into pity – the imagination and suffering. From what we know of the imagination from Chapter I, it is not surprising that this impersonal force should effect the intersubjective identification. The imagination belongs to neither 'I' nor 'you', yet in Rousseau's account seems capable of making them interchangeable. There is a strong affinity between his description here and his account of reverie. The verb 'transporter' and the phrase 'hors de lui' signify departures from self in both instances. But if the 'outside' of reverie is an atemporal level of identity which Rousseau wants to claim as his own, pity leads to an 'outside' which is within time and the human sphere; namely, to another person. The two 'outsides' need not be mutually exclusive. It could be that the 'outside' of reverie, seemingly so remote from the normal experience of time and from other individuals, is a source of self-imitation and change, the source of the process whereby he constructs and appropriates his own identity. The function of the imagination in reverie thus would strongly resemble its function in the identification of pity, with the major difference that the 'other' of the intersubjective experience can be neither constructed nor appropriated.

But most important in this account is the social function of the imagination. Man is not social by nature, according to Rousseau, and pity adds nothing to his nature which was not already present in 'amour de soi'. Yet, with pity, the social world begins. This leads to the unusual conclusion that the imagination is the key to social development. Though not a basis or foundation, it serves as a sort of social catalyst. Society becomes intrinsically aesthetic, by implication. The arts, and the theatre especially, become an important social force. 'Celui qui n'imagine rien ne sent que lui-même', Rousseau states; 'il est seul au milieu du genre humain' (Essai, p.121).

The imagination would not have to perform such heavy duty if Rousseau had begun by giving a social instinct to natural man. But he does not. Nor does he give much direct assistance in following up this unusual conclusion. The imagination remains one of the hazier concepts among the already complex set of notions that mediate between Nature and Culture. Rousseau never explicitly defines it, and certainly not in the way suggested here.

In Book IV of *Émile*, one major clue about the imagination concerns its connection with the senses, and this eventually leads to Rousseau's emphasis on suffering. Together, the imagination and the senses produce sensibility. Different mixtures and priorities produce varying results. Comparing Émile's education to that of other children, the author states:

Les instructions de la nature sont tardives et lentes, celles des hommes sont presque toujours prématurées. Dans le prémier cas les sens éveillent l'imagination; dans le second, l'imagination éveille les sens. (IV: 495)

The senses should trigger the imagination rather than vice versa, according to Rousseau. But the two are linked, whichever comes first. The way in which the physical movement of walking stirred the imagination of the *rêveur* exemplifies this contact. But here are further remarks on the subject:

l'enfant n'imaginant point ce que sentent les autres ne connoit de maux que les siens; mais quand le prémier dévelopement des sens allume en lui le feu de l'imagination, il commence a se sentir dans ses semblables . . . (IV: 504)

La source de toutes les passions est la sensibilité; l'imagination détermine leur pente. (IV: 501)

An awareness of the strong link between the senses and the imagination, or *how* one feels, leads quickly to the possibility of organizing *what* one should feel. By stirring certain senses and not stirring others, the imagination may develop in one rather than another direction. Determining the direction of sentiments then lies within reach of the educator. Such a theory would undoubtedly have been elaborated in the abandoned work, *La Morale sensitive*, or *le Matérialisme du sage* (I: 409). It underlies, in any event, the educational practice detailed in *Émile,* and is especially visible in these lines:

Mais l'homme est-il maître d'ordoner ses affections selon tels ou tels rapports? Sans doute, s'il est maitre de diriger son imagination sur tel ou tel objet, ou de lui donner telle ou telle habitude. (IV: 501)

Rousseau, it becomes increasingly clear, has a vested interest in promoting a particular sort of development, which he describes as 'natural', but which in fact includes several normative assumptions. His rather extraordinary insistence on equating the virtuous and the natural is an indication of the choices he makes in allowing certain sentiments while rejecting others. For inasmuch as every sentiment develops from 'amour de soi', his theory admits that they are all natural:

En ce sens toutes (passions) si l'on veut sont naturelles. Mais la plupart de ces modifications ont des causes étrangéres sans lesquelles elles n'auroient jamais lieu, et ces mêmes modifications loin de nous être avantageuses nous sont nuisibles, elles changent le prémier objet et vont contre leur principe; c'est alors que l'homme se trouve hors de la nature et se met en contradiction avec soi. (IV: 491)

What constitutes a 'cause étrangére', or distinguishes an advantageous change from a harmful one? Only within a normative framework is it possible to appreciate Rousseau's emphasis on suffering, the second important factor in the identification which brings man into society. Suffering arouses the imagination in a particular and very limited way, and is invoked to promote *amitié* while discouraging *amour*. 'Le prémier sentiment dont un jeune homme élevé soigneusement est susceptible n'est pas l'amour, c'est l'amitié', Rousseau states (IV: 502). This injunction is closely tied to a second principle in the education of Émile: 'souffrir est la prémiére chose qu'il doit apprendre' (IV: 300).

Why should suffering be displayed to affect the imagination? Pity, the social sentiment which this interaction generates, does require this sort of experience – one is not likely to pity a happy person. But Rousseau might conceivably have chosen another sentiment – envy, pleasure, hatred, joy, even love – and a different initial step would have been required. His choice reveals at least two basic assumptions, both of which directly influence his version of *amitié*.

The first assumption is that suffering is a fundamental condition of man's being. This strong claim is difficult to summarize. One could say that man suffers individually from incompleteness, or from the impossibility of ever achieving a permanent coincidence between personal and social existence. Suffering, the major symptom of man's distance both from himself and from others, is also what binds him to them; and this condition would hold for all men, not just for Rousseau or for the ideal student he rears in *Émile*. There he supports his position with these words:

Tout attachment est un signe d'insuffisance: si chacun de nous n'avoit nul besoin des autres il ne songeroit guéres à s'unir à eux. Ainsi de nôtre infirmité même nait nôtre frêle bonheur. Un être vraiment heureux est un être solitaire: Dieu seul joüit d'un bonheur absolu; mais qui de nous en a l'idée?

Il suit de là que nous nous attachons à nos semblables moins par le sentiment de leurs plaisirs que par celui de leurs peines; car nous y voyons bien mieux l'identité de notre nature. (IV: 503)

From 'l'identité de notre nature' in human suffering stem several important attributes of Rousseau's conception of *amitié*. Friends are always equals for him. As 'semblables', they enjoy reciprocity of affection (at the level of social relations this mirrors the reversible order of time within the world of reverie). Full reciprocity, based on the common bond of suffering, makes for the same sort of immediate contact we noticed in the initial stage of pity. Individual identities can even become transferred from one person to another in extreme cases. The exchange of roles between the two leading female characters near the end of *La Nouvelle Héloïse*, when Claire acts out all the symptoms of Julie's illness and Julie appears calm and healthy, is one such transfer.

Rousseau's first assumption about suffering has a plausible if normative ring. Autobiographical descriptions of *amitié* from *Les Confessions* demonstrate his consistency here – for instance, Rousseau's exasperation with the apparent suffering of his good friend Grimm because of unrequited passion for as actress. In order to produce an impression of heartbroken grief, Grimm 'tomba tout subitement dans la plus étrange maladie', Rousseau recalls. 'Cette belle passion mit Grimm à la mode; bientôt il passa pour un prodige d'amour, d'amitié, d'attachement de toute espéce' (I: 370).

Grimm's shrewd acting is a sign of bad faith in Rousseau's eyes. He feels that *he* knows what it means to suffer, and that it should bring people together in an unselfish way. His certainty resounds in the repeated phrase, 'j'étois né pour l'amitié' (I: 362;1124;426). Thus, when he recalls a childhood anecdote about unjustified suffering (the account in Book I of an accidentally broken comb) the inseparable 'cousin Bernard' must become part of the story. 'Mon cousin dans un cas à peu prés semblable' receives the punishment simultaneously with Rousseau (I:20). 'L'amitié qui nous unissoit étoit si vraie', the author narrates, that the cousins lie together in bed afterwards, screaming furiously and locked in an embrace which makes them more one person than two.

But even in this confusion of identities, one of the two friends predominates; and it is Rousseau. He states that his cousin 'se mettoit en fureur à mon exemple, et se montoit, pour ainsi dire, à mon unisson' (I: 20). This predominance reveals a second normative assumption in Rousseau's exposition — his demand that one word to control the accidental, and to escape from the pain of existence. This corresponds to the second stage in pity noted earlier, and is equally difficult to countenance. In any spectacle of suffering, the individual in pain is inferior to the person who witnesses and identifies with it. The process of identification is in this sense not just based on a shared relation to 'être', but also on the relative freedom of one of the individually involved. He retains a social awareness all his own, a 'sensibilité surabondante' within the pity he discovers for the sufferer; and his relative autonomy (which is precisely what Rousseau denies man in presenting suffering as the important factor in human affection) makes the friendship 'volontaire et doux' (IV: 514).

This paradox in the discussion of *Émile* is a consistent development of the author's basic insight in the second *Discours,* that inequality comes into being with the social order. Pity, inaugurating that order in the context of human passions rather than in a political or economic sense, makes men 'equals' and identical in suffering only to the extent that they are already and necessarily unequal in it.

The effects of this second assumption in Rousseau's own friendships tend to be less than attractive. In his adult life, he turns equality into a demand for 'estime', and the relative freedom of one friend into the proposition that both are independent from and owe nothing to one other. Rousseau also makes use of reciprocity between 'semblables' to displace his own suffering on to others, as shown in a letter to Mme d'Épinay, the female friend and admirer who built the country house at l'Ermitage for him. Here are some of Rousseau's 'règles de l'amitié':

J'exige d'un ami bien plus encore que tout ce que je viens de vous dire; plus même qu'il ne doit exiger de moi . . . En qualité de malade, j'ai droit aux ménagemens que l'humanité doit à la foiblesse et à l' humeur d'un homme qui souffre. (C.C. IV: 199–200)

This appropriation of the human condition as an individual prerogative leads Rousseau to make extraordinary demands of his friends, and inevitably alienates him from their affection. But even during that tumultuous period when he is forced to leave l'Ermitage, when most of his close friends are ignoring or discarding him, we find Rousseau writing another, exalted letter on the subject to a new acquaintance, Sophie d'Houdetot.

L'amour de soi-même, ainsi que l'amitié qui n'en est que le partage, n'a point d'autre loi que le sentiment qui l'inspire; on fait tout pour son ami comme pour soi, non par devoir, mais par délice, tous les services qu'on lui rend sont des biens qu'on se fait à soi même.
(C.C. IV: 394)

All in all, the process whereby 'amour de soi' develops into 'la pitié' is by no means as straightforward as Rousseau would have the reader believe in *Émile*. Suffering, the median term between the senses and the imagination in his account of social sensibility, affects the pitier in conflicting, even contradictory ways. As we follow the paradoxes of pity into examples of *amitié* in Rousseau's life, it appears at once a profoundly social and a superficially individual sentiment. With pity, man enters the social order. But he barely enters it. After the initial identification, pity involves a person extrinsically and without cost to himself in the suffering of another. Rousseau's version of the sentiment rarely if ever leads to action to alleviate pain, but sooner to reflection on his own suffering, or to gladness at being able to share and displace it. Faced with the first alternative, that of alleviating pain, Rousseau tends to retreat into the solitary certainty of his own physical misery. 'J'ai toujours mieux aimé souffrir que devoir', he admits in *Les Confessions* (I: 168).

In the account in *Émile*, part of the attraction of suffering lies in the fact that its sensible effect mortifies rather than awakens the imagination. The imagination therefore does not develop of its own accord, as it will in *amour,* and Rousseau maintains one of the central tenets in the education of the student — that the limits of his imaginative world remain coextensive with those of his actual world — through Émile's entry into the social order (IV: 298; 304–5). This major achievement sidesteps the implication we noted earlier — the social sphere does *not* become an aesthetic, theatrical domain. Offered the spectacle of suffering, the imagination simply converts 'amour de soi' into pity, and then, like a catalyst, disappears from the equation.

This absolutely indispensable but limited use of its wide, impersonal force insures a closed economy to affective development, and allows Rousseau to propose the direct and 'natural' lineage for *amitié*: 'l'amour de soi, ainsi que l'amitié qui n'en est que le partage . . .' Even if it can be made to look plausible, the proposition that friendship should be a refined form of self-preservation is not entirely coherent, and Rousseau's account is ingenious rather than convincing. In it, suffering has become wholesome, in order that the individual 'I' may remain intact and 'intègre' in his social identity (IV: 249)[3]

*Conclusions*

Although it would be fruitless to try to reconcile the tensions in Rousseau's version of *amitié,* we might do justice to the unity of his sentiment by invoking a new concept and perspective – convention. Friendship is conventional in the etymological sense of the word: individuals 'come together' in it. Conventions are social, not natural agreements between people, and this fact points to the knot in the issue. For pity is the primary convention in Rousseau. He proposes it as a natural convention, forging the transition from Nature to Culture. To this extent, he cheats – though perhaps not more than the concept of convention already permits. The reflections of a different critic are helpful here.[4] Levin recalls a French definition of convention as an 'accord tacite pour admettre certaines fictions ou certains procédés', especially 'fictions du théâtre'; and he argues that convention allows 'a central place where the disparity of art and nature seems to disappear'. This definition certainly applies to Rousseau's version of *amitié*. The sentiment is conventional because it brings individuals together in the social order, but also because it allows important fictions to pass as realities – the fiction that men are equal, for instance. In this second sense, *amitié* and pity do bridge Nature and Culture, since they let Rousseau retain, in immanent fashion, the former fiction within the latter, social sphere. The tacit acceptance of the fiction Nature is what makes it a norm, and only the social espousal of the norm keeps human interactions from seeming thoroughly artificial and theatrical.

But convention, Levin continues, is a form of 'collective style'; and here we may pin-point where Rousseau cheats unduly. He uses the convention of *amitié* to put by fictions that are individual rather than social, and thereby attempts implicitly to equate personal and collective style. In this manner, he abuses friendship. The effort to gain recognition on individual terms rejoins another, larger effort to realize the norms of the imaginative world of reverie as objectively valid. In the author—reader dialogue of the autobiography, these are one effort, as the reader becomes Rousseau's *ami* and 'semblable', with all the demands attendant upon this status. We have worked here to prepare for this issue in Chapter V. A second section can further this preparation, examining the second of his 'idoles de mon cœur', *amour*.

### Amour

Rousseau's version of *amour* does not lend itself to the genetic analysis which he gives in the case of *amitié*. The few direct remarks about love in *Émile* serve mainly to dissociate the sentiment from any basis in natural 'amour de soi', and to place it in the very different register of 'amour-propre'. *Amour* instead becomes an issue in the romance between Émile and Sophie, in Book V. Its narrative, almost novelistic treatment there follows a strange contract of *amitié* between the Mentor and Émile, in which the young man has given up all claim to determine whom he will love. The Mentor chooses the name of Émile's future spouse. *Amour* is effectively subjugated to the authority of *amitié* before it even has a chance to develop.

Why this discomfort with *amour*? How is it different from *amitié*, and why does Rousseau find it so threatening that he has to bring it under the control of friendship? Two different parts of his work — the early play *Narcisse*, and his own relationship with Sophie d'Houdetot, as described in *Les Confessions* — provide the best indications here.

### Narcisse

The play, *Narcisse ou l'Amant de lui-même*, is one of Rousseau's earliest literary pieces. He claims in a preface that it was written at the age of eighteen, or as early as 1730 (II: 959). The work in fact underwent major revisions, with an undetermined amount of help from Marivaux, before its two performances at the Comédie-Française in 1752 (II: 1860).[5]

*Narcisse* plays on the comedy of mistaken identity. Valère, engaged to Angélique but more interested in dress and manners, falls in love with his own image when he sees it retouched to appear like a woman. This visual device is intended in jest to shock him out of his vanity and self-indulgence. But it only exacerbates the flaw. Valère leaves no stone unturned in his efforts to find the 'lady' in the portrait and declare his love. His indecisiveness about whether to return to Angélique (who loves him dearly), or to renounce her in favour of the non-existent woman, forms the comic tension of the play.

The theme of mistaken identity is compounded by a sub-plot in *Narcisse*. A love affair between Lucinde (Valère's sister) and Léandre (Angélique's brother) also labours under a misapprehension. Lucinde loves Léandre, but thinks that he is named Cléonte. The male characters in the play thus have dual identities. Valère loves a feminine rendering of himself; his sister Lucinde is in love with Léandre, but as Cléonte. *Narcisse* wrings some mirth out of these contradictions, and ends merrily when the mistakes are discovered and corrected, and the couples unite in marriage.

Though *Narcisse* is not one of Rousseau's major works, if offers provocative insights into his version of *amour*. One of these is its emphasis on the sense of sight. After Valère has seen the retouched portrait, and while he searches Paris for the woman be believes he sees there, his fiancée Angélique sighs, 'Il s'est vu par mes yeux' (II: 995). The meaning here is fairly straightforward: to fall in love with the person in the portrait, Valère must see himself through the eyes or with the sight of another person who is in love. Angélique herself seems to understand this phenomenon and is unworried by it – she calls it 'le vice universel de son age' (II: 995). Valère's mistake is presented as merely one instance of 'amour-propre', Rousseau's sentimental *bête noire*.

The solution for this 'universal vice' leads to the intersection in Rousseau's thought where self-love (or loving oneself as other, like Valère) meets love for another person. In the decisive scene of the play, Angélique takes centre stage and dangles before her confused lover the possibility of finding the person in the portrait. *She* will introduce Valère to the person he loves – that is, to himself. This scheme she fulfils by restoring his love for her. Playing on the ambiguity that the portrait both is and is not Valère, Angélique praises the 'woman' represented there, all the while intending her praise for him (II: 998-1002). The curiosity that this feint arouses in Valère turns into jealousy when Angélique pretends also to be in love with another man (her brother, Léandre – II: 1013). The self-infatuated hero of *Narcisse* is finally so befuddled by Angélique's manipulation of his passion that he renounces the portrait and returns to her; that is, he moves from mistaken identity to himself, and from narcissism to love for someone truly different from himself.

This version of *amour* is by no means simple, and a closer look at its cause – the portrait – may help to clarify things. Valère's confusion is primarily a visual mistake. 'Il s'est vu par mes yeux', as Angélique has stated. But a linguistic affiliation also is indicated here by the mix-up of names in the sub-plot. A play on words by the drunken servant, Frontin, makes this explicit. 'Tenez', he states in perplexity,

c'est un portrait . . . metamor . . . non, metaphor . . . oui, metaphorisé. C'est mon maitre, c'est une fille . . . Vous avez fait un certain mélange. (II: 1006)

Valère's visual 'mélange' corresponds in rhetorical terms to a metaphor. Does Rousseau's work not provide a second, less comic instance of one person being two individuals at once? The linguistic aspect of this situation is not fully developed until the *Dialogues,* when, as a result of a similar misunderstanding, 'J.J.' is haunted by a double who both is and is not himself. The projection in the autobiography is not so charming as it is in *Narcisse.* But the basic error is the same, and Rousseau will deploy the same energy in writing, trying to dissociate himself from a monstrous image, that Valère uses in his search through Paris to find the non-existent beauty. If metaphors referred directly, both monster and beauty would evaporate. The search would end.

In *Narcisse,* Valère can fall in love with the portrait only because he sees the person represented there as different from himself. His narcissism is not immediate. If it were, narcissistic *amour* would be no more than a cultural version of natural 'amour de soi', and would have to be understood as an internalized, intrapersonal form of pity and *amitié.* Quite the contrary, Valère does not identify with the portrait. Frontin and Lucinde state this clearly:

Frontin:  Il est devenu amoureux de sa ressemblance.
Lucinde: Quoi! sans se reconnaître?
Frontin:  Oui, et c'est bien ce qu'il y a d'extraordinaire.

(II: 1006)

The woman in the portrait is different from Valère. Or, to put the situation in Angélique's perspective, Valère sees himself there, but through eyes which are not his own. Some form of otherness, in any event, mediates the narcissistic relationship he maintains toward himself.

Given these circumstances, Angélique's shrewdness lies in turning them to her own advantage, without changing Valère's passion in any substantial way. 'Il n'est pas juste que je vous chasse de chez vous', she admits, accepting his terms (II: 1002). Her own attraction to the portrait – as Valère, of course – precludes the possibility of jealousy on her part. Her strategy is then to feign indifference to him, and to rouse his jealousy by bringing in another possible suitor. During the penultimate scene of the play, Angélique presents Valère with an ultimatum – herself *or* the portrait – and he chooses the actual women.

The penultimate scene is decisive in *Narcisse* for two different reasons. The mediating 'other' of *amour* takes the concrete form of a rival lover, who introduces a new set of eyes and who forces Valère to see Angélique through them. The rival's presence permits yet another transfer of passion through sight. This undoubtedly hastens Valère's sudden change of heart. Second, Angélique controls the stage, and becomes the first female character in Rousseau's work to assume that submissive yet dominant tone that he will lend in greater depth to later heroines.

But the oddest aspect of the scene is a line from Angélique after Valère has made his choice: 'Vous pourrez juger de ma reconnaissance par le sacrifice que vous venez de me faire' (II: 1015). How can the act of giving up a portrait for a living woman be considered a sacrifice unless Valère's narcissism is itself taken as a serious rival to love? When Léandre, the nominal rival, recognizes Valere in the portrait ('Oui, ma foi, c'est lui'), Valère replies, still unknowing,

Qui, lui? Dites donc, elle. C'est une femme à qui je renonce comme à toutes les femmes de l'univers, sur qui Angélique emportera toujours. (II: 1015)

*Amour* in *Narcisse* is ultimately presented as a choice, in which one renounces the infinite possibility of loving oneself *as* other, in favour of loving oneself *through* a single other person. 'Ingrat', Angélique scolds, 'avois-je tort de vous dire que j'aimois l'original de ce portrait?' 'Et moi je ne veux plus l'aimer que parce qu'il vous adore', Valère responds (II: 1016). He will continue to love himself, by implication, but Angélique becomes the mediating 'third party' to his desire. Valère's obsession with himself is channelled through his love for her. The final line, the moral of the comedy, sums up the arrangement: 'quand on aime bien, on ne songe plus à soi-même' (II: 1018).

What about Angélique? What the nature of *her* love might be, why she should be in a position to effect this change, are yet new questions.

Perhaps it is best not to ask them. Working within circumstances of non-reciprocation, she turns them to her advantage and achieves a workable degree of mutual affection. The basic structure of Valère's folly, in any event, remains unchanged. His narcissism is intact. But the unending range of women he would require to satisfy his desire for himself as other comes into single focus through the decisive choice for Angélique. It is interesting to note that the infinite possibility associated with love in its first, narcissistic stage is perfectly compatible with a unique 'objet d'amour'.

'On a fait l'amour aveugle parce qu'il a de meilleurs yeux que nous', Rousseau states in *Émile* (IV: 494). The implied conclusion of *Narcisse* undercuts this statement. To promise mutually is to effect reciprocation, and to restore sight. But Valère makes his choice *before* he discovers his error. His promise involves risk and uncertain circumstances. Valère must act while still under his illusion. Angélique's use of the word 'sacrifice' has more than a comic effect.

Rousseau himself provides the best counter-example to Valère, and expresses in his life and works a different choice. 'Croyez-moi, Monsieur', the servant Marton urges ironically before the decision, 'choisissez le portrait; c'est le moyen d'être à l'abri des rivaux' (II: 1015). One of the effects of this choice is a change from the conception of *amour* presented in *Narcisse*.

## Sophie d'Houdetot

In Book IX of *Les Confessions,* narrating the drama of his residence at l'Ermitage in 1757, Rousseau also recounts the story of his passion for Sophie d'Houdetot. He describes their affair as his sole experience of love. 'Je fus pris à l'air romanesque de celle-là', he says of one of Sophie's visits to him at his country home,

> et pour cette fois ce fut de l'amour. Comme il fut le prémier et l'unique en toute ma vie et que ses suites le rendront à jamais terrible à mon souvenir, qu'il me soit permis d'entrer dans quelque detail sur cet article. (I: 439)

Rousseau's statement here is confirmed by an earlier remark – 'il étoit écrit que je ne devois aimer d'amour qu'une fois en ma vie' (I: 360). Apparently, Sophie alone deserves the title of 'objet d'amour', 'Maman', Thérèse, Mme de Larnage and other women notwithstanding. What are the circumstances of this unique passion? How does he get involved with Sophie?

The 'novelistic air' mentioned above provides an important clue to Rousseau's *amour*. When Sophie first visits him, he is fully immersed in an imaginative world, and has begun writing *La Nouvelle Héloïse,* the first major elaboration of his 'autre monde' (II: 12).

Au plus fort de mes douces rêveries j'eus une visite de Mad^e d'Houdetot, la prémiére qu'elle m'eut faite en sa vie ... Cette visite eut un peu l'air d'un début de roman. Elle s'égara dans la route. (I: 431–2)

This initial contact is an accidental departure from the normal course of events. And although the bad autumn weather and Sophie's stranding invite on Rousseau's part a warm welcome and a significant lending of clothes ('il fallut changer de tout' – I: 432), the encounter is a preliminary one. It plants a seed in Rousseau's mind, as it were, a memory to accompany him during the continued writing of the novel.

When Sophie makes a second visit, Spring has arrived and Rousseau is even more excited by his work.

Le retour du Printems avoit redoublé mon tendre délire, et dans mes érotiques transports j'avois composé pour les derniéres parties de la Julie plusieurs lettres ... Précisément dans le même tems j'eus de Mad^e d'Houdetot une seconde visite imprévue. (I: 438–9)

The major appeal of both visits stems from the way they register within the imaginative world Rousseau is constructing in *La Nouvelle Héloïse.* The sentiment of *amour,* when it finally surfaces, corresponds directly to his involvement in the well-advanced written work. In quite explicit terms, Rousseau describes how Sophie becomes involved in it as well.

Elle vint, je la vis, j'étois ivre d'amour sans objet, cette ivresse fascina mes yeux, cet objet se fixa sur elle, je vis ma Julie en Mad^e d'Houdetot, et bientôt je ne vis plus que Mad^e d'Houdetot, mais revêtue de toutes les perfections dont je venois d'orner l'idole de mon cœur. (I: 440)[6]

The matter-of-fact tone of this quotation indicates Rousseau's general lucidity about the relationship between imagined and real objects of love. Like *amitié, amour* requires the imagination to develop. But the second sentiment develops very differently from the first. If the imagination acts as a catalyst between two friends, it serves as a foundation for the relationship of lovers. In Rousseau's case, the catalyst is Sophie herself. He falls in love with the actual woman only because she corresponds to an imaginary ideal. The author's infatuation with 'his' Julie thus prepares the way for the infatuation with Sophie, just as Telemachus will provide the image whereby a later Sophie (in *Émile*) falls in love. Love, for all the uniqueness of its object, requires a model. A literary model is most appropriate, but in any event it must be linguistic, as indicated by the fact that the mere name, 'Sophie', chosen by the Mentor, suffices to determine the love of Émile.

Without the immediacy of *amitié, amour* complicates the process of identification between individuals. For although the person who is the actual object of love must be unique, he or she is somehow not the most essential part of the sentiment. Sophie d'Houdetot happens upon Rousseau while he is composing *La Nouvelle Héloïse,* and becomes his loved one primarily because his imagination focuses its activity on her. The process of identification is not entirely uncontrolled – his imagination is already focused on the figure of Julie, and this constitutes a form of pre-selection. Furthermore, Rousseau would never have experienced the sentiment as he did if Sophie had not visited him, and in this sense her actual presence, as well as the unusual circumstances surrounding it, supports the love. But Sophie's personal presence is accidental and implicitly impersonal – an 'égarement' which intrudes from outside on the novel that Rousseau is elaborating. He quickly turns the actual woman into an imagined presence, or applies the world of his novel to her, as much as either procedure is possible. He even repeats the 'égarement' in reverse in a later text, when Émile and the Mentor are drenched in a thunderstorm and make their way unawares to the home of the fictive Sophie, there to change clothes and discover love. The scenarios of Rousseau's experience as described in *Les Confessions* and of the fictional repetition in *Émile* agree about the non-essential aspect of the loved person.

Instead of identification, one could almost speak of non-identification in *amour*. The literary or linguistic model mediating between the sentiment of the lover and the object of his love insures that they will never fully coincide. *Amour* relates to its object indirectly, through what Rousseau terms an 'autre univers', or world of the imagination. We first noticed this phenomenon in Valère's relation to the altered portrait, inasmuch as he does not identify with the woman portrayed there. In Rousseau's personal experience, however, the process of non-identification ends differently from *Narcisse*. He does not succeed, and does not really want to succeed, in making love reciprocal.

Il n'y a point de véritable amour sans enthousiasme, et point d'enthousiasme sans un objet de perfection réel ou chimérique, mais toujours existant dans l'imagination. (IV: 743)

The 'objet de perfection . . . chimérique' in Rousseau's love affair is none other than Sophie herself, whose 'real' perfection derives from what the imagination confers upon her. Julie, the fictive character from Rousseau's novel, is the primary source of his sentiment for the actual woman. Such dependence on an image opens an irreducible distance within the intimacy of *amour,* in direct contrast to the proximity of friends. Within the world of *La Nouvelle Héloïse,* the novel, this point is made as clearly as possible. Writing to Julie about his inability to love Claire as he loves her, Saint-Preux states:

Mon cœur, content de ses charmes, ne leur prête point son illusion; je la vois plus belle que je ne l'imagine et je la redoute plus de près que de loin: c'est presque l'effet contraire à celui qui me vient de vous, et j'éprouvois constamment l'un et l'autre à Clarens. (II: 677)

Several different perspectives may shed light on this conception of *amour.* In an epistemological sense, Rousseau's love for Sophie involves the same mistake which lent comic proportions to *Narcisse.* The mistake is essential to the sentiment, since *amour* develops through the confusion of an imagined model of love with an existing person, and on the assumption that they can be one and the same. Rousseau embraces the error. 'Qu'est-ce que le véritable amour lui-même si ce n'est chimere, mensonge, illusion?' he asks 'On aime bien plus l'image qu'on se fait que l'objet auquel on L'applique' (IV: 656). The metaphorical structure of language (we shall see later) tends to encourage the epistemological confusion. In linguistic terms, the confusion consists of taking a figure for an actual referent. It is not by chance that the model for love should be literary or linguistic.

But it would be yet another order of error to equate the 'mistake' of *amour* with meaninglessness. Mistakes can be eminently significant, especially romantic ones. Love opens a new window on existence, bringing it into contact with the world of the imagination. For Rousseau, this world is the source of value. He consistently reminds us that *amour* creates moral values as it effects an interchange between imagined and actual objects of love. 'Tout n'est qu'illusion dans l'amour, je l'avoue', he remarks,

mais ce qui est réel, ce sont les sentiments dont il nous anime pour le vrai beau qu'il nous fait aimer. Ce beau n'est point dans l'objet qu'on aime, il est l'ouvrage de nos erreurs. Eh! qu'importe? En sacrifie-t-on moins ses sentimens bas à ce modéle imaginaire? (IV: 743)

Rousseau does not specify the sort of values which love engenders. He seems instead to be describing a mechanism for the production of values, rather than any value in particular. This is an important qualification – an abstract understanding of sentiments does not always suffice. Although mistaking an actual person for an imagined ideal may add a valuable dimension to experience, this version of *amour* makes it wholly impracticable. Rousseau's insistence that it be neutralized, or brought under the sway of *amitié*, stems from an awareness that love necessarily escapes his control. Even lucidity has its limits. 'La préférence qu'on accorde on veut l'obtenir; l'amour doit être réciproque', he states in *Émile* (IV: 494). But the word 'should' implies an imperative rather than a reality, and the practice of love is devastatingly non-reciprocal. In theory, the impossibility of the sentiment stems from the fact that it is based in the imagination. How can an imagined object of love ever become fully real? The carefully constructed torments of *La Nouvelle Héloïse* dramatize this dilemma in fiction. In the affair with Sophie d'Houdetot, the dilemma takes the form of the prior commitment on her part to Saint-Lambert. 'Bientot je ne vis plus que Made d'Houdetot', Rousseau has stated about the transfer of passion from the character of Julie. Then he directly continues his thought: 'Pour m'achever, elle me parla de St. Lambert en amante passionée. Force contagieuse de l'amour!' (I: 440). The presence of Saint-Lambert, which effectively means the absence of Sophie as far as Rousseau is concerned, is an essential undercurrent to the affair. 'Nous étions ivres d'amour l'un et l'autre; elle pour son amant, moi pour elle' (I: 443–4). Saint-Lambert's role is to make Sophie as distant and unreachable as Rousseau's cherished image, fueling the passion. In fact, he also gives Rousseau an excuse to avoid sex. Speculation that he never availed himself of Sophie's physical responsiveness indicates that Rousseau would have had to invent Saint-Lambert, or someone like him, if the person had not already existed.[7] His imagination cannot permit the love to be consummated. 'Je la trouvois si aimable aimant St. Lambert', he admits,

que je m'imaginois à peine qu'elle eut pu l'être autant en m'aimant moi-même, et sans vouloir troubler leur union, tout ce que j'ai le plus véritablement désiré d'elle dans mon délire étoit qu'elle se laissât aimer. (I: 461–2)

In *amour*, Rousseau does not require the 'retour' he demands so excessively of friends. At its most powerful for him, love functions in one direction, and follows the successive pattern mentioned earlier in the different context of reverie. Rousseau loves Sophie who loves Saint-Lambert . . . When generalized, the sequence is infinite and irreversible, and places the fulfilment of love outside the grasp of each individual lover along the line.

## Conclusions

This scenario is a disquieting one. Rousseau's version of *amour* runs counter to normal expectations about what the sentiment should be. It also runs counter to *Narcisse,* where the act of promising sealed off the imagination and effected a reciprocation between lovers. But the non-reciprocal nature of *amour* is consistent with Rousseau's remarks here. Whether Saint-Lambert loves someone other than Sophie, for instance, is not a material consideration. Nor is the fact that in other contexts and definitions love signifies a harmonious happiness. For Rousseau, it signifies 'une vigueur inépuisable et inutile' (I: 445), because of the impossibility of identifying a person loved with an imagined model of love.

Moral values can arise from the effort to make the person and the model coincide, but the effort itself is fruitless. Rousseau's 'autre univers' remains an *ought* rather than an *is*. This leads him quickly to conclude that it *is not*. 'Est-ce ma faute si j'aime ce qui n'existe pas?' Sophie asks in *Émile* after discovering the image of Telemachus that will determine her love (IV: 762). Aside from *Narcisse*, Rousseau leaves one with this question in all his works. Whether within the imaginary world of *La Nouvelle Héloïse* or in the events at l'Ermitage in 1757 that follow on his own affair with Sophie d'Houdetot, 'aimer ce qui n'est pas' has unfortunate consequences. In his life, it separates Rousseau from long-standing friendships – from Mme d'Épinay, Grimm, and Diderot – and arouses the first symptoms of his incipient paranoia. In his novel, it causes the death of the fictive heroine, Julie. Such disasters are a good indication of the unnaturalness of his conception of *amour* and of its lack of connection with 'amour de soi'. It leads, not to the conservation and preservation of the impassioned person, but to a destructive expenditure of energy.

## Contrasts and Combinations

Let us now consider *amour* and *amitié* together. While very different, the two sentiments are not entirely separate. A single person may feel both. They may even complement one another in a given situation.

*Amour* and *amitié* can be distinguished first of all in terms of their different relations to the imagination, and by the type of identification (or non-identification) they involve. The imagination is an extrinsic catalyst in *amitié*. Its indispensable but limited function makes friends aware of their profound identity, and allows them to establish a convention of free, equal and reciprocal partnership. In *amour,* the imagination acts as a sort of intrinsic, final cause. It makes identification between lovers indirect at best, impossible at worst. Love isolates individuals, and creates in them an awareness of singularity and uniqueness in relation to an imaginative model.

*Amitié* implies a symmetrical, reciprocal, and essentially circular relationship, based on identity. In Rousseau's account, it develops directly and 'naturally' from 'amour de soi', within a closed system. This closure is most evident in the dovetail between suffering and the instinct of self-preservation, which enables Rousseau to invoke the imagination without its illusory, impersonal force. *Amour*, on the other hand, implies an asymmetrical, non-reciprocal relationship, based on difference. It displays an 'unnatural' or open economy – which goes hand-in-hand with its transcendent character, and with the debilitating fact that the lover is possessed instead of in control. Rousseau's version of love demonstrates the haphazard and gratuitous aspects of affection.

Can these differences between *amour* and *amitié* be brought into line with the discussion in Chapter I of reverie? *Amour*, for instance, at first resembles the second, elaborative stage of reverie, since it requires a developed imaginative model through which sentimental value can be conferred on an actual person. And *amitié*, to the extent that it requires the immediate 'transport' of identification, resembles the initial, instantaneous stage of reverie.

Such comparisons are misleading. The closed order of *amitié*, which circumscribes two friends within one fundamental identity, benefits the world of reverie in its elaborated mode. The recognition which Rousseau confers and receives in friendship is of a type which allows him to take a reverie for reality. A friend, for him, already belongs to his 'autre univers'. Grimsley has this point in mind, perhaps, when he states: 'It is because the other is necessary for the preservation or elaboration of this private image of himself that Jean-Jacques clings so desperately to the ideal of friendship'.[8]

*Amour,* though it presupposes a developed imaginative world as a model for sentiment, finally resembles the first stage of reverie. For in the application of the model to an existing person, the accidental, impersonal substructure of the reverie experience once again becomes visible. No matter how much Rousseau may pursue his mistaken identification, a lover will never belong to his 'autre univers'. He always returns to the discrepancy between actual and imagined worlds. *Amour*, as it heightens his awareness of this discrepancy, undercuts the world of reverie and shows it to be a fiction.

*Amour* and *amitié* thus offer and deny different froms of confirmation which are essential to Rousseau's imaginative life. Inasmuch as it frustrates the coincidence of experience and imagination, the sentiment of love disrupts the enclosed, personal elaborations of reverie. Neither the sentiment nor the person loved will ever be circumscribed within a text, the literary form of reverie. But to the extent that it persists outside Rousseau's control and appropriative power, *amour* fuels the imaginative process and generates new possibilities of elaboration. The dialectic of value must work in two directions: not only does the imagined model of love confer value on the actual object of the sentiment, but the presence of the actual person gives value to the model itself. *Amour* thus authorizes the world of reverie, providing a source of recognition which cannot be found within that world. In Rousseau, love is not just a dialogue between two persons, but a dialogue between the actual world and the third party to *amour,* the imagination.

*Amitié,* which shares the closed economy of the world of reverie, is able to confer value only on the negative basis of suffering. But it serves a different, equally important function for Rousseau. Although he needs objective recognition for the world of reverie from an external, independent point of view, he also wishes to be recognized on terms which remain internal to that world. A friend must therefore toe an ambiguous line between independence from Rousseau and submission to him. The immediate effusion of sentiment in *amitié* blurs the problem of recognition. Should an *ami* begin to assert his own needs, however, or to contradict Rousseau's, the problem reappears in the high drama of betrayal and rejection.

Rousseau's desire to combine the two sentiments stems from his wish to confer value on friendship while keeping love within safe bounds. In his relationships with others, fulfilling this aim usually involves a move from dual to triadic interactions.[9] Trios come in two basic configurations. The first is similar to the opening triad in *La Nouvelle Héloïse*, involving a man and two women. Lover of one woman and friend of the other, Rousseau (or Saint-Preux) luxuriates in indecision in their dual presence. *Amour* is not consummated, but *amitié* is enhanced, and the tension of being at the border between them satisfies him more than could either sentiment alone.

A second sort of trio involves a relationship between two lovers and a third, supposedly disinterested *ami,* who surveys and regulates their affection. In the Mentor of *Émile,* Rousseau offers the most developed version of a role filled also by Wolmar in *La Nouvelle Héloïse,* by Rousseau to a limited extent in the last stages of the affair with Sophie d'Houdetot, and by Claude Anet to an even lesser extent in the *ménage à trois* with 'Maman' at Chambéry. The Mentor plays no direct part in the love of Émile and Sophie; in fact, he presents himself as a stern moralist and circumspect proponent of *amitié.* But his omniscience disguises a debilitating lack of contact with any profound affection, and he needs *amitié* more for personal solace than for the help it supposedly offers the lovers. The Mentor's friendship with Émile allows for surreptitious participation in his passion, not as a rival, but in the voyeuristic manner of the Devin. Once again, Rousseau treads a border, enjoying inclusion in *amour* while unruffled and apparently self-sufficient in *amitié*

## A Third Sentiment: Madame de Warens and Writing

What, more precisely, is the border area between *amour* and *amitié*? Can it be characterized without reference to them? In Book III of *Les Confessions,* Rousseau gives a first positive indication here, while recounting his first extended stay at Chambéry with Mme de Warens. 'Me voila donc enfin établi chez elle', he states. He goes on to describe a new and more profound sentiment:

Quoique cette sensibilité de cœur qui nous fait vraiment jouir de nous soit l'ouvrage de la nature et peutêtre un produit de l'organisation, elle a besoin de situations qui la développent. Sans ces causes occasionelles un homme né très sensible ne sentiroit rien, et mourroit sans avoir connu son être. Tel à peu pres j'avois été jusqu'alors, et tel j'aurois toujours été peut-être, si je n'avois connu Made de Warens, ou si même l'ayant connue, je n'avois pas vécu assez longtems auprés d'elle pour contracter la douce habitude des sentimens affectueux qu'elle m'inspira. J'oserai le dire; qui ne sent que l'amour ne sent pas ce qu'il y a de plus doux dans la vie. Je connois un autre sentiment, moins impétueux peutêtre, mais plus délicieux mille fois, qui quelquefois est joint à l'amour et qui souvent en est séparé. Ce sentiment n'est pas non plus l'amitié seule; il est plus voluptueux, plus tendre; je n'imagine pas qu'il puisse agir pour quelqu'un du même sexe; du moins je fus ami si jamais homme le fut, et je ne l'éprouvai jamais près d'aucun de mes amis. Ceci n'est pas clair, mais il le deviendra dans la suite; les sentimens ne se décrivent bien que par leurs effets. (I: 104)

Rousseau describes this unusual sentiment hesitantly, first in contrast to both *amour* and *amitié*, then through its 'effets' during his stay with Mme de Warens. The discursive difficulty is bound up with the subject matter. In the company of another person, Rousseau is discovering the 'sentiment de l'existence' that he experiences individually in the 'extase' of reverie. He cannot state the sentiment when it is shared any more directly than he did in the *caesura* in his reverie passages. 'Maman', incidentally, is the one person in whose company reverie is possible (I: 105; 107).

Why should Mme de Warens be the other person? One can only acknowledge her importance in the opening instalment of *Les Confessions*, where Rousseau *de facto* makes her the greatest determining influence in his life. The maternal aspect of the relationship adds an element of psychological drama to it — Mme de Warens is a lover of sorts, but more significantly she is the protector of Rousseau's extended childhood. As interesting as the actual relationship, however, is how Rousseau conceives of the sentiment which it provokes and sustains.

In the tenth 'Promenade', the unfinished text written just before his death, Rousseau returns to describe his 'prémiére connoissance avec Made de Warens'. He states that, with her, 'Je vis longtems prolonger pour moi cet état delicieux mais rapide où l'amour et l'innocence habitent le même cœur' (I: 1098). Elsewhere he comments in the same vein: 'l'innocence de mœurs a sa volupté qui vaut bien l'autre, parce qu'elle n'a point d'intervalle et qu'elle agit continuellement' (I: 138).

For Rousseau, innocence is the guarantor of continuity. To love innocently is to share all the voluptuousness and value of *amour* without its disruption and threat of non-reciprocation. It is to become aware of a profound and shared identity in 'être' without the pathos of suffering involved in *amitié*. And in Book V of *Les Confessions*, just before narrating his 'séjour . . . (de) bonheur et dc l'innocence' at 'les Charmettes' (I: 224), Rousseau describes this sentimental relation in its most developed state, in a passage that replies directly to the passage from Book III:

S'il y a dans la vie un sentiment délicieux, c'est celui que nous eprouvames d'être rendus l'un à l'autre. Notre attachement mutuel n'en augmenta pas, cela n'étoit pas possible; mais il prit je ne sais quoi de plus intime, de plus touchant dans sa grande simplicité. Je devenois tout à fait son œuvre, tout à fait son enfant et plus que si elle eut été ma vraye mére. Nous commençames, sans y songer, à ne plus nous séparer l'un de l'autre, à mettre en quelque sorte toute notre existence en commun, et sentant que reciproquement nous nous étions non seulement necessaires mais suffisans, nous nous accoutumames à ne plus penser à rien d'étranger à nous, à borner absolument notre bonheur et tous nos desirs à cette possession plus essencielle qui, sans tenir aux sens, au sexe, à l'age, à la figure tenoit à tout ce par quoi i'on est soi, et qu'on ne peut perdre qu'en cessant d'être. (I: 222)

Although Rousseau refers to Mme de Warens here, she hardly figures as a distinct person. With an 'existence en commun' and 'possession mutuelle', they are no more than one identity. The paradox of reverie lay in the simultaneity of identity and transition. In the shared 'sentiment de l'existence', it lies in the ideal of a maternal lover, with whom he can maintain through time the delicious ambiguity of singularity in duality, independence within dependence. The most succinct expression for this pattern in Rousseau is the word 'double', or 'doublement'. 'Insensiblement je me sentis isolé et seul dans cette même maison dont auparavant j'étois l'ame et où je vivois pour ainsi dire à double', he will say after the spell with 'Maman' has been broken (I: 266). But the sentiment he eventually loses with her will reappear in another guise — not in an interpersonal relationship, but in the special relationship which he begins to establish as an author. In the writing activity, and especially in the writing of the autobiography, Rousseau is again at ease. 'En me livrant à la fois au souvenir de l'impression receue et au sentiment présent je peindrai doublement l'état de mon ame . . .' (I: 1154).

The developing direction in this analysis, from reverie to 'Maman' and further to the writing activity, follows a continuous and consistent movement in Rousseau. The indeterminate 'sentiment de l'existence' is present at each level — reverie is its individual manifestation, the relationship with Mme de Warens an interpersonal one. And if the process of creating a text can be considered an objectification and literary shaping of reverie, it also allows Rousseau to sustain the 'possession mutuelle' described above. Writing in fact becomes the primary way for him to sustain the sentiment. Whatever his claims, he is not self-sufficient in reverie. Nor does his ideal of shared innocence with 'Maman' last through time. Rousseau holds to these experiences primarily through the constructions and elaborations of memory and of the writing activity.[10]

## Conclusion: Pygmalion

*Pygmalion*, Rousseau's treatment of the myth about a sculptor who tries to bring a statue of a woman to life, best dramatizes the author's relation to his written work. This pantomime piece works at the boundary between gesture and language, natural and conventional signs, and is directly concerned with the antagonism between Art and Nature. It was written, furthermore, at a crucial point in Rousseau's career, late in 1762, when the great elaborative expansion of fictive and theoretical works that precede the autobiography has come to an end. *Pygmalion* marks the critical stage in the move to autobiography, when Rousseau is not satisfied to forfeit his own happinesss to the happiness of a work that is independent of him, and works instead to identify himself within his aesthetic creation.[11]

The moment in *Pygmalion* which casts light on the present discussion occurs when the statue, Galathée, comes to life. Galathée undergoes an uncanny birth and change of substance — stone becomes flesh, the inorganic the organic. Before this awakening, the statue is only a 'monument' to perfection, too perfect to exist in this world, and therefore most unwordly (I: 225). It embodies the completeness of an aesthetic world, the fulfilment of the sculptor's desire. But Galathée, for all this, nonetheless falls short of actual existence. 'Éparne cet affront à la nature', Pygmalion pleads before the transformation occurs, 'qu'un si parfait modele soit l'image de ce qui n'est pas' (II: 1229).

From the perspective of the present chapter, the 'non-being' of the statue poses a problem among two persons, the sculptor and the woman in the stone. 'Oui, deux êtres manquent à la plénitude des choses', as Pygmalion states. It is therefore possible to interpret Galathée's entry into existence as a paradoxical combination of *amour* and *amitié*, as the interpersonal version of the 'sentiment de l'existence', but now highlighted in Rousseau's or the artist's relation to his aesthetic creation rather than to Mme de Warens. Seen in this way, her awakening is an exchange of being: Galathée moves from non-being to being, from what *is not* to what *is,* through the efforts of Pygmalion. 'Je t'ai donné tout mon être', he states at the end of the short text, 'je ne vivrai plus que par toi' (II: 1231).

But *Pygmalion* can also be viewed in a light which helps to bring Chapters I and II into a coherent juxtaposition. If Galathée's birth is a shared identification among two persons, it is also a 'réveil', the instant of awakening in reverie, in which the primary identification is not between two persons, but between the illusory and the real. Galathée moves from illusion toward reality, Pygmalion from reality toward illusion. From different starting points, they meet in one 'Moi', at a point somewhere between illusion and reality, or even prior to such a distinction. The stage directions given by Rousseau for the pantomime are significant in this regard; one finds the words 'transport', 'avec extase', 'transporté' — the vocabulary of reverie — alongside the 'passion' of Pygmalion.

In *Pygmalion*, therefore, the separation between solitary reverie and interpersonal fulfilment is not so great as it might have seemed. Identification with other persons seems possible through identification with oneself in a created, aesthetic work. The resolution in reverie of 'un etre qui manque à la plénitude des choses' is fully comparable to that of 'deux etres qui manquent à la plénitude des choses'. Reading the autobiography, where Rousseau repeats the effort of Pygmalion, we shall examine his attempted identification in its three rhetorical stages. But first we must follow his transformation of the intuition of reverie into an articulated imaginative universe, give critical authority to the notion of a world of the text, and witness how the author slowly accomplishes his transfer of being to it. Only then will we be justified in making an equation between the experiential structures of the past two chapters and the rhetorical structures of the final two. Between them lies the move to autobiography.

# III

## THE MOVE TO AUTOBIOGRAPHY

Our discussion of Rousseau's work thus far has examined selected aspects of his life rather than the several accounts of it that he will give in the autobiography. The author's role, implicit throughout, has not yet been the primary topic. To examine it more directly, we now change tack, and look specifically at those aspects of Rousseau's writing activity which precede and make possible the autobiographical works.

If a writer is different from the person who writes, we should also make a distinction between the writer and the autobiographer. Rousseau demonstrates such strong self-expressive tendencies in all his works that it is easy to view the autobiography as a direct, 'natural' extension of his life and early writings. The personal tone that pervades his fiction, drama, and even the theoretical works, and the repeated episodes, described in *Les Confessions,* where he recounts his 'petite histoire' to a sympathetic listener, all point to an apparent spontaneity between living and writing, between experience and autobiographical narration.

But Rousseau does not become a writer until midway through his life, and an autobiographer only in the final stage of his career. Eighteen years separate his sudden entry into the literary world, in 1749, from his revision of the first extended segment of the autobiography, in 1766. To turn a tendency toward self-expression into a definite rhetorical option is obviously a lengthy and complicated process. It involves virtually all of Rousseau's authorship before *Les Confessions.*

### Biographical Background

Rousseau's varied career as a writer divides roughly into three general periods. The first, between 1749 and 1756, begins with the 'inspiration subite' on the road to Vincennes (I: 1135), his quasi-religious conversion to writing. This period establishes Rousseau's position as a social critic, actively living and speaking from within society. A second period, between 1756 and 1762, begins with his withdrawal from Paris to the country, and ends with the flight into exile after the publication of *Du Contrat social* and *Émile*. In relative seclusion at l'Ermitage and at Montmorency, Rousseau exists mainly in order to write, and elaborates the critical impulse of his early writings into a fully articulated literary vision and theoretical stance. The development of his career is accompanied by a growing association with aristocratic patrons, and a rupture with many long-standing personal friends The third period, from 1762 onwards, is a retreat into a series of apologetic writings, of which the autobiography is a major part. Rousseau's decision to write about himself increasingly isolates him, leading finally to a stage where his social commitments extend little beyond a basic commitment to written language.[1]

## 1749–56

As Rousseau describes it, the force informing the impassioned rhetoric of the *Discours sur les sciences et les arts* in 1749 derives from the discovery of 'un autre univers' (I: 351). But the beginning of his writing career also coincides with another, much more down-to-earth relationship, namely the establishment of a permanent 'ménage' with Thérèse la Vasseur.

Thérèse's importance to Rousseau deserves attention. 'Il falloit, pour tout dire, un successeur à Maman', he remarks in Book III. 'Je trouvois dans Thérèse le supplement dont j'avois besoin' (I: 331–2). Unlike Mme de Warens, Thérèse rarely enjoys the favour of the author's imaginative recollection. To the end of his life she shares his daily existence. Thérèse's intellectual gifts are so limited that Diderot and Grimm, Rousseau's best friends before 1756, conspire simply to free him from what they consider a constricting relationship.[2]  But her physical presence is undoubtedly important, permitting a stability without which Rousseau might never have written his major works. As helper and eventually as nurse, for sheer human contact, Thérèse is indispensable to him. Rousseau even states at one point, 'J'ai toujours regardé le jour qui m'unit à ma Thérèse comme celui qui fixa mon être moral' (I: 413). Man does not live by imagination alone. It is significant that the two begin to share a household just as his talents fall into place.

More significant in this period is the awakening of an imaginative force in Rousseau when, in 1749, he reads the prize essay question put by the Académie de Dijon: 'Si le rétablissement des sciences et des arts a contribué à épurer les mœurs'. The full scope and import of the movement of Enlightenment are at question here, and Rousseau senses a decisive opening. For the first time he finds his voice as an author. Earlier interests and projects have been peripheral, if promising: a theory of musical notation, an unperformed opera and play, some writings on music. They depend on the tenuous support of patrons, or link him with the 'philosophes' and the *Encyclopédie*. The 'inspiration' that Rousseau experiences while walking to visit Diderot (imprisoned at Vincennes in 1749 for his own writing), provides him with a platform he will henceforth call and sustain as his own.

In the first *Discours* Rousseau takes up a critical stance, rather giving his intuition a positive elaboration as an 'autre univers'. A consistent emphasis on *this* world is evident from the start. Rousseau is more interested in the existing than in the ideal, and his imagined worlds, whatever purpose they are made to serve or in whatever rhetorical mode they are presented, always grow out of an exhilarating dissatisfaction with the present. Sketchy as his Utopian vision may be in 1749, it is nonetheless fully 'autre'. In his first major work, Rousseau delivers a broader critique of the Enlightenment than any other contemporary writer.

In 1750, when the first *Discours* wins the prize competition and is published, Rousseau strongly desires public recognition. Claiming that the arts and sciences contribute to moral degeneration, not advancement, the basic argument of his first work could be said to invite attention. But the essay is only a first step. Rousseau attracts further attention by a 'réforme personelle' (I: 362), his very social repudiation of the social mores of the time. The reform is ostensibly made to bring his everyday behaviour in line with his written statements. 'Pour me faire écouter il falloit mettre ma conduite d'accord avec mes principes', he states (I: 416). The process of organizing a personal existence around the theory and strictness of a piece of writing – an autobiographical process, in the end – has already begun.

The description in *Les Confessions* of this personal transformation is quite revealing. A sudden illness, perhaps induced psychosomatically by the unexpected success of the essay, raises the spectre of impending death. (Bodily disorder is a recurring feature of every crisis in Rousseau's adult life, from the ailment at 'les Charmettes', at the age of twenty-six, onwards.) According to Rousseau, the illness 'me fit faire de serieuses reflexions sur mon état' (I: 361). Among the decisions carried out on his return to health, Rousseau resigns an undemanding, well-paid post given him by an influential patron, and takes up the repetitive, manual labour of copying music. Here begins a strange sub-career, which runs parallel to the author's creative writing, later extends to the transcription of his own texts, and which, in the case of music copying, amounts to over eleven thousand full sheets of intricate notation before Rousseau abandons the activity near the end of his life.

But the process of decision-making is as unusual as this particular decision. Rousseau comes to it in the 'délire' of his illness.

Ces idées se fermentérent si bien dans ma tête avec la fiévre, elles s'y combinérent avec tant de force, que rien depuis lors ne les put arracher, et durant ma convalescence je me confirmai de sang froid dans les résolutions que j'avois prises dans mon delire. (I: 362)

Just as the sudden, involuntary reverie on the road to Vincennes informs the critical eloquence of the first *Discours,* Rousseau's decision to reform his moral stance crystallizes in a period of feverish hallucinations. Force and illusion combine once again, grounding personal identity as an 'abnormal' state. Rousseau himself must have been struck by the parallel with earlier, equally aberrant episodes of his life. In *Les Confessions* he describes his behaviour during the 1750–6 period and at the same time reminds us of Vaussore de Villeneuve, Dudding, or other temporary pseudonyms:

Qu'on se rappelle un de ces courts moments de ma vie où je devenois un autre et cessois d'être moi; on le trouve encor dans le tems dont je parle; mais au lieu de durer six jours, six semaines, il dura prés de six ans . . . (I: 417)

This characterization of the 'réforme personnelle' connects Rousseau's capacity for change with his ability to imitate a model. In the pseudonymous episodes, Rousseau acts out roles with attributes which he himself would like to possess. While the pseudonyms in one sense conceal his actual identity and shield him from recognition, they also allow him to enter into the possible, desired identity. Rousseau's gift for role-play is such that his identity is frequently indistinguishable from the role assumed, and real change occurs. The 'réforme personnelle' is an extended instance of this phenomenon. 'Je ne jouai rien,' Rousseau states, 'je devins en effet tel que je parus' (I: 416).

The personal transformation after the first *Discours* involves a crucial new element — the act of writing — which is not present in earlier pseudonymous episodes. The process of change remains the same: Rousseau continues to identify with a role, and in 1752 loses himself

in it as much as he did in 1732. But the nature of the assumed role
has altered. Rousseau has become his own model, and constructs his
identity in accordance with texts he has written. He 'imitates himself',
rather than characters from other novels of figures from his past.
Rousseau has internalized the process of change, since his own work
as an author now offers him the role to be enacted. Such freedom from
external models leads him to the conclusion that his behaviour during
this period is simply an expression of personal identity, not pseudonymous. It engenders an illusion of control and a feeling of individual
potency akin to the intuition of total possibility experienced by the
rêveur. Writing is reverie-made-public, like the performance of *Le Devin
du village,* but permits Rousseau to shape his act in a private, enclosed
sphere.

One can hardly overestimate the importance of the new order of
self-invention which begins when Rousseau becomes an author. Able to
choose a role which is already himself, he persists in the 'réforme
personnelle' for 'pres de six ans'. Even in the first *Discours,* before
setting down a word of autobiography, he establishes a close correspondence between text and life. He also invents perhaps the most
fundamental and paradoxical of his notions, without which the autobiography is inconceivable – 'mon naturel'. At once radical and conservative, 'mon naturel' will allow Rousseau to change himself at will
while nonetheless remaining true to his identity. 'J'étois vraiment
transformé', he states; that is, 'transformed', but in such a way that he
is more 'truly' himself than ever (I: 416). Can one ask for a better
manifestation of difference disguising itself as personal identity than
this sustained episode?

As the act of writing begins to give literary shape to the imagined
space of reverie, public esteem or displeasure reach Rousseau through
his work. He is recognized when the first *Discours* receives praise and
blame, or, at one further remove, when the adoption of his own direc-
tives causes notoriety and makes him a renegade. Success eventually
places him squarely in the spotlight. The performances of his *Devin,*
in 1752, and the scandal surrounding his *Lettre sur la musique
Française,* in 1753, begin to undermine Rousseau's inflated self-
assurance. With the production of *Narcisse,* late in 1752, he already
demonstrates a desire to retreat.[3] He withdraws the play after two
moderately successful performances, quite convinced that it is a failure
despite a favourable audience response.

Rousseau is quick to note and make use of the public and private faces that come with being a successful writer. As early as 1750, writing to Voltaire, he signs a letter: 'J.J. Rousseau, citoyen de Genève' (I: cvi). The epithet is intended primarily to set Rousseau apart in Voltaire's mind from another author of the same name. But it also reveals Rousseau's new-found concern for civic responsibility and for his own past. He makes a trip to Geneva in 1754 in two capacities — to return to the community he abandoned at sixteen, but to return as the successful author of the *Discours sur l'origine et les fondements de l'inégalité*. He dedicates this new work to the citizens of Geneva using this same signature.

The second *Discours* combines serious-minded exposition with the provoking thesis that inequality among men is a social, not a natural phenomenon. Conceived in 1753 and written early in 1754, it raises Rousseau's standard of work above the flashy quality of the first *Discours,* and succeeds in infuriating Voltaire (among others). There is a thematic as well as a coincidental link with the return visit to Geneva. Rousseau's writing also makes a 'retour' — to a full-fledged vision of 'natural', uncorrupted man. The description of 'un État qui n'existe plus, qui n'a peut-être point existé, que probablement n'existera jamais, et dont il est pourtant necessaire d'avoir des Notions justes pour bien juger de nôtre état présent' (III: 123), is Rousseau's first elaboration of the Utopian perspective informing his critical voice. *Natural* man he portrays — not yet *a* natural man, nor *himself* as natural man. The conception is original and the exposition philosophically rigorous, inasmuch as social virtues and vices are excluded from the State of Nature in any but a virtual way. Altogether, the second *Discours* must be considered a seminal eighteenth-century piece.

In a somewhat unrealistic parallel, the trip to Geneva involves a symbolic return to what the author is beginning to consider natural about himself. The independent city-state eventually comes to represent for him a civilized version of the natural state that he describes unsentimentally in this piece of writing. In 1754, Rousseau re-enters the Church, assumes his rights as a Genevan citizen, and achieves a sort of social and personal reconciliation. Life and work are again juxtaposed.

If one can judge the year 1755 from the limited space devoted to it in *Les Confessions,* Rousseau enjoys a happy interval between the Geneva visit and his move to l'Ermitage in 1756. The scant reference for this period suggests a change of tempo from the contestation of the early works, a regrouping of ideas and force, and a shift of direction. One important sign of a new start is the contact made in Geneva with the Amsterdam publisher, Marc-Michel Rey, who will print most of Rousseau's later texts. On his return to Paris, the author submits the manuscript of the second *Discours* to Rey. He no longer depends on assistance from others in making basic publishing arrangements, as in the printing of the first *Discours*, which Diderot handled. Rousseau has established himself to a degree inconceivable in 1749, and is ready to consolidate his position as an independent writer.

## 1756–62

In the spring of 1756, Rousseau, Thérèse, and her mother settle in a house built expressly for Rousseau by Mme d'Épinay, ten miles from Paris.[4]  Subsequent autobiographical remarks indicate that the main reason for the move are the numerous writing projects which Rousseau has begun or is projecting at this time. In addition to a general wish for the solitude of the countryside, he leaves the city in order to be able to devote himself to writing.

*La Nouvelle Héloïse,* significantly, does not figure on the list of the author's projects. The inception of the epistolary novel, the first major work to take form after the move, is particularly interesting in that it connects with the inception of the autobiography. Before casting his fictional scenario, and the characters of Julie, Claire, and Saint-Preux, Rousseau turns to episodes involving women from his own past. Primary among them is 'le diné du Château de Toun' (I: 426), which will eventually be recounted as 'l'idylle des cerises' in Book IV of *Les Confessions*. 'Bientôt je vis rassemblés autour de moi', Rousseau recalls,

tous les objets qui m'avoient donné de l'émotion dans ma jeunesse, Mlle Galley, Mlle de Graffenried, Mlle de Breil, Made Basile, Made de Larnage . . . jusqu'à la piquante Zulietta . . . (I: 426–7)

According to a thesis of H. de Saussure, a number of fragments describing women memorable to Rousseau and classed among the 'Ébauches des *Confessions*' date from this spring of 1756.[5] But among these written recollections, a fragment describing 'le diné du Chateau de Toun' is conspicuously absent. The similarities between the participants in the episode from the author's past and the main characters of *La Nouvelle Héloïse* lead one to surmise that the possible 'ébauche' is not so much missing as simply transmuted into the fictional mode of Rousseau's developing epistolary novel. His remark in *Les Confessions* about his relation to the male figure in the triad – 'Je m'identifiois avec l'amant et l'ami le plus qu'il m'étoit possible' (I: 430) – supports the speculation.

Two different remarks might be made about this initial textual grafting between fiction and autobiography in Rousseau. First, the author's move to autobiography begins quite early, even before the major fictional and theoretical expansion of his writing career gets underway. If the more fragmentary 'ébauches' date from 1756, the first evidence of autobiographical writing occurs almost seven years before the *Lettres à Malesherbes,* and a full ten years before the revision of the first six books of *Les Confessions.* Much of Rousseau's writing in the intervening period could then justifiably be considered as fictional expressions of an autobiographical intention which the author has not yet directly recognized.

But one must also remark the fact that Rousseau's autobiographical intention, blossoming as it may have been in the spring of 1756, does not last through the heat of the summer. The impulse immediately side-steps into fiction, and will not re-emerge with any consistency until 1762, at the end of this second period. Though he may begin with a non-fictional and autobiographical intention, Rousseau realizes it only after a lengthy elaboration in a different rhetorical mode. The pattern in question here is important, and similar in structure to the personal appropriation of theoretical principles in the 'réforme personnelle'. It now occurs at a purely textual level, however. Rousseau will be able to write the autobiography largely because he has already constructed a fictional world from which he can borrow an articulate sense of value, and through which he can actively identify himself and his past. Fiction leads the way to autobiography. This order of development is not merely particular to Rousseau, nor exclusively chronological. It informs the more general relationship between the novel and autobiography in the eighteenth century, the latter appropriating from the former its expressive tools and techniques.[6]   P. Lejeune, commenting on the precedence of fiction, states, 'la sincérité s'apprend; l'originalité s'imite'.[7] Rousseau disregards this in his conservative claims about 'mon naturel', and when he begins to write the autobiography itself. But he is acutely aware of it in earlier texts. He maintains a studied uncertainty about the priority between fiction and reality in the 'Préface Dialoguée' to *La Nouvelle Héloïse.*

In the spring and summer of 1757, the author's love affair with Sophie d'Houdetot adds a further permutation to the interchange between imaginary and actual worlds. The affair acts as the immediate catalyst in a long-brewing misunderstanding between Rousseau and three of his closest friends, Diderot, Grimm, and Mme d'Épinay. Temperamental and philosophical differences separate him from them; personal shame at his behaviour in the affair heightens his sense of isolation. The ensuing, melodramatic rupture forces a hasty departure from l'Ermitage at the end of the year, and shakes Rousseau profoundly. Loss of intimacy from these friendships undoubtedly undermines his confidence in himself, no matter how much he subsequently projects blame for the split on external causes.

Already imaginatively over-extended, Rousseau might at this point have turned back to the actual world for stability. Instead he immerses himself in writing. As the editors of *Les Confessions* suggest, the personal turmoil surrounding and stemming from the rupture may delay the start of the autobiography, in that Rousseau uses the inter-vening fictional and theoretical works to find a moral bearing and sense of security necessary for him to write more directly about himself (I: xviii–xix).

At the very end of 1757, Rousseau moves to nearby Montmorency. Here he lives for the next four and a half years, completing almost all the remaining major works published during his lifetime. Although very much alone, he is not really isolated – the Maréchal de Luxem-bourg and his wife seek his acquaintance, and from 1759 onwards be-come patrons. After 1760, the Prince de Conti begins to fulfil the same role. These aristocrats show themselves to be more discreet in their understanding of Rousseau than previous friends and benefactors. Presumably, their expectations and demands of him are less direct than those of equals, like Diderot and Grimm. Rousseau communicates with them primarily as artist to patron, through the mediation of the written work. His private readings of *La Nouvelle Héloïse* for Mme de Luxembourg illustrate this new type of relationship.

Continuing generosity throughout this period is crucial to the author's production. Thérèse's practical presence is matched by gratifying recognition from several of the leading families in France. Rousseau's writing proceeds apace. Among his gifts, exercised fully between 1756 and 1762, is an astounding capacity for work. One after the other, the texts move from his desks into print.

The first to appear, the *Lettre à d'Alembert*, combines aspects from both periods of his authorship, and constitutes a sort of turning-point between them. On the one hand, the work remains in a critical mode reminiscent of the first *Discours*, as Rousseau argues from his original thesis against the establishment of a theatre in Geneva. But the text strikes a new, para-autobiographical tone, which the author is the first to notice. 'J'étois rentré dans mon élément', he states about the writing (I: 501–2). 'C'est ici, car la Julie n'étoit pas à moitié faite, le prémier de mes écrits, où j'aye trouvé des charmes dans le travail'. One reason for this new-found pleasure? Rousseau involves himself personally in the text, even if unconsciously so. 'Sans m'en appercevoir j'y décrivis ma situation actuelle', he remarks in Les Confessions (I: 495–6).

By the end of 1758, Rousseau completes La Nouvelle Héloïse; in early 1761 printed copies reach Paris. The novel achieves an immediate and lasting success, and the author's positive role as a public figure reaches its peak during 1761. At the same time, however, he remains personally entrenched in the closed, aesthetic world which he has created. The unstinting care and elegance with which he transcribes complete copies of the long text for Sophie d'Houdetot and Mme de Luxembourg attest to his attachment to the work. He produces these copies at a nominal fee, and in one sense simply transfers the mechanical 'métier' of music copying to his fiction. But the activity itself undoubtedly gratifies him, and should be interpreted as an effort to prolong the imaginary world of the text and to extend it into his own life. Rousseau in fact emulates Saint-Preux, copying the letters of Julie within the novel, and ensures contact at a distance with the two women most important to him at this period of his life. Not the least of his 'work', from 1758 onwards, involves the copying and recopying of his own texts.

The project of the Lettres morales, a one-way correspondence with Sophie d'Houdetot begun and abandoned in late 1757 and early 1758, is resuscitated in Émile, where Rousseau elaborates and fulfils his need to instruct an 'ami' with an imaginary, male, and more pliable student. The treatise on education, as it is recognized in more objective terms, is written and completed alongside a second project, dating from before the visit to Geneva, and less personal in tone. It takes the final form of Du Contrat social. The two texts constitute his most sustained and direct attack on the two corner-stones of Church and State in mid-eighteenth-century France – the religious doctrine of original sin, and the political doctrine of the divine right of the monarchy. Published in close succession, they appear after a delay in the printing of Émile, and after Rousseau's first bout of frenzied paranoia. While he imagines a conspiracy to distort *Émile*, the real threat is elsewhere. The unfortunate but hardly unexpected reaction to the works arrives in June 1762, when their author, inexplicably, has become as calm as he was earlier agitated. 'J'épuise en quelque sorte mon malheur d'avance', as he states in *Les Confessions* (I: 585). Despite connections with the Luxembourgs and the Prince de Conti, Rousseau is a public figure in his own right, and the authorities hold him responsible for his unortho-doxies. They condemn and burn the books; he escapes arrest by fleeing, and departs from Montmorency in the direction of Geneva.

Throughout the seven years from 1756 to 1762, the fragmentary autobiographical intention of the first Spring at l'Ermitage slowly develops to a point where Rousseau can act on it directly. In 1759 or 1760, he begins to collect documents and letters pertaining to his past and present. He even begins to copy his own letters. At the end of 1761, he receives a specific external stimulus, a letter from Rey, the publisher, urging him to write an account of his life (*C. C.* IX: 368–9).

Rousseau's first major step to autobiography occurs early in 1762, with the apparently informal, remarkably graceful *Lettres à Malesherbes*. These are written during yet another severe illness, in the recurrent expectation of death. The author desires, before dying, to explain 'les vrais motifs de ma conduite' and 'mon état moral dans ma retraite' (I: 1138). The link between the beginning of the auto-biography and the imminence of death is an important one, as is the fact that Rousseau begins what will become a long-winded enterprise in letter form, directly addressing his remarks to a respected and indulgent reader. Taken together, the two circumstances support his curious conviction that, in 1762, he renounces literature for 'la sphére étroite et paisible pour laquelle je me sentois né' (I: 515). In Rousseau's mind, autobiography will involve a type of writing unrelated to his literary pursuits between 1749 and 1762. He no longer has to think, or to invent; he will simply 'write himself'. An uncritical presupposition of this order is conceivable only in a writer who is in the process of creating a genre unto itself, or transforming an old genre into a completely new mould. The autobiography itself will be the best gauge of this naïve yet lucid attitude.

In the next chapter, we shall return to Rousseau in the final period of his writing career, just as, later in this chapter, we shall return to many of the pre- and para-autobiographical texts just mentioned. But let us now turn from biographical considerations to investigate the more general significance which writing has for Rousseau. More exactly, what motivates him to construct and to try to live his life in a world of the text?

## The Construction of a Textual World

The terms 'imaginative universe' and 'textual world' have surfaced from time to time in my discussion, employed in an interchangeable and as yet undefined manner. They are hardly confined to this reading of Rousseau. Whenever a critic wants to refer to a global unity of an author's works, or to the background and range of intention from which particular works are said to emerge, a term such as 'imaginative universe' inevitably appears. Since the techniques of New Criticism in America (since the 1930s, at least), close attention has been paid to the internal mechanisms of a work, as opposed to its representational, 'realistic' dimension. If the work suffices unto itself and is an immanent source of meaning, the critic does not need to leave its boundaries (even to refer to the author) to interpret it. The attribute of enclosed coherence can be detached easily from the individual work, given more general status, and something like a textual world comes into existence.

My own use of this notion will take the form of a demonstration of its scope and limits within Rousseau's works. By reconstructing in progressive stages the way in which he creates his textual world, I hope to bring the notion into sharp relief and make it a believable concept. The strategy here comes from the autobiographer himself, and is only as valid as his project.[8] It is intended to give my reading unity while marking a transition from experiential to rhetorical structures. The need for such a concept stems from the self-referential aspect of any sort of autobiographical analysis – whether of Rousseau's life by the author, or of Rousseau's work by the critic. Each undertaking involves a specular moment when unity (of personal identity) and understanding (of the autobiography) seem possible. Parenthetically, this is why the opportunities and pitfalls of autobiographical writing parallel and shed light on those of interpretation in general.

### 'Jouissance' and Distance – Memory and the Pont du Gard

The first question one must ask when examining the construction of a textual world is: why does Rousseau write? One possible line of response is that writing gives him pleasure.

Since Rousseau himself emphasizes 'l'extrême difficulté que je trouve à écrire' and 'la peine qu'ils [mes manuscrits] m'ont coûtée' (I: 114), the gratification of writing must be of an unusual sort. 'Pleasure' is used in this context to suggest the sense of the French word 'jouissance'. It implies an indefinite erotic experience, not gratification in a specific sexual object. In fact, the act of writing fosters 'jouissance' in Rousseau because of the distance between the author and the actual world around him. To take this distance is the first step in his creation of a textual world.

A striking demonstration of the connection between distance and 'jouissance' occurs in Book VI of *Les Confessions*, in Rousseau's description of the journey where he encounters Mme de Larnage. A young man at this stage of the narrative, the author recalls the affair as the most successful sexual episode of his life. 'Je puis dire que je dois à Made de Larnage de ne pas mourir sans avoir connu le plasir', he states. 'Je me gorgeai, je m'enivrai des plus douces voluptés. Je les goutai pures, vives, sans aucun mélange de peines, ce sont les prémiéres et les seules que j'aye ainsi goutées . . .' (I: 253). The seductive and enlivening powers of this older woman come at a fortuitous moment, both for Book VI, which lags badly before the sexual adventure, and for the young Rousseau, who is physically lagging and on his way to Montpellier for medical treatment. 'Le medecin qu'il me falloit' reaches him sooner than anticipated. Not to be denied,

voila Made de Larnage qui m'entreprend, et adieu le pauvre Jean Jaques, ou plustot adieu la fiévre, les vapeurs, le polype, tout part aupres d'elle, hors certaines palpitations qui me restérent et dont elle ne vouloit pas me guérir. (I: 249)

So much for Rousseau's psychosomatic illness! Mme de Larnage reads his symptoms properly and treats him to a better, more direct expression of desire – erotic enjoyment. The author leaves no doubt about this aspect of 'jouissance' in the episode.

Where, one must ask, is the distance?

An obvious, inviting indication of distance is Rousseau's persona during the affair.

En se familiarisant il falloit parler de soi, dire d'où l'on venoit, qui l'on étoit. Cela m'embarrassoit; car je sentois très bien que parmi la bonne compagnie et avec des femmes galantes ce mot de nouveau converti m'alloit tuer. Je ne sais par quelle bisarrerie je m'avisai de passer pour Anglois. Je me donnai pour Jacobite, on me prit pour tel; je m'appelai Dudding, et l'on m'appela M. Dudding. (I: 249–50)

With disarming simplicity, reflected in the syntax of *Les Confessions*, the young Rousseau introduces himself to his travelling companions under a new name. The selected pseudonym places him in the favourable role of a melancholic English aristocrat. It combines an assumption of social standing with an acceptable, even romantic explanation of his illness. Melancholy, a spiritual disease of the wealthy, signifies nothing more than a diverted or unrequited sexual impulse. The supposed 'bisarrerie' of Rousseau's behaviour is thus less pronounced than he would have the reader believe. Whether consciously or unconsciously picked, the name 'Dudding' implies a highly appropriate role for the young traveller's needs. It makes his suffering elegant.

If one takes the persona as an indication of distance, it is possible to argue that Rousseau's pleasure derives largely from his masking of himself. This departure from everyday identity would provide the distance necessary for sexual gratification. A reading or argument can be valid without being entirely appropriate, however. It is no doubt true that Rousseau becomes a man, in the sexual sense of the word, only when he is an 'other' man, and that the pseudonym is as necessary for their erotic enjoyment as is the insistence of Mme de Larnage. In fact, his misrepresentation probably heightens the passion of the affair. But the force of this explanation diminishes considerably when one examines the distinction between 'real' self and 'fictive' self apparently at play in the episode. To justify the equation between persona and distance, this opposition must hold. And as we saw in the 'réforme personnelle', the distinction tends to dissolve in the actions of Rousseau. When he plays the role of Dudding, the young man becomes the character, without ceasing to be as much Rousseau as he ever was. Criteria of truth and falsity, fictive and real, may well apply in the perspective of his fellow travellers, viewing him from outside. They do not apply to 'Rousseau', whose personal identity is suspended in a process of change which does not allow for such clear-cut oppositions.

The description in *Les Confessions* demonstrates this suspension best of all. Comparing his sudden self-confidence directly after the affair to his earlier lethargy, Rousseau declares, 'Je n'étois plus le même homme' (I: 263). Sexual fulfilment can induce this feeling of transformation, but to whom does the phrase refer? Not to Dudding – it is meant to refer to Rousseau, whoever and wherever he might be. If he is 'not himself' going into the affair with Mme de Larnage, he is no more himself coming out of it. Rousseau does not recover a stable personal identity until a later stage in the episode, and even then he will not so much recover it as construct it anew in the order of memory.

We should instead begin our argument at the moment of separation.

Enfin je la quittai . . . j'achevai ma route en la recommençant dans mes souvenirs, et pour le coup très content d'être dans une bonne chaise pour y rêver plus à mon aise aux plaisirs que j'avois goûtés, et à ceux qui m'étoient promis. (I: 255)

The end of the sexual affair marks the beginning of Rousseau's reconstitution of the experience in memory. Memory is a new sort of affair, involving a series of substitutions and a change of temporality from the encounter with Mme de Larnage. Rousseau first of all attributes his ease of recollection to the unaccustomed luxury of a 'bonne chaise'. But the comparative in the description ('plus à mon aise') also suggests an implicit contrast between the carriage as the site of memory and the various sites of the affair itself, and a primacy of the act of memory over the act remembered. If a 'bonne chaise' in eighteenth-century France is as much a symbol of sexual power and conquest as its twentieth-century equivalent, the automobile, these substitutions become very plausible. Among literary parallels, Mme Bovary and Leon come readily to mind, or, better yet, Laurence Sterne's Mr Yorick, travelling in *A Sentimental Journey through France and Italy*, who pauses in his *désobligeant* in Calais, catches sight of a pretty woman, and puts his carriage into a see-saw while setting down her description in his journal. The enclosed comfort of a vehicle which travels finely and rapidly through space lends itself to the temporal travel of memory. It is difficult to determine whether Rousseau, in the current episode, is more pleased by the past erotic event or by the equally erotic process of transforming it in his mind.

Other remarks in *Les Confessions* confirm the suggestion above. Speaking of his affection for 'Maman', Rousseau states, 'Je la quittois pour venir m'occuper d'elle; autre caprice que je n'excuse ni n'explique, mais que j'avoue, parce que la chose étoit ainsi' (I: 181). He distances himself from the presence of the actual woman in order to come to her more fully in the presence of her image. Instead of being a hardship, separation is but the first step towards greater enjoyment.

In the episode with Mme de Larnage, the priority of imagined over lived experience concerns only the process of memory. But it will apply just as well to the writing activity, which presupposes a comparable distance. 'Je me souviens qu'une fois Made de Luxembourg me parloit en raillant d'un homme qui quittoit sa maitresse pour lui écrire', Rousseau remarks. 'Je lui dis que j'aurois bien été cet homme-là, et j'aurois pû ajoûter que je l'avois été quelque fois' (I: 181). This line of thought recalls Rousseau's behaviour with Sophie d'Houdetot, in which his constant shuttle from expectation to remembrance and back again precludes any actual, physical consummation. It also recalls the fictional character Saint-Preux, in *La Nouvelle Héloïse*, whose passion for Julie is sustained and fulfilled primarily by the writing and copying of letters – from Meillerie, from Paris, even from within the same house. Taken to its extreme, Rousseau's preference for memory over the experience itself creates a ludicrous situation.

Any penchant in excess is ludicrous, however, and the sequence presented in Book VI of *Les Confessions* in fact helps to clarify the question of personal identity. In *Émile*, Rousseau makes memory the key to a coherent and unified sense of self. The most basic discriminations arise only at this level of experience, in his view, no matter what distance memory presupposes from an actual event.

C'est à ce second dégré que commence proprement la vie de l'individu: c'est alors qu'il prend la conscience de lui-même. La mémoire étend le sentiment de l'identité sur tous les momens de son existence, il devient véritablement un, le même, et par conséquent déja capable de bonheur ou de misére. (IV: 301)

Later in *Émile* he reiterates the same thought in somewhat different terms.

Ce que je sais bien c'est que l'identité du *moi* ne se prolonge que par la mémoire, et que pour être le même en effet, il faut que je me souvienne d'avoir été. (IV: 590)

When personal identity is conceived as a temporal prolongation held together by the continuity of memory, the reasons for the young Rousseau's pleasure at remembering his affair become clear. Only in retrospect does the event become in any sense his. Until he gives it meaning for himself, Mme de Larnage embodies a powerfully ambivalent force. In one sense, she returns him to himself, renewed, cured of illness, and initiated into the mysteries of the body. But in another sense, she is a threat. For the change in Rousseau's personal identity can occur only through a disruption of this same identity, and engenders an instability of which the pseudonym is the most specific symptom. Although he needs this external, threatening force, Rousseau also wants to neutralize it. Leaving Mme de Larnage permits himself to return to himself, and to incorporate the transformation which she precipitates into a continuous identity. Her presence in memory is no longer physical; it is the presence of a significant image, held in a subjective space.

'J'achevai ma route en la recommençant . . .' – we must conclude that, for Rousseau, the affair with Mme de Larnage begins to take on meaning after it is over. The substitution of the 'bonne chaise' is a first stage in this process. But it is not the last. For the image of Mme de Larnage still possesses Rousseau, and informs his fantasy in the future tense ('plaisirs . . . qui m'étoient promis'). At this point, since he still plans actually to return to her, the episode is not fully closed. The first stage of memory therefore gives way to a final substitution and more extreme process of recollection. These consign both the woman and Rousseau's image of her to an intense oblivion. The paragraph in Book VI narrating the separation continues in a single movement from 'enfin je la quittai' to the description of a second experience, as unusual as the affair itself. Rousseau recounts:

On m'avoit dit d'aller voir le Pont du Gard; je n'y manquois pas . . . C'étoit le premier ouvrage des Romains que j'eusse vu. Je m'attendois à voir un monument digne des mains qui l'avoient construit. Pour le coup l'objet passa mon attente, et ce fut la seule fois en ma vie. Il n' apparte-noit qu'aux Romains de produire cet effet. (I: 225)

Mme de Larnage and the Pont du Gard: two superlatives ('la seule fois de ma vie') in one week. The first is a companion of physical intimacy; the second, a monument in 'silence' and 'solitude', 'au milieu d'un desert' (I: 256). They are not just parallel and sequentially distinct events in Rousseau's trip to Montpellier. The young traveller moves from the intimate company of another individual to an edifice built on an impersonal scale. One replaces the other, in a contrast which dramatizes the shift from living experience to writing. This shift can occur implicitly, in memory, or explicitly, in *Les Confessions*:

On se demande quelle force a transporté ces pierres énormes si loin de toute carriére, et a reuni les bras de tant de milliers d'hommes dans un lieu où il n'habite aucun . . . Je me perdois comme un insecte dans cette immensité . . . Je restai là plusieurs heures dans une contemplation ravissante. Je m'en revins distrait et rêveur, et cette rêverie ne fut pas favorable à Madame de Larnage. Elle avoit bien songé à me prémunir contre les filles de Montpellier, mais non pas contre le Pont-du Gard. On ne s'avise jamais de tout. (I: 256)

The juxtaposition of presence and absence in Rousseau's text, of bodily warmth and the overpowering remains of a dead civilization, could not be more striking. Flesh has become stone – the qualitative transformation which we noticed in reverse order in the birth of the statue in *Pygmalion*. There Rousseau conveyed the drama of an aesthetic object which enters the order of actual existence. He moves now in the opposite direction, transforming lived experience into the 'other world' to which Galathée belonged. Though only a few days in the past, Mme de Larnage is like a monument, pertaining to a level of memory at which Rousseau effectively 'forgets' the actual woman in order better to 'remember' her. His distance from the affair is now absolute, and he demonstrates the true measure of his 'jouissance' through his wonder at the Roman relic, which he appreciates by transferring his sympathies from the lady. He may evoke her charms, praise her generosity, revere her sexual favours. But he will not return to her. The obstensible qualms which he mentions later to justify his change of heart – qualms about the fifteen-year-old daughter, or about being found out in the Dudding role – are self-congratulatory and quite secondary to the reverie by the Pont du Gard.

A comparison with *Pygmalion* helps to show the symbolic importance of the sequence we have followed in Book VI. By 'substitution', we do not mean to suggest that the Pont du Gard simply takes the place of Mme de Larnage in Rousseau's affections. Instead, it symbolizes the paradoxical filiation between aesthetic and actual orders of experience. To Rousseau, the actual woman has become as foreign to lived experience as his very aesthetic conception of Roman times, when great men built great monuments, and supposedly lived in peace and prosperity. But, at this aesthetic level, the affair gains a definite clarity and continuity, which permit Rousseau to make his way to it whenever he desires, and especially when he wants to write about it. At the point of no return, a new sort of return becomes possible. For the monument, like any symbol, functions in several different ways simultaneously. It separates the lovers, marking the moment when the young man leaves behind Mme de Larnage, and disaffects himself from his affair with her. In the form of a bridge, however, it also symbolizes a continuity across this distance, a more fundamental memory, and a greater 'jouissance'. When the specific function of the bridge is mentioned, the text provides a very telling image for this continuity.

What is apparently a bridge, Rousseau states, is in fact an 'aqueduc' — a stone edifice designed to convey flowing water (I: 256). Ensuring the connection between living flesh and written stone, there is the flowing of the author's memory. If the aqueduct symbolizes a qualitative transformation, it also shows a symbolic passage from past to present, from one moment of experience to another. It links Rousseau to the affair, even as it separates him from it. His high sense of playfulness and satisfaction as he relives the experience in the narration of *Les Confessions* is the best evidence of this paradoxical connection.[9]

If this particular demonstration of the connection between distance and 'jouissance' in one episode is convincing enough to allow for generalization, we have made a major step toward understanding why Rousseau should want to transform the world of lived experience into a textual world. Only in an aesthetic mode does he fulfil the promise of wholeness implicit in his life, and construct an affective order of time which he can call personal and his own.[10] That Rousseau himself chooses to individualize this process does not invalidate it, nor alter its basic implication — namely, that lived experience is participation in an open creation, which calls for recreation and temporary completion and closure in a work of art. This position, both an assumption and an implication of our reading, is necessary to justify a positive explanation of the paradox of *Pygmalion*, and of its counterpart in Book VI. At its fullest, experience must already be in some sense aesthetic, just as the genuine work of art provokes and sustains a dialogue with life. Rousseau does not forsake experience in the unusual sequence of events which we have followed. Distancing himself, he endows them with significance, producing a small unity of personal value which is the greatest source of 'jouissance' in the episode.[11]

## Renunciation and Control

The complementary concepts of renunciation and control also help to account for Rousseau's construction of a textual world. They are, in part, ramifications of the 'jouissance'/distance connection. Through renunciation the author establishes distance from the actual world. The control he is then able to exercise in imaginative space is an additional source of pleasure. Both terms shed new light on the motivation to write.

The act of renunciation is inextricably bound up with pleasure in Rousseau, and is not always noticeable in its own right. At the surface

of the episode just considered, for instance, the young Rousseau's
denial of Mme de Larnage is less direct than our symbolic reading
makes out – the two are travelling companions, bound to separate
Renunciation occurs only in his decision not to return to her, and thus
remains implicit. Rousseau's fictional works point more directly to the
basic importance of renunciation. The dictum about Julie – 'l'art de
jouir est pour elle celui des privations' – is perhaps the most succinct
expression of the general tendency visible in Saint-Preux's relationship
with Julie, Bomston's with Laure, or Émile's with Sophie. Through his
characters, Rousseau never tires of promoting renunciation as the way
to (delayed) gratification.

For Rousseau himself, renunciation has the curious effect of dis
appearing into the elaborate edifice of his own form of 'jouissance' –
the delayed gratification of the written work. His reasons for building
a textual world on this basis are in any event not exclusively sexual
More importantly, they stem from a particular manner of taking in o
comprehending experience. Consider the continuation of Rousseau's
earlier description of his difficulty and pain in writing:

Non seulement les idées me coûtent à rendre, elles me coûtent même
à recevoir. J'ai étudié les hommes et je me crois assez bon observateur
Cependant je ne sais rien voir de ce que je vois; je ne vois bien que ce
que je me rappelle, et je n'ai de l'esprit que dans mes souvenirs. De
tout ce qu'on dit, de tout ce qu'on fait, de tout ce qui se passe en ma
présence, je ne sens rien, je ne pénétre rien. Le signe extérieur es
tout ce qui me frappe. Mais ensuite tout cela me revient: je me rappelle
le lieu, le tems, le ton, le regard, le geste, la circonstance, rien ne
m'échappe. Alors sur ce qu'on fait ou dit je trouve ce qu'on a pensé
et il est rare que je me trompe. (I: 114–15)

The tone of these remarks is characteristically extreme. The final
affirmation resembles the outspoken phrase, 'je sens mon cœur', at the
start of Les Confessions. But Rousseau refers here to persons and
objects outside himself, and the gist of his message is that presence i
incompatible with meaning. Articulated in the contrapuntals of 'tout'
and 'rien', the passage argues that delay and distance are necessary fo
comprehension. In the present moment, possessed by a 'signe
extérieur', Rousseau discerns nothing: 'je ne pénétre rien'. In memory
however, 'tout cela revient'. This is an abstract version of the affai
narrated in Book VI of Les Confessions. Rousseau moves from sig
to meaning, from 'dire' to 'penser', and possesses the event by under

standing it. 'Rien ne m'échappe.' The present moment has passed, but its significance has been retained.

For Rousseau, renunciation of the actual present is a preliminary to conferring more lasting duration on it in an order of meaning. The negative aspect of this moment in his creative act should not be under-estimated. Something is lost, or seems to be lost, in the process of turning away from the present. But Rousseau renounces with the positive intention of attaining the entirety of what he initially denies himself. And in return for his self-imposed limitation, he gains an expanded power of control.

If renunciation tends to disappear within Rousseau's textual world, the complementary concept of control is on the contrary all too visible. Pervasive, vast in scope, it cannot be reduced to specific instances without turning the author into a clumsy behavioural scientist.[12] And since Rousseau exercises control largely in an imaginative rather than an actual domain, to interpret him in this manner is to confuse the issue. We might fruitfully examine his exercise of control under two different headings, defensive and elaborative.

Rousseau exercises control defensively in order to determine the image of himself which he offers to others for recognition. This is a protective and almost automatic reflex. It has only an indirect connection with the notion of a world of the text which we are investigating. But it certainly influences his decision to write, and should be mentioned. Several lines from *Les Confessions* convey Rousseau's reasoning. 'J'aimerois la societé comme un autre', he states,

si je n'étois sur de m'y montrer non seulement à mon desavantage, mais tout autre que je ne suis. Le parti que j'ai pris d'écrire et de me cacher est précisément celui qui me convenoit. Moi présent on n'auroit jamais su ce que je valois, on ne l'auroit pas soupçonné même. (I: 116)

Presence and meaning continue to be incompatible, but the moment of incomprehension which is part of Rousseau's way of giving sense to the world now afflicts the judgements whereby others appreciate him. Renunciation in this case simply signifies his withdrawal from social life, in order to craft in writing a version of identity which corresponds to his own feeling of personal worth. The juxtaposition of 'écrire' and 'me cacher', however, is not fortuitous. Constructing a textual world, Rousseau shows his identity only to the extent that he also hides it, in a dialectic of self-revelation and self-concealment which we first noticed in the performance of *Le Devin du village*.

The desire to present oneself in the best possible light is certainly not restricted to Rousseau, nor to any writer. Every person undergoes the same process of reconciling the image he has of himself with that which others have of him, whatever the specific images involved may be. But Rousseau, more than most, desires to achieve a reconciliation on his own terms. His decision to write cannot be separated from the strong impulse to protect himself against misunderstanding. In constructing a textual world, he establishes an imaginary space of immediate recognition, where image and reality are not at odds. The need to control extends on to the printed page, where Rousseau gives scrupulous attention to every detail, including his own, idiosyncratic punctuation.[13] The imaginary reconciliation eventually rebounds upon him forcefully in direct proportion to his controlling effort (as in the *Dialogues*). The social nature of language then asserts itself and Rousseau discovers that he is 'tout autre' even within the circuit of his own writings.

The second, more interesting direction in which Rousseau exercises control is elaborative – he trades his renunciation of the actual present, whether in the temporal sense of the present moment or in the social sense of the actual presence of other individuals, for the freedom to work possibility into a world of his own design. Although it is difficult fully to dissociate the defensive from the elaborative use of control, they are quite different. Control as elaboration reflects the constructive nature of Rousseau's writing activity, and continues the positive explanatory framework begun in our discussion of 'jouissance' and distance. We can approach it best through an anecdote from Book I of *Les Confessions*, where the elaborative process of memory is taken up directly within the writing activity.

### *'La grande histoire': Writing*

Rousseau recounts 'la grande histoire du noyer de la terrasse' at a pivotal moment in Book I. Aside from its intrinsic interest, it is the first story narrated for purely personal pleasure, the first explicitly *selected* episode in the autobiography. In the narrative sequence of Book I, Rousseau recounts it after the episode of the broken comb has brought injustice to Bossey. A 'veil' covers the countryside, nostalgia overcomes the author. As if suddenly realizing that he can never return to the imagined, whole innocence of childhood, Rousseau focuses with poetic precision on scattered details from the past – powerful but isolated debris of memory – evoking them as single and sharply etched images.

After this recitation of happy objects and lost composure, he goes on to add, 'Je sais bien que le lecteur n'a pas grand besoin de savoir tout cela, mais j'ai besoin, moi de le lui dire' (I: 21). The *need* to write about the past coincides with the author's awareness of an irreversible entry into time. 'Toutes les petites anecdotes de cet heureux age' then surge to mind, demanding expression, and Rousseau, mock-serious, makes a bargain with the reader: one story for the five he could tell: 'Je vous fais grace des cinq, mais j'en veux une, une seule; pourvû qu'on me la laisse conter le plus longuement qu'il me sera possible, pour prolonger mon plaisir' (I: 22).

Expelled from the paradise of childhood, the author's first act is to narrate an anecdote. He responds to his feeling of a loss of time in experience by prolonging the pleasure gained in the time required to tell a tale. The story of the 'noyer de la terrasse' is the tale chosen, and the fact that it constitutes an apparently gratuitous, peripheral addition to the autobiography partially justifies our approach to it.[14] This approach consists of reading the *énoncé*, the content of the story, in the light of Rousseau's stated need to recount any story. I read it as an allegory for the process of writing in general. In its shift of attention from what is written to the act of *énonciation*, this critical approach mirrors the shift from life to text which we are following in the present chapter.[15]

It is not surprising that a story chosen to prolong the pleasure of the author as he recounts it should itself be a story about a similarly prolonged activity – the construction of an 'aqueduc' (I: 22–4). The anecdote is too long to quote fully, but its plot is fairly simple. M. Lambercier, a childhood guardian, has planted a walnut tree on the terrace at Bossey to provide shade. Rousseau and his cousin, fascinated by the daily watering of the tree, decide to plant one of their own. With great pride they secure a willow sapling, and watch it grow. But the process of watering which initially caught their fancy soon presents a problem. Water is scarce and remote. To conserve their planting, they conceive the idea of a tunnel to lead water from the nut tree when it is attended to by M. Lambercier. After great effort and prolonged labour, they complete the plan. The watering hour arrives, the duct functions perfectly – until the joyful shouts of the boys attract the attention of M. Lambercier. He notices, becomes angry, and destroys the tunnel, 'criant à pleine tête, *un aqueduc, un aqueduc*' (Rousseau's emphasis).

The tale, which at this point might have turned into a saga of punishment (like the episode of the broken comb, with which this narrative sequence begins), ends instead on a humorous note. The boys plant another tree elsewhere, and take to repeating the absurd cry of 'aqueduc'. Time moves ahead without pain or loss. When Rousseau closes the anecdote, it is by moving the narrative quickly forward to 1754, and to his visit to Geneva, when 'un de mes plus agréable projets . . . étoit d'aller à Bossey revoir les monumens des jeux de mon enfance, et surtout le cher noyer' (I: 22–4).

Having selected it for the telling, Rousseau narrates his anecdote with far more zest than this summary can suggest. But the elements for a reading are present in our outline. One sense of the tale concerns the authority of M. Lambercier, the paternal figure at Bossey. Rousseau imitates his act of planting a tree, and thereby effectively engages in a sexual challenge: who can grow bigger faster? The trees are an appropriate symbol at the level of the *énoncé*, since Rousseau is a mere stripling at the time of the anecdote, growing and sprouting in much the same manner as his willow sapling.

But although the trees are an essential feature of the story, they are not its most important element. It is the watering which fascinates the boys, and which Rousseau pin-points as the centre of the tale.

Chaque jour, ardens spectateurs de cet arrosement, nous nous confirmions mon cousin et moi, dans l'idée très naturelle qu'il étoit plus beau de planter un arbre sur la terrasse qu'un drapeau sur la bréche; et nous résolumes de nous procurer cette gloire, sans la partager avec qui que ce fut. (I: 22)

The boys' desire to plant their tree stems from their observation of the watering, and no sooner have they staked their claim, as it were, than a lack of water presents the second, more significant challenge in the story. Rousseau describes at length the efforts made to construct the tunnel and to divert the flow of water from the 'noyer' to the 'saule'. He emphasizes the difficulty, the delays, the expectation, and suspense. This work provides him with his major pleasure within the story. 'Rien ne nous rebuta. *Omnia vincit labor improbus*' (Labour conquers all), he states (I: 23). The process of constructing a water-course thus functions in the anecdote as the analogue of the delay, work, and gratification of constructing a written text. For the pleasure which Rousseau desires to receive from telling the story occurs within it at the exact moment when water flows freely from one tree to another.

A peine achevoit-on de verser le prémier seau d'eau que nous
commençames d'en voir couler dans notre bassin. A cet aspect la
prudence nous abandonna; nous nous mîmes à pousser des cris de
joye. (I: 23)

The over-reaction of M. Lambercier and the specific word which
characterizes it – 'aqueduc' – confirm the importance of the flowing
water. They confer recognition on the boys' initial challenge, even as
the tunnel is destroyed. Anyone can plant a tree, but who can build
an aqueduct? To judge from Book VI, only the Romans produced such
monuments. And yet here, in Book I, the autobiographer has succeeded
in giving a small episode from his past all the grandeur of the Pont du
Gard. As they escape the wrath of M. Lambercier to plant a tree elsewhere, the boys recall their triumph in these terms, 'répétant entre nous
avec emphase: *un aqueduc, un aqueduc*' (I: 24). Rousseau uses the
word eight times in all as the story reaches its climax and comes to a
close.

Although the most evident link here is coincidental, it is instructive
to compare the episodes in Books I and VI. In each, Rousseau faces a
sexual challenge, and indirectly, by distance or by work, achieves
satisfaction. In each, pleasure is capped when an 'aqueduc' (of whatever
size) symbolizes the continuity of the experience. When he encounters
a monument to which Mme de Larnage cannot compare, Rousseau
leaves her to the past. But the Pont du Gard, which marked their
separation, also reminds us that he can return to her in memory
whenever he desires.

The elements of the story in Book I are similar, but the direction
and register in which the story unfolds now have changed. Just before
'la grande histoire du noyer de la terrasse', the child Rousseau has
reached a point of no return, and the author himself is excluded from
the past. As author, Rousseau's recourse is to recount for his own
pleasure a tale which allegorically conveys the elaborative power and
control of writing. Through a textual act, he replaces himself in the
past. Better yet, he makes the past present. The aqueduct serves in both
instances as a concrete image for the bridge between past and present.
And the water flowing along it, which will eventually become a
dominant element as his textual world takes on determinate shape and
constancy, symbolizes the temporal continuity which this world
affords.

It is important for our argument not to confuse an allegorical with
a reductive approach to the text. Rousseau clearly does not say all that

my analysis imputes to him, and it makes no sense to spoil a good story by tying down all its constituent parts in a one-to-one correspondence with a supposed 'deeper' meaning. The analysis we are slowly developing must justify itself by its coherence, by which I mean the degree to which it is able to hold different elements and levels of meaning in a fruitful tension. In this we emulate Rousseau. The tension in 'la grande histoire du noyer de la terrasse' is not just between the elaborations and prolongations within the story and those in the act of recounting it, as though one could be reduced to the other. It is primarily the tension of Rousseau's pleasure as he holds the various parts of himself − child, writer, the temporal difference and sexuality of both − together in the act of writing. Constructing a textual world in which he is at once absolutely distant from and immediately present to himself, Rousseau maintains this tension through time, and satisfies his major desire.

We shall only gradually appreciate the importance of allegory in Rousseau's move to autobiography and in the autobiography itself. But it is possible to indicate a fundamental connection between allegory and time. Generally speaking, this rhetorical category corresponds in structure to the duality of the instant, examined in Chapter I. Like the labour of the child described in Book I, the construction of a world of the text is a lengthy process; it is the second, elaborative stage of reverie transposed into the register of writing. The elaboration itself, however, has its source in a primary, instantaneous intuition of possibility. As Rousseau states, in one description of the inspiration in 1749, 'A l'instant de cette lecture, je vis un autre univers' (I: 351). The instant contains an entire imaginative universe, or offers the possibility of creating such a universe. In the indeterminacy of pure possibility, Rousseau's imaginative universe quite literally *is not*. A pregnant image of memory, the modulations of sense in a told tale, come into existence only because a person renounces the actuality present in the instant, steps into the open possibility which is also present there, and fashions it into some form of text.

In constructing a text, therefore, Rousseau retains the virtual significance of his life in an articulate order of meaning. In so doing he alters his relation to time. Anyone who has enjoyed a book can appreciate the fact that it has its own time, separate and different from the time of everyday experience, yet not entirely separate, and often more powerful and fulfilling. The apparently unnecessary anecdote from Book I is an example of this phenomenon, seen from the author's point of view. As he writes, Rousseau experiences time on his own terms, because he engages it, at least initially, in the mode of possibility. His choice to live through writing, aesthetic in its basic intent, is closely connected to the desire to overcome a temporal destiny. For we must consider the virtual 'is not', the possibility which the author exploits, in two very different lights. In one sense an opportunity for creation, in another it is temporal loss, an absence, ultimately a sort of death within life. The aesthetic response to this existential dilemma is to convert non-being into the life of the work.

Here we must tread very carefully. For what is the relation between the life of the work and the life of its author, or between the world of the text and the world of experience? According to our thesis, it is within his textual world that Rousseau elaborates the identity which he calls personal and his own. And yet this same elaboration has a vein of impersonality running through it. We cannot affirm that the aesthetic conversion of experience fundamentally changes the temporal destiny of an author. The duality of the instant extends into the work itself, disjoining it from its creator even as it offers him the possibility of giving meaning to his existence. Life and work can never be fully identified. And since it is the property of an authentic work to express this existential situation in its own terms, we might anticipate that allegory will be the rhetorical category whereby Rousseau renders the time of his life in the first text of the autobiography.[16]

Rousseau's word for the temporal aspect of the aesthetic conversion is 'prolonger'. It suggests the sense of personal duration that he experiences in writing and achieves in the text.[17] But the word also implies that, for him, the text develops as a continuous extension of the time of everyday experience. Rousseau becomes intransigent in this attitude only in the autobiography, which he begins after having elaborated a highly determinate aesthetic vision in earlier texts. By then, however, he no longer engages time in a possible mode; he feels more at home in the world of the text than in the world which he has renounced. He wants to identify himself with his vision.

## Completeness

Thus far, we have referred to Rousseau's imaginative universe as a virtual domain, 'outside' and separate from the actual experience renounced in order to construct it. But as we follow the active elaborations of memory and writing in the passages from Books I and VI, possibility begins to assume body and form. We can imagine the 'other world' of reverie gradually acquiring a definite structure and personal character in a textual world. The interpretation here attempts to trace the emergence of this world, rather than to analyse any of its specific traits. The trait most specific to Rousseau, however, is perhaps his fervent personal espousal of his fictions as he elaborates them. The sense of personal identity which most men and women construct in the actions and relationships of their lives, he constructs in the act of writing. Rousseau's choice does not change the fundamental terms of his existence, but it certainly changes the register in which he lives it. From our readings, a shift from experiential to rhetorical structures should be partly visible. Soon we shall explore the author's textual world as an 'inside', enclosed, and apparently complete domain, where writing is act, and rhetoric a guide to experience itself.

One crucial question remains to be answered before this final step in our analysis. Why should Rousseau construct an entire world in language? We refer to it as a finished entity, in a conceptual description not justified by the passages analysed thus far. They show the author engaged in an activity, a process of construction; this is very different from showing a textual world as a completed totality. What motivates Rousseau toward this end? How and why does he want to reach it?

*Émile* provides perhaps the most telling principle and rationale for Rousseau's effort. We have seen that he works to control time by creating the temporal order of the text. But he also works to control desire in the name of happiness. As the Mentor states:

En quoi donc consiste la sagesse humaine ou la route du vrai bonheur? Ce n'est pas précisement à diminuer nos desirs . . . Ce n'est pas non plus à étendre nos facultés . . . mais c'est à diminuer l'excés des desirs sur les facultés, et à mettre en egalité parfaite la puissance et la volonté. (IV: 304)

Un être sensible dont les facultés égaleroient les desirs seroient un être absolument heureux. (IV: 304)

In Rousseau's definition of 'le bonheur', force is equivalent to will, and human desires do not exceed the human capacity to satisfy them. This ideal of equilibrium is the source both of his most conservative tendencies and of his extraordinary will to power. Taken to its logical conclusion, the position requires that the limits of the world be or become coextensive with the limits of the individual within it (and the equivocation between 'be' and 'become' produces an intense alternation between conservatism and the need for radical change). Force and will are balanced in the conception of natural man presented in the second *Discours*, but only because the will as such has not yet been developed. Similarly, the educational methods employed by the Mentor in *Émile* maintain the balance primarily by denying the student any will of his own. The key to the Mentor's policy, significantly, is the imagination:

C'est l'imagination qui étend pour nous la mesure des possibles soit en bien soit en mal, et qui par consequent excite et nourrit les desirs par l'espoir de les satisfaire . . . Le monde réel a ses bornes, le monde imaginaire est infini; ne pouvant élargir l'un retrécissons l'autre; car c'est de leur seule différence que naissent toutes les peines qui nous rendent vraiment malheureux. (IV: 304–5)

The imagination upsets the delicate equilibrium between human desires and human powers; and the Mentor does not hesitate to contradict Rousseau's own childhood experience, as related in *Les Confessions*, on behalf of his principle. Withhold the development of the imagination, he argues, as long as possible. Not coincidentally, one of the major tasks implied in this dictum concerns the relationship between language and the world. This is one area in which it appears that control may fruitfully be exercised:

Reserrez donc le plus qu'il est possible le vocabulaire de l'enfant. C'est un très grand inconvénient qu'il ait plus de mots que d'idées, qu'il sache dire plus de choses qu'il n'en peut penser. (IV: 298)

Like the excessive desire generated by the imagination, the surplus implicit in a symbolic non-individual use of language must be kept within the bounds of what is represented.

En général ne substituez jamais le signe à la chose que quand il vous est impossible de la montrer. Car le signe absorbe l'attention de l'enfant, et lui fait oublier la chose réprésentée. (IV: 434).

*Émile* suggests here that language shares the volatile nature of the imagination, and recommends a balance between word and world, like that between force and will. Following Austin, we might label it a constative balance. If each word is no more than an index, exhausting its meaning through its relation to a referent, it becomes possible to promote or to achieve happiness on a linguistic basis.[18]

But the text of *Émile*, which argues for this elementary though pervasive form of control, is in fact a more sophisticated version of the same principle. To ensure happiness by restricting the imagination and by keeping words in constative balance with the world is one option. But what option remains when, as in Rousseau's case, the imagination is fully inflamed at the age of six, generating more desire and more vocabulary than can ever be fulfilled or matched in the world? (I: 8; 62.) Though crudely put, the question leads to a fundamental aspect of Rousseau's move to autobiography: his Promethean exercise of will in writing. For he retains the basic principle of *Émile* − that the limits of the world coincide with those of the individual in it − and acts upon it in a way quite different from the Mentor. Instead of submitting language to the world, Rousseau creates a world through language. The constative ideal flip-flops into its opposite, a performative ideal. Both assume the completeness and totality which are built into Rousseau's goal of happiness. His positive imaginative exercise of control in the construction of a world of the text finds its mirror image in the total control employed by the Mentor in his 'negative' education of Émile.

### 'L'Élysée': the World of the Text

With the issue of completeness laid down at least in theory, we might test the notion of a textual world in a specific example from Rousseau's text, the description of Julie's garden in Part IV of *La Nouvelle Héloïse*. It forms the second of two long letters which Saint-Preux writes, shortly after returning to Clarens, to his *ami* and faithful reader, Milord Edouard.[19] The name of the garden and its unusual location within Clarens indicate its emblematic status. 'L'Élysée' is not of this world; it belongs in the 'other world' of the author's imagination. Despite its proximity to the rest of Clarens, despite the sense of open space which Saint-Preux receives once he has entered it, the garden remains invisible and detached from its actual surroundings. 'Ce lieu, quoique tout proche de la maison est tellement caché par l'allée couverte qui l'en sépare qu'on ne l'apperçoit de nulle part', Saint-Preux writes (II: 471). Within but not contained by Clarens, 'l'Élysée' constitutes a world unto itself. It is the most complete and rigorous instance of Rousseau's textual world to be found within his writings. What is it like? How does it work?

It is not by chance that a fictional work should be the immediate source for a complete version of the author's imaginative universe. In contrast to earlier passages, which conveyed progressive stages in the constructive process, and which come from *Les Confessions*, the end-point of the process, a textual world in its totality, can be expressed only in a work of fiction. Because *La Nouvelle Héloïse* is itself an expression of an 'other world', and 'l'Élysée' a secondary haven within the haven of Clarens, Julie's garden is doubly removed from any form of actuality. Rousseau therefore benefits from an exceptional opportunity to reflect on his imaginative enterprise as if it were a closed whole. We shall return later to this simple but basic point, but at present it is helpful when one considers the two major external sources for the conception of the garden. The informal, apparently natural landscape of the English garden – the source most frequently mentioned by critics – certainly constitutes an important historical reference for understanding 'l'Élysée'. In a lengthy discussion between Saint-Preux and M.de Wolmar, Rousseau definitely favours the English garden against the authoritarian, rigid lines of the Classical French garden. However, we must not conclude from this one source that Julie's garden refers primarily to nature, or to a reality outside the text.[20] A second, less mentioned source for the same passage is the *Roman de la rose*, from which Rousseau draws not only many of the specific details of 'l'Élysée', but also its character as an enclosed, separate space. This literary source places the description of the garden in an intertextual network and implies that it refers, not to nature, nor to an historical phenomenon, but to another written work. That the *Roman de la rose* itself should lie within the allegorical tradition of medieval romance is but a further confirmation of the fact that we are entering a linguistic, stylized, and imaginative domain.[21]

The prerequisite for indulging oneself in the sumptuous detail of 'l'Élysée' is, predictably enough, a renunciation. In terms of the plot and character development of *La Nouvelle Héloïse*, Saint-Preux and Julie must renounce their *amour*; in terms of the symbolic topoi of the novel, their renunciation involves the rejection of another type of landscape and locale, Saint-Preux's. In Part I, the young lover has been forced to retreat to the mountains across the lake, and the countryside around him expresses the torment of his passion. 'Ce n'étoit pas seulement le travail des hommes qui rendoit ces pays étranges si bizarrement contrastés', he writes Julie from Meillerie;

La nature sembloit encore prendre plaisir à s'y mettre en opposition avec elle-même, tant on la trouvoit différente sous divers aspects. Au levant les fleurs du printems, au midi les fruits de l'automne, au nord les glaces de l'hiver: elle réunissoit toutes les saisons dans le même instant, tous les climats dans le dans le même lieu, des terrains contraires sur le même sol, et formoit l'accord inconnu par tout ailleurs des productions des plaines et de celles des Alpes. (II: 77)

The temporal and emotional contradictions reflected in Meillerie run their course in the first half of the novel, when the sublime disorder of *amour*, of differences united in one 'instant', is given full sway. But when Saint-Preux returns to Clarens in Part IV, the tempo of the novel has changed. He comes as a friend, and Julie has married Wolmar, the dispassionate husband required of her by her father. 'L'Élysée' is in many respects the token of the lovers' renunciation. Julie conceives of the garden during walks with her father; it replaces the 'bosquet' of the lovers' first kiss in Part I; in Part VI, Wolmar himself feels called upon to rebuke Saint-Preux, after his indiscreet mention of the 'bosquet', 'Apprenez à respecter les lieux où vous êtes; ils sont plantés par les mains de la vertu' (II: 485).

But although renunciation is the starting point, the *sine qua non* of Julie's garden, this negative aspect seems to vanish as soon as one discovers the unexpected beauty and freshness inside it. Saint-Preux's first impression is that he has reached 'le lieu le plus sauvage, le plus solitaire de la nature', so unspoilt is 'l'Élysée' (II: 471). When Julie reminds her visitor that the site was an uncultivated, dry plot of land only seven years earlier, during his first stay at Clarens, he is understandably bewildered.

Ma foi, lui dis-je, il ne vous en a coûté que de la négligence. Ce lieu est charmant, il est vrai, mais agreste et abandonné; je n'y vois point de travail humain. Vous avez fermé la porte; l'eau est venue je ne sais comment; la nature seule a fait tout le reste et vous-même n'eussiez jamais sû faire aussi bien qu'elle. (II: 472)

Julie replies: 'Il est vrai . . . que la nature a tout fait, mais sous ma direction, et il n'y a rien là que je n'aye ordonné' (II: 472). For all its unspoilt appearance, 'l'Élysée' is in fact a highly artificial construction. Nature is present, but only to the extent that Julie harnesses it to her own ends. With the same sort of performative power which Rousseau uses to establish a world of language, she creates a domain so complete and artful within the enclosure of the garden that it can be mistaken for nature. 'L'Élysée' reflects her wishes, is ordered according to her design, is finally no more than an extension of herself. Since nature works under Julie's control, the transformation has required a minimum of cost and labour on her part. The human work required to construct the garden thus disappears, such that art becomes a second nature, providing all the effects of a Meillerie, but without its contradictions.

After walking through and examining the garden, Saint-Preux begins to understand its workings. His bewilderment diminishes. But one feature, the most important of all, continues to puzzle him. 'Je comprends à présent tout le reste', he tells Julie, 'mais ces eaux que je vois de toutes parts' (II: 474).

Water is indeed a key aspect of the garden. There was no water in the area before 'l'Élysée' was created (II: 472). And the beauty of the garden is not only enhanced, but depends on the complex water flow throughout it.

Toutes ces petites routes étoient bordées et traversées d'une eau limpide et claire, tantôt circulant parmi l'herbe et les fleurs en filets presque imperceptibles; tantôt en plus grands ruisseaux courans sur un gravier pur et marqueté qui rendoit l'eau plus brillante. On voyoit des sources bouillonner et sortir de la terre, et quelquefois des canaux plus profonds dans lesquels l'eau, calme et paisible réflechissoit à l'œil les objets. (II: 474)

After Julie indicates the source of the water (which we shall examine in a moment), Saint-Preux explains how so much is accomplished with so little effort in the garden.

Je vis alors qu'il n'avoit été question que de faire serpenter ces eaux avec économie, en les divisant et réunissant à propos, en épargnant la pente le plus qu'il étoit possible, pour prolonger le circuit . . . Ces mêmes ruisseax courant par intervalles sous quelques larges tuiles recouvertes de terre et de gazon au niveau du sol formoient à leur issue autant de sources artificielles . . . Enfin la terre ainsi rafraichie et humectée donnoit sans cesse de nouvelles fleurs et entretenoit l'herbe toujours verdoyante et belle. (II: 474)

The 'economy' of 'l'Élysée' is based on the careful control of a single element, which branches and interconnects in a complex, prolonged 'circuit' through the garden. That water is this element should come as no surprise — it was an implicit presence in the Roman aqueduct in Book VI of *Les Confessions*, and the object of Rousseau's fascination and labour in the childhood anecdote from Book I. The omnipresence of water in Julie's garden calls now for more deliberate consideration.

In a work entitled *L'Eau et les rêves*, Gaston Bachelard develops a premise which may aid the present reading. 'Pour qu'une rêverie se poursuive avec assez de constance pour donner une œuvre écrite,' Bachelard states, pour qu'elle ne soit simplement la vacance d'une heure fugitive, il faut qu'elle trouve sa *matière*, il faut qu'un élément matériel lui donne sa propre substance, sa propre règle, sa poétique spécifique.

In Bachelard's thesis, the imagination feeds directly on impressions from the natural world, material intuitions which Rousseau would call sentiments, not sensations. When a *rêveur* becomes an author, he employs these material intuitions to give body and duration to his imaginative vision. The 'constance' of the natural element is a key to the transformation of reverie into the more sustained and articulate form of the text.

If we may follow the hypothesis that water serves as the 'matière' through which Rousseau gives literary shape and body to his reverie, the intricate 'circuit' of rivulets, streams and springs in Julie's garden provides a consistent, adequate image for the unity and complexity of the textual world which results from this process. Passages from other texts certainly support this interpretation. One thinks of the reveries by the Lac de Bienne, described in the fifth 'Promenade'. The surrounding, indeterminate body of water embodies in this instance the end-point of Rousseau's authorship, when his imaginative universe dissolves back into the natural element through which it first took form. More aptly, in the present context, one recalls the importance accorded to water in the description of the transition between Nature and Culture in the *Essai sur l'origine des langues*.[22] 'Cet age heureux', as Rousseau calls the transitional stage, is in fact not so much a period of time as an instant of abrupt change. But his major aim as a writer is to give duration to this 'in-between' in the imaginative space of the text. And 'l'Élysée' offers an image of the author's textual world in its most refined and complete form, when its various parts are held together in a prolonged, paradoxical state of unity and separation, matching the profound suspension of time in the second half of *La Nouvelle Héloïse*.

Within the bounds of the textual enclosure, as within Julie's garden, the principles of happiness set forth in *Émile* can be said to hold. But Saint-Preux's initial question must first be answered: what is the source of the water? The description of 'l'Élysée' at this point shows the limits of Rousseau's textual world, and goes beyond them. Julie replies:

Elles viennent de là, reprit-elle, en me montrant le côté où étoit la terrasse de son jardin. C'est ce même ruisseau qui fournit à grands fraix dans le parterre un jet d'eau dont personne ne se soucie. M.de Wolmar ne veut pas le détruire, par respect pour mon pere qui l'a fait faire: mais avec quel plaisir nous venons tous les jours voir courir dans ce verger cette eau dont nous n'approchons guére au jardin! Le jet d'eau joue pour les étrangers, le ruisseau coule ici pour nous. Il est vrai que j'y ai réuni l'eau de la fontaine publique qui se rendoit dans le lac par le grand-chemin qu'elle dégradoit au préjudice des passans et à pure perte pour tout le monde. Elle faisoit un coude au pied du verger entre deux rangs de saules; je les ai renfermés dans mon enceinte et j'y conduis la même eau par d'autres routes . . .

. . . Nous descendimes par mille détours au bas du verger où je trouvai toute l'eau réunie en un joli ruisseau coulant doucement entre deux rangs de vieux saules qu'on avoit souvent ébranchés . . . Presque à l'extrémité de l'enceinte étoit un petit bassin bordé d'herbes, de joncs, de roseaux, servant d'abruvoir à la voliere, et derniere station de cette eau si précieuse et si bien menagée. (II: 474−5)

The water coursing through l'Élysée has its source outside the private enclosure, in a 'jet d'eau' constructed at great expense by the Baron d'Étange. Though this source supplies her own garden, Julie's remarks leave little doubt as to how the reader is meant to regard the Baron's amusement. Disused at present (like the 'bosquet' from Part I of the novel), it is saved from destruction only by M. de Wolmar, who in modified form has assumed the paternal role in the household through his marriage to Julie. The 'jet d'eau' is foreign to the exceptional intimacy of 'l'Élysée', and interests outsiders. These it can interest only at their own expense; for in the run-off toward the lake, by the 'fontaine publique', the water from the terrace fountain 'degrades' the open pathway, and is wasted for everyone. Much better, the passage seems to suggest, that Julie has diverted the stream, put it to use in the gentle waterplay of her own garden, and even incorporated one portion of the run-off, that part running between two lines of willow trees, directly into her own garden.

Despite the separation and closure which make it so attractive, 'l'Élysée' and its intricate water system are therefore made possible only by a link to an open, relatively rude water source. In the context of our previous analyses, the opposition between open and closed economies corresponds to the very different functions of the imagination in the first and second stages of reverie, and in *amour* and *amitié*. And if we follow Bachelard's thesis, this correspondance is not simply fortuitous. The water inside and outside 'l'Élysée' would be a material embodiment of the imagination – the force which informs and is shaped in Rousseau's textual world. The description of Julie's garden confirms our earlier distinctions within a complex system of spatial relationships within the fictional world of *La Nouvelle Héloïse*. How does one make sense of them?

The figure of the Baron d'Étange is an obvious starting point. His role in the epistolary novel is a limited but crucial one, much like the role of the 'jet d'eau' in the passage above. The reader learns very little about him directly, since the Baron only writes one letter. That letter epitomizes his purpose in the novel: it is a demand that Saint-Preux renounce Julie. To the extent that the father keeps the lovers separate, he contributes vitally to the production of the text, which consists mainly of letters written to bridge the distance that he imposes. But Rousseau rarely brings the Baron to the fore, and as a result it is easy to neglect him. What little one learns about him indirectly, through the letters of others, suggests a die-hard aristocrat, 'inconstant et volage' (II: 323), who breaks easily into violence. His one attack on Julie, followed by a near-incestuous scene of reconciliation with her, precipitates her miscarriage, denies Saint-Preux paternity, and considerably influences the development of the novel (II: 174, 178; 345). This explicit act of force tends to get diffused in the virtuous and sentimental mood of the major characters, however. Once the Baron has succeeded in making Wolmar the husband of his daughter, he disappears, enveloped in a 'procès' unrelated to Clarens. The Baron's implicit presence in the fountain just outside Julie's garden is one of the few references to him in the second half of the novel.[23]

The spatial separation between the 'jet d'eau' and 'l'Élysée', and especially Julie's tone as she indicates the connection between the two, make clear that this father figure has no place within Rousseau's textual world. But although he must be kept at a distance from the well-watered, interlaced beauty of the garden, the father is also the final source of its value. 'A grands fraix', someone must work to bring water. If Julie herself expends little time and effort in creating her haven, it is only because the Baron d'Étange has already provided the indispensable element. The parallel with 'la grande histoire du noyer de la terrasse', where the paternal figure was also a source of water, underlines an undeniable sexual aspect of the symbolic configuration of 'l'Élysée'. Julie's father, the one truly male character in *La Nouvelle Héloïse*, expresses himself, in the remaining trace of his presence at Clarens, in an extremely masculine manner. The 'jet d'eau' shoots skyward and, via a 'fontaine publique', rushes without delay to the

lake below. Saint-Preux and Wolmar pale beside this spectacle of
arbitrary passion. The rational Wolmar functions in the novel as a
surrogate for the Baron, keeping his fountain intact without ever
demonstrating his energy. Saint-Preux, to whom the role of castrated
Abelard is implicitly given in the title of the work, is all too quick to
accept the burden of renunciation continually forced upon him.
Despite their obvious differences, furthermore, these two characters are
alike in fundamental ways. Each comes to Clarens without property;
each is without a proper name ('Wolmar' and 'Saint-Preux' are
pseudonyms); and each depends for identity on his relationship to
Julie. Instead of being father figures, Wolmar and Saint-Preux sooner
resemble the domesticated, severely trimmed trees which stand guard
in two rows over the 'joli ruisseau' where Julie incorporates the stream
directly into her garden.

In contrast to the 'jet d'eau' outside, the garden is a reassuring
maternal haven. A fitting symbolic expression of the type of relationship which it offers can be found in the large community of birds which
make their home there. 'Cela est charmant', Saint-Preux remarks when
he discovers that the Wolmars have not caged the birds. 'Je vois que
vous voulez des hôtes et non pas des prisonniers.' 'Qu' appelez-vous
des hôtes?' Julie quickly rejoins. 'C'est nous qui sommes les leurs'
(II: 476).

Since the word 'hôte' signifies both guest and host, Julie's reply
is in a sense unnecessary. Rousseau is himself sensitive to the ambiguity,
as he says in a note added to the 1763 edition of the novel. Calling
attention to Julie's inexact use of the word, Rousseau states that 'hôte'
is 'corrélatif de lui-même' (II: 476, note a). But the author does not
change the diction of his character. It indicates well the reciprocal roles
of giver and receiver inside the garden. In the slightly larger context of
*La Nouvelle Héloïse*, the relation between the bird community and the
Wolmars is a microcosm of the harmonious interchange between master
and servant at Clarens. In a yet broader framework, it is one further
instance of the reversibility of interest and identity in Rousseau's
version of *amitié*.

Saint-Preux, ever-curious, asks how the keepers of 'l'Élysée' are able
to enjoy the company of so many 'habitans volontaires' and receives
a lengthy reply from M. de Wolmar on various procedures of animal
husbandry. The explanation concludes on an explicitly political,
familial note. 'Voila comment la patrie des peres est encore celle des
enfans, et comment la peuplade se soutient et se multiplie', Wolmar

pontificates (II: 477). This statement is quite suggestive, given the fundamental lack of agreement between father and child in the first half of the novel, and the political overtones of the second. Once the Baron d'Étange has forced the issue of renunciation and left the scene, an improbable reconciliation flourishes across generations and across unequal levels in family and community. It is a long step from Julie's garden to Rousseau's political theory, but inasmuch as the latter belongs to the textual world for which 'l'Élysée' is a symbol, his contractual mode of politics pertains directly to the convention of *amitié*, and to the constructive, controlled uses of artifice and language visible in this setting.[24]

What, finally, is involved in the distinction between the maternal and paternal aspects of 'l'Élysée', in the claim that Rousseau's textual world is a closed maternal haven separate from, but dependent on, an open-ended paternal source outside its boundaries? The distinction enjoys strong support when the spatial configuration of the garden is interpreted in the light of characters and events from *La Nouvelle Héloïse*. But it is also helpful not to remain entirely within the terms of Rousseau's epistolary novel, in order to avoid turning descriptive insights into a causal explanation. If one makes the error of identifying Rousseau with a specific character or characters (and Julie is the most plausible single candidate), it quickly follows that his writing enterprise is no more than an effort to achieve unity with a maternal figure. This interpretation may have its applications, but 'l'Élysée's adequacy as an emblem of the author's imaginative universe suggests a wider significance. This may have more to do with Rousseau's experience of time and of language than with the specific characters and spatial setting involved in the description of the garden.

The beginning of another major pre-autobiographical text, *Émile*, is relevant here. 'O mére tendre qui sus t'écarter du chemin', Rousseau exhorts early in that work,

... fais de bonne heure une enceinte autour de l'ame de ton enfant. Cette enceinte un jour sera ton azile, un autre en peut marquer le circuit, mais c'est à toi de planter la barriére. (IV: 58)[25]

In outline, this passage repeats the symbolic configuration of 'l'Élysée'. The Mentor, the author's narrative spokesman who lays out the apparently natural 'circuit' of education in *Émile*, combines the functions of Julie and Wolmar in *La Nouvelle Héloïse*. He is no less paternal or maternal. Plot and characters aside, what is at stake in both works is a structure of reversibility or reciprocity fostered within the confines of an enclosed, carefully tended space – the 'azile' mentioned above, or Rousseau's world of the text. To the extent that particular texts involve various characters, the question of family relations, or social inequality, reciprocity takes the forms of *amitié*, mother-child harmony, or political reconciliation. But these very different thematic issues are all linked. They are written dramatizations of Rousseau's intuition in reverie, of the forceful coincidence between the virtual and the actual, of the instant when time itself seems to become reversible. The pairing of the Mentor and Émile, the spatial setting of Julie's garden, and even the word 'hôte' reveal a single fundamental concern.

## Conclusions

The structure of reciprocity that I have singled out as a feature of Rousseau's textual world takes on meaning and value only when embodied in individual contexts, characters, and aesthetic dramatizations. The reading here does not account for differences across particular texts or for developments within Rousseau's career. The repetitive mode of his temporal intuition, whether in the lived experience of reverie or in its dramatization in writing, goes hand-in-hand with changes in personal attitude and in the genre and rhetorical mode of his texts. These deserve attention in their own right. We followed some of Rousseau's shifts of attitude in the biographical section of the present chapter. The shifts of genre and rhetoric within his textual world will be analysed presently.

Another qualification goes to the centre of the exposition here. It concerns the issue of completeness. The very fact that Rousseau is continually engaged in writing, from 1749 onwards, and involved with very different types of texts and instances of reciprocity within them, demonstrates clearly that his textual world never reaches the degree of totality and stability which an abstract presentation inevitably implies. We have analysed 'l'Élysée' according to the principle of happiness in *Émile*, as though it embodied the author's imaginative universe as a finished whole, a complete entity. But although completeness may be implicit in the concept of a world of the text, or within the boundaries of 'l'Élysée', does it obtain in the practice of Rousseau's life and writings?

At this juncture we might return to an earlier point, that a work of fiction is the immediate context for Saint-Preux's description of the garden. Here also one must consider both the inside and the outside of 'l'Élysée'. Julie's garden is set in a fictional work, which itself manifests the closure and totality to be found within 'l'Élysée'. These attributes belong to *La Nouvelle Héloïse* inasmuch as it is a work, separate from its author. Consonant with the analysis of reverie, where Rousseau's profound sense of wholeness occurred at a depersonalized level, the attribute of wholeness passes into the elaborated text, the aesthetic object, when he realizes his intuition in the act of writing. It does not derive from, nor truly sustain, the personal identity of the author.

This thought runs counter to an equally important strand in our argument. For Rousseau is undoubtedly involved in the work, as he is in reverie. It is in the text, I have claimed, that he elaborates his 'autre monde'. He desires its unity and consistency as his own. The life of the author is in fact so intimately bound up with his aesthetic construction that it is easy to confuse the two, and to make the completeness of the work a part of personal identity. Since the unity and consistency of 'l'Élysée' is imaginative, however, and belongs to the life of the work, not to Rousseau, it is possible to call this transfer a 'mistake'. The author's life and identity are fundamentally open. They demand an elaboration and creation of sense such as we find in the extended circuit of the garden. Otherwise it would be impossible to distinguish between life and art; Rousseau would lose his connection with other individuals; the process of elaboration itself would end, or enter a mechanical, deterministic cycle of repetition. In terms of the spatial imagery in Saint-Preux's description, the 'jet d'eau' outside 'l'Élysée' is an open, foreign source, without which the intricate network of streams and water-play within the enclosed, private sanctuary would run dry.

The double edge in this interpretation may seem to warrant either pessimism or a surreptitious, childish optimism. The latter predicament is outlined in a return visit to the garden which Saint-Preux makes alone. He describes it at the end of his letter. 'Avec l'empressement d'un enfant je suis allé m'enfermer', Saint-Preux writes. He quickly resorts to a vocabulary of fantasy. In 'l'Élysée', 'l'homme de goût qui vit pour vivre, qui sait jouïr de lui-même', enjoys 'la jouissance de la vertu'; 'on peut s'y plaire soi-même', 'se plaire avec soi-même' (II: 482, 484, 487). The thread of self-complaisance in Rousseau's work is strong enough to cause many readers and critics to reject both the author and the work. It is nowhere more evident than in these lines.

But Rousseau's dualism is not so strict that it becomes a sterile pessimism or an immature optimism. Instead, it encourages the active constructive process which we have analysed throughout this section, and which has been present in each of the passages discussed. No matter how far the young traveller separates himself from Mme de Larnage, the 'aqueduc' will vividly bring her back to him in memory. No matter how distant the author of *Les Confessions* feels himself from the past of the tunnel digger at Bossey, the present act of writing brings the two together. No matter how arbitrary the 'jet d'eau' of the Baron d'Étange, the water from it finds a way to Julie's garden, and to the textual world of her creator. Rousseau makes this passage, the passage of water, of the imagination, and through time; but he makes it in the elaboration of a work, in the creation of a temporal duration of which fiction is a constituent element.

The major tension in this interpretation is unresolved. I present the notion of a textual world as a necessary fiction, indispensable for the autobiography and for our analysis of it. But it can never be made complete. The tension arises from the fact that Rousseau constructs his sense of personal identity in a domain and under conditions which are not themselves personal. His personal identity is an image. Subsequent chapters have thus to chart Rousseau's continued development, when the 'autre monde' of his imaginative universe and 'this world' of his actual existence come into contact in the writing of the autobiography.

Though unresolved, our discussion has at least followed Rousseau into the act of writing. As an author, in the process whereby he brings the structures of lived experience into focus within a textual world of his own design, he demonstrates the sense of a brief statement — a rhetorical question from Bachelard:

De l'homme ce que nous aimons par-dessus tout, c'est ce qu'on en peut écrire. Ce qui ne peut être écrit mérite-t-il d'être vécu?[26]

### Pre-autobiographical Rhetoric

When Rousseau reviews the major circumstances of his life in 1756 in Book IX of *Les Confessions* in order to help the reader understand the saga of l'Ermitage, he includes a lengthy summary of his works in progress at the time. Texts have become an appreciable, even determining influence on his existence: if he had written this text instead of that one, the reader is told, the story might have turned out differently. Had the *Écrits* of l'Abbé de Saint-Pierre been but worthy of more attention, there would have been no time for the dreaming from which emerged *La Nouvelle Héloïse* . . .

The notion of a textual world and mode of existence allows us to consider seriously this otherwise whimsical proposition, and to examine Rousseau's move to autobiography from the perspective of the texts which precede it. Autobiography arises as an option for Rousseau the writer only after he has elaborated an imaginative universe in which he can find his identity. Our brief biographical section sketched several external aspects of this elaboration. The analysis just concluded has attempted to clarify some of the motives which lead him to construct a world of the text, how it takes form and consistency in a life, and what it might look like as a completed whole. The world of writing now begins to rival the world of experience. When Rousseau attempts to make them coincide, in the autobiography, the distinction between rhetorical and experiential structures will be difficult to maintain. But our analysis has yet to examine in what specific ways Rousseau develops his textual world. Before we examine how he identifies himself in and through it, we must observe this rhetorical development.

## Genre and Expression

Rousseau's writing covers a remarkable range of genres. Drama, social theory and criticism, musical theory, fiction, and pedagogy all claimed his attention at different times. If he did not remain for long in any one genre, the author is equally at home, when he wants to be, in all of them. He disregards only poetry. Apart from a few youthful and undistinguished verses, Rousseau creates his lyrical effects through discursive prose.

Since different modes of writing allow an author varying expressive possibilities, Rousseau's use of one genre rather than another provides an important index of the development of his imaginative universe. It is significant, for instance, that musical and dramatic genres are his primary artistic interest before 1756. Arriving in Paris in 1742, Rousseau carries the *Projet concernant de nouveaux signes pour la musique* and an unfinished comedy, *Narcisse*. Both will have matured and, in different form, have reached the public by the time of his departure for l'Ermitage. But to neither does the author return with any concentration thereafter. The *Dictionnaire de musique*, published in 1765, comprises an expanded version of articles which Rousseau wrote for the *Encyclopédie* in 1749. His late musical compositions serve mainly as a personal distraction, like the interest in botany.

*La Mort de Lucrèce*, a promising and serious-minded dramatic sequel to *Narcisse*, breaks into fragments early in its development, in 1754. Only in *Pygmalion*, the short but important pantomime of 1762, does Rousseau briefly return to and combine these early artistic interests.

It is possible to interpret the development of the social criticism and overtly political writing along similar lines. First awakened during the Venice sojourn of 1743–4, and the occasion for his initial literary success, Rousseau's theoretical interest in political and social life tends to be subsumed within fictional genres after 1756. There is one major exception to this tendency – *Du Contrat social*. Yet when we examine the author's own comments on the matter in *Les Confessions*, the impulse, if not the final labour, for the work stems from the earlier period:

J'avois encore deux ouvrages sur le Chantier. Le Prémier étoit mes Institutions Politiques. J'examinai l'état de ce livre, et je trouvai qu'il demandoit encore plusieurs années de travail. Je n'eus pas le courage de le poursuivre et d'attendre qu'il fut achevé pour executer ma résolution. Ainsi renonçant à cet ouvrage, je résolus d'en tirer ce qui pouvoit se détacher, puis de bruler tout le reste, et poussant ce travail avec zèle, sans interrompre celui de l'*Émile*, je mis en moins de deux ans la derniere main au *Contrat social*. (I: 516)

The 'résolution' in question – to give up writing books (I: 515) – leads Rousseau to salvage rather than to expand a work which, dating from 1754, belongs already to his past (I: 394, note 10). Although we may well regret this decision, since it isolates *Du Contrat social* from both the context and the more extensive text in which it was initially conceived and might have been interpreted, Rousseau's words suggest that one regard the work alongside the less famous *Dictionnaire de musique*, as a reworking and refinement of previous material. Later texts of political interest, primarily the *Lettres écrites de la montagne, Projet de constitution pour la Corse,* and *Considérations sur le gouvernement de Pologne* are either specific applications of theories articulated in *Du Contrat social*, or polemical self-justifications of the author himself. Rousseau never abandons social and political writing (as he did in drama), nor trivializes it (as in the case of music). But his theoretical interest in the field ceases to renew itself at a relatively early stage in his writing career.

Given this shift of interest, which occurs in 1756, and which,

Rousseau claims in commenting on the *Lettre à d'Alembert*, extends even to his writing style (I: 503), it seems reasonable to focus attention on works written thereafter. Of these, two stand out. *La Nouvelle Héloïse* and *Émile* embody the author's imaginative universe at its fullest, and offer an extended and sustained vision of reality. The first achieves this mainly in its development of the network of relationships which make up the closed community of Clarens; the second through the Mentor/Émile pairing, which constitutes a self-enclosed and (with the inclusion of Sophie) self-perpetuating island of naturalness. Because the autobiography will employ many themes and formal configurations which Rousseau elaborates in these two texts, they are highly relevant to it. *La Nouvelle Héloïse* and *Émile* contain both indirect and direct autobiographical references, so much so that a liberal definition of autobiography might authorize one to name and analyse them as preliminaries to *Les Confessions*. As it is, their para-autobiographical status invites interpretation from the perspective of Rousseau's life and later texts. Examples quickly come to mind: Saint-Preux and Wolmar as Rousseau's ambivalence between unrealized passion and impotent moralizing in his affair with Sophie d'Houdetot; the Mentor's attitude toward Émile as that of Rousseau to his ideal self, or to the reader; Julie as a prefiguration of the Rousseau of the *Rêveries*. The interpretative possibilities, some of them fascinating, are more than plentiful.

There are good reasons to approach the pre-autobiographical texts in a more restrained manner, however. Most importantly, we must avoid anachronism. All of Rousseau's writing, looking back from the autobiography, can be seen to contain strong autobiographical elements. The author's personal involvement in even the earliest texts easily leads one to interpret them as incomplete versions of an intention which comes into its own with *Les Confessions*. One freely reconstructs a 'development' in the chronology, of which *La Nouvelle Héloïse* and *Émile* would be major stages, aimed at reaching a 'final stage' which has already been predetermined. The move to autobiography would then occur along a seamless, teleological line, until the author realizes a potential he has supposedly possessed throughout his writing.

As Rousseau writes, however, he surely discovers his intention, and creates new rhetorical possibilities for himself with each successive text. His autobiography, if present as a tendency from a very early age, is possible as an elaborated work only at a certain juncture of his writing career. Then it is not exhausted in one textual form, but generates a rhetorical momentum all of its own, according to particular tensions which do not obtain in earlier writings. The moment for interpretation of the autobiographical implications of *La Nouvelle Héloïse* and *Émile* will arrive if and when, examining the autobiography itself, we can use them to expand and confirm analysis of problems which arise there. At present, let us trace a path within the pre-autobiographical texts where Rousseau's tendency turns into a willed (even if unconsciously willed) decision to take up a rhetorical option. This will involve some mention of his abandoned and unfinished texts which shed light on his rhetorical development.

### Dialogue: Letters and Readers/Fiction and Reality

It is possible to focus discussion of the many pre-autobiographical works on two different but interrelated issues. The first concerns the tension between the poles of fiction and reality. Rousseau first introduces this polarity in the second *Discours* in his account of the transition between a hypothetical, fictional version of natural man and the reality of social inequality. *La Nouvelle Héloïse*, the first text to take shape after the author's decision to leave Paris (though not the first to be published), consciously plays one side off against the other: are the letters 'real' or fictional? The 'real' beginning of *Émile*, contrasted with its fully fictional ending, is a later example of the same tension.

The second issue concerns the position of the reader in Rousseau's texts between 1756 and 1765. A glance over the list of works published during this period reveals a simple but rather remarkable fact. With the exception of *Émile* and *Du Contrat social*, every major text takes the implicit or explicit form of a letter. On the one hand, Rousseau uses the convention of the public letter – for example, his *Lettre à d'Alembert*, *Lettre à Christophe de Beaumont*, and *Lettres écrites de la montagne*. These are very different texts, but share the fact that they reach two audiences simultaneously – the man (or work) to whom they are addressed as a response, and all the bystanders who read them. (The unsent *Lettres morales* and the unfinished *Lettres à Sara* remain private and unpublished, though not from any lack of willingness on Rousseau's part.) *La Nouvelle Héloïse* and *Émile et Sophie*, on the other hand, are two epistolary novels that rely on letters for plot development and dramatic effects. In the case of *La Nouvelle Héloïse*, the significance of Rousseau's choice of the epistolary form is increased when one considers the possible competitors contemporary to its inception. Neither *Les Amours de Claire et de Marcellin* nor *Le Petit Savoyard*, two abandoned projects, is cast in the letter form in which Rousseau feels so free to write during this period. Why, we must ask, does his writing develop in this way?

Because *La Nouvelle Héloïse* is Rousseau's major work in the epistolary form (as well as the most influential in the eighteenth century), critical mentions have been made of the aptness of the letter form (II: xxxiv–xxxvi). In a genre popularized by the English novelist Richardson, Rousseau projects his own personality through his letters. The use of 'personnes interposées', most evident early on in his plays, thus continues into Rousseau's later writing. But an epistolary form allows him to engage one voice at a time, in a discursive prose unconstrained by the conventions of drawing-room conversation or theatrical dialogue. The author can speak through a variety of voices while developing each one at length, uninterruptedly. In contrast to a play like *Narcisse*, which required public production and performance, Rousseau is now out of sight, alone in the silence of l'Ermitage while everywhere in the text.

The most important aspect of the letter form is not restricted to *La Nouvelle Héloïse* but is present in almost all the works I have referred to above. It is the dialogical structure that a letter automatically confers on the text. A letter is always addressed to someone, whether to Milord Bomston, the faithful *ami* and reader of Saint-Preux's fictional missives from Clarens, or to Christophe de Beaumont, a real interlocutor. A published letter reaches its reader only indirectly. We read Saint-Preux through Bomston, and are asked to listen in on the debate between Rousseau and Christophe de Beaumont. Because one reader is already identified as the addressee of the letter, the actual reader of the text has a freedom mirroring Rousseau's. Both remain disengaged from the world of the text, even as they may choose to be deeply involved in it.

This preponderance of the letter form is closely linked to our first issue, the tension between fiction and reality. Constructing or defending a textual world in his various epistolary works, Rousseau occupies a virtual position 'behind' them. To him corresponds an equally virtual reader, who is not identified with the reader which the text specifically denotes. Two levels of communication are thus implied. When examined closely, this duality concerns not only the two-tier, dialogical structure of the letter, but also the two categories of fiction and reality. In Rousseau's apologetic letters against Beaumont and Tronchin, the tension between fiction and reality occurs in the context of debate: who is right and who is wrong, who true and who false? In *La Nouvelle Héloïse*, it takes the different form of an indecision as to whether the letters in the novel are 'real' or not, whether Rousseau is editor or author. The question, odd as it may seem today, was tantalizing to readers in 1761.

By looking at the relation between fiction and reality in connection with Rousseau's uses of the epistolary convention, I unfortunately omit *Émile* from direct consideration. *Émile* can be said to resemble a letter only in one early sentence – 'c'est à toi que je m'addresse, tendre et prévoyante mére' (IV: 245). But the tension between fiction and reality surfaces strongly in other ways. What begins as abstract pedagogy slowly becomes a full-fledged novel. As Émile takes a name and assumes an identity of his own, Rousseau's voice fades into that of the Mentor. The student is at once general and fully individual; the Mentor both is and is not Rousseau. Only when Sophie is introduced does the text resolve the indecision in favour of the novelistic, and lead into a fully fictional, though unfinished epistolary sequel, *Émile et Sophie*.

It is not necessary, therefore, to discuss Rousseau's playful handling of fiction and documentary solely in terms of his use of the letter form in many pre-autobiographical texts. This approach is useful mainly because it is the most inclusive way to consider the wide range of texts involved. But, given the approach, it is possible to focus discussion on one specific text which exemplifies the issues in question – the second preface to *La Nouvelle Héloïse*, the 'préface dialoguée' between the author/editor of the novel and 'un homme de goût et de lettres' (II: 1342), 'R' and 'N'. Rousseau composed this short piece after completing the novel, in 1759. It comes directly between *La Nouvelle Héloïse* and *Émile*, the two main pre-autobiographical works.

I consider the 'préface dialoguée' to be exemplary because its two protagonists are the author and reader who remain 'behind' the authors and recipients of the letters in *La Nouvelle Héloïse*, and because they discuss no less than the issue of the real or fictional status of the work. 'Cette correspondance est-elle réelle, ou si c'est une fiction?' (II: 11) is the provocative question of 'N' at the outset of the dialogue.

## The Preface in Dialogue

In the Preface, Rousseau develops the fiction/reality distinction through the two notions of a 'Portrait' and 'un Tableau d'imagination'. 'N' defines them:

Un Portrait a toujours son prix pourvu qu'il ressemble, quelqu'étrange que soit l'Original. Mais dans un Tableau d'imagination, toute figure humaine doit avoir les traits communs à l'homme, ou le Tableau ne vaut rien. (II: 11)

If the letters of *La Nouvelle Héloïse* are real documents, written by real people, the text is a 'Portrait'. The novel would then cease to be fiction, and would have to be considered as a non-literary text, the autobiography of its characters. The peculiar style, content, and repetitiveness of the letters would be explained and validated in relation to the personalities of their authors, rather than by aesthetic standards. 'Un Tableau d'imagination', on the other hand, belongs to the category of fiction, and is constructed in relation to a 'modele commun' (II: 12). 'N''s distinction implies different criteria of judgement and appreciation. A 'Portrait' derives its force from the singularity and difference of the individual who portrays himself. The value of the 'Tableau d'imagination' derives from its capacity to represent 'l'humanité', as a novel contains characters with whom, in principle, all its readers can identify (II: 12).

'R' and 'N' judge *La Nouvelle Héloïse* from both perspectives, debating its merits without deciding 'N''s initial question.

N – Mais surement ce n'est qu'une fiction.
R – Supposez.                                                            (II: 12)

or:

R – Vous jugez ce que vous avez lu comme un Roman. Ce n'en est point un.                                                             (II: 13)

The uncertainty stems from 'R''s basic unwillingness to state to which category the text belongs. When pressed by 'N' to explain why he avoids answering, 'R' replies. 'Pour cela même que je ne veux pas dire un mensonge' (II: 28). This reply seems to suggest that either answer would be a lie, that the question does not admit of a final answer. When 'N' rejoins, 'Mais vous refusez aussi de dire la vérite?', 'R' quickly returns the issue to the reader's court: 'Comment osez-vous faire une question que c'est à vous de résoudre?' (II: 28).

This strategy is obviously not without its 'préciosité' and guile. Rousseau's preface-in-dialogue raises a question in order to say that it will not, or cannot, answer it. And in the meantime the author both attracts and disarms critical attention to his work. But the importance of his remarks extends beyond these immediate considerations. For the status of *La Nouvelle Héloïse* is placed directly in line with that of the first half of the second *Discours*, which Rousseau constructs fictitiously – 'Commençons donc par écarter tous les faits . . .' (II: 132) – only to proclaim its indispensability as a criterion of judgement for the present – 'dont il est pourtant necessaire d'avoir des Notions justes pour bien juger de nôtre état présent' (III: 123). In both texts, he wants to have it both ways, combining the liberties of the fabulist with the severities of the realist and moralist. The inhabitants of the State of Nature and of Clarens exist only as fictions, in 'l'autre monde' (II: 12). Yet this is a world which, Rousseau claims, influences one's capacity to live in this world.

The preface-in-dialogue also significantly anticipates the terminology of the autobiography. The 'Préambule de Neufchâtel', an early and important introduction to *Les Confessions*, will take up the distinctions of 'R' and 'N', without respecting their scrupulous indecision. 'Je veux tâcher que pour apprendre à s'apprecier, on puisse avoir du moins une piéce de comparaison; que chacun puisse connoitre soi et un autre, et cet autre, ce sera moi' (I: 1149). Rousseau's method for achieving this end is to conflate the 'Portrait' with the 'modele commun': in the autobiography, he promises to provide both 'l'image' of himself, and himself as 'modelle' (II: 1149). The terminology is almost identical across the two texts. It shows how the autobiographer is no longer content to use fiction as a mere guide, or even as a regulatory aid for judgement.

In *La Nouvelle Héloïse* and in other pre-autobiographical texts, Rousseau elaborates his 'autre monde' without yet making it *his* world. The natural man of the second *Discours* acquires personality and multiple social skills in the characters of the epistolary novel. He becomes a natural man, in a community of others like him. But Rousseau, the author, remains in a virtual position outside the letters which compose the textual world of the novel. Partly as a result of this rhetorical strategy, the work can oscillate between fiction and reality, in a seriously hypothetical mode.

N – . . . Certainement, si tout cela n'est que fiction, vous avez fait un mauvais livre: mais dites que ces deux femmes ont existé; et je relis ce Recueil tous les ans jusqu'à la fin de ma vie.

R – Eh! qu'importe qu'elles ayent existé? Vous les chercheriez en vain sur la terre. Elles ne sont plus.

N – Elles ne sont plus? Elles furent donc?

R – Cette conclusion est conditionelle: si elles furent, elles ne sont plus. (II: 29)

It is not exactly correct to say that the preponderance of the epistolary form in Rousseau's writing between 1756 and 1765 accounts for the creative tension between fiction and reality in the works of this period. The author's rhetorical choice obviously reflects his own expressive needs more than it creates them. But the present argument suggests that this choice does create the possibility of a new and different rhetorical choice at a later stage in Rousseau's life. Between the two poles of fiction and reality, in the state of a suspended conditional which he believes he resolves in the autobiography, the pre-autobiographical works make a bridge from a theoretical version of natural man to the full-bodied self-conception of *Les Confessions*. The move from the abstract to the personal in the account of Émile's education is one illustration of this extended pre-autobiographical development.

A more detailed discussion here would show how, in successive texts from 1756 onwards, Rousseau develops the voice, and even the actual expressions that he eventually employs in the autobiography. *Émile et Sophie*, among the last of the para-autobiographical texts composed before expulsion and exile, in 1762, is astonishingly close to the autobiography in tone. One gets the strong impression that Rousseau leaves the work unfinished because he would quite simply prefer to be narrating the story of his own childhood in Geneva rather than the adventures of a fictional character.[27]

The most important rhetorical aspect of the move to autobiography is not similarity or borrowing between texts. The key element is Rousseau's changing attitude as author to the hypothetical mode in which he constructs his imaginative universe. The works which best demonstrate this change are the *Lettres à Malesherbes* and *Pygmalion*, both written in the transitional year of 1762. In the first, Rousseau combines the epistolary convention of the pre-autobiographical period with his first major autobiographical statement. In the second, he depicts in pantomime an artist's effort to bring his aesthetic creation to life in this world – his own situation at the time. When Rousseau emulates Pygmalion, the autobiography is underway, and the tension between fiction and reality begins to take the rhetorical forms which we shall investigate in the next chapter.

## Language

One further issue remains to be investigated before we read Rousseau's autobiography — namely, language. Given an increasing emphasis on what has been termed the world of the text, it is important to possess some understanding of the medium through which the autobiographer confronts himself and his reader. Rousseau's acts as a writer are linguistic acts. While we have followed and given an explanation for his choice to live in and through the writing activity, we have not yet examined how language itself may affect his project.

The *Essai sur l'origine des langues*, a posthumously published work which has drawn major attention in recent years, contains much of Rousseau's direct reflection on language.[28] *Émile* also includes within its theory of education an implicit theory of language. Two aspects of language presented in these works have an impact on Rousseau's autobiography. The first is the figural basis of linguistic signification; the second, Rousseau's notion of 'la langue des signes qui parlent à l'imagination' (IV: 645). My brief analysis of them here aims to indicate significant points of contact between Rousseau's language theory and his autobiographical writing practice.

### Figural Naming

A primary thesis in the *Essai* affirms that language has its origin in human passions rather than human needs (*Essai*, p. 89).[29] Rousseau distinguishes between 'gestes' and 'paroles', between physical movement and voice, and asserts that all the needs of natural man could be fulfilled through gestural communication. 'Besoins moraux' or 'passions' (p. 95), on the other hand, are the reason for the invention of speech. Like sentiment, or moral sensation, the passions are among the attributes which distinguish man from animals. It is natural, in Rousseau's view, that language should derive from this human and moral source.

To invoke 'des besoins moraux, les passions' (p. 96) requires a further clarification of Rousseau's argument. What, more exactly, are the passions? Analysis of two of the more prominent among them, *amour* and *amitié*, indicates that they represent a highly ambivalent and even contradictory attitude on Rousseau's part. Furthermore, we know that the world of the text encourages the closed, intimate reciprocity of *amitié*, to the exclusion (but with the use) of *amour*. Language has its origins in the passions, we are now told; but it would be helpful if we could specify which, and how. The theory of language in the *Essai* could then shed useful light on the efforts of the autobiographer.

Rousseau, after the general statement of his thesis, does not directly offer much help in this regard. 'Ce n'est ni la faim, ni la soif, mais l'amour, la haine, la pitié, la colère, qui leur ont arraché les premières voix', he states (p. 96). This list of passions, if not complete, is certainly too diverse to answer our question. 'Amour' and 'pitié' both figure equally on it.

But a second thesis, 'Que le premier langage dut être figuré' (p. 97), contains an indirect response:

Comme les premiers motifs qui firent parler l'homme furent ses passions, ses premières expressions furent des tropes. Le langage figuré fut le premier à naître. Le sens propre fut trouvé le dernier. (p. 97)

Rousseau supports his claim here not by rejecting the notion of 'un sens propre' – which is essential for a figured expression – but by asserting that the initial 'sens propre', or referent, of a word is the passion which it expresses rather than the object which it represents. He expounds:

... pour m'entendre il faut substituer l'idée que la passion nous présente au mot que nous transposons; car on ne transpose les mots que parce qu'on transpose aussi les idées: autrement le langage figuré ne signifierait rien. (p. 97)

The best way to understand what Rousseau means by 'passions' in this context is to look at the example he chooses to illustrate his notion of figural language.

In the natural state, Rousseau states, a man meets other men. Man's first reaction, fright, leads him to see them as larger than himself; he names them 'giants'. The name for men is thus originally the name for the passion which they provoke in the namer. Later, after repeated meetings, the namer realizes his error and invents another name – 'man'. 'Giant' is left as an expression of the idea in the first encounter, the mistaken idea of passion which has now been corrected. 'Voilà comment le mot figuré nait avant le mot propre, lorsque la passion nous fascine les yeux, et que la première idée qu'elle nous offre n'est pas celle de la vérité' (p. 98).

This example is deceptively simple; one of its more disturbing features is the implicit suggestion that *fear* is the primary social emotion. P. de Man, who has carefully examined the *Essai*, argues that this is incidental, an error on Rousseau's part.[30] I am not so sure. The apparently neutral example from a relatively early piece of writing has to be considered in the light of the author's later paranoia.

But the example does make its point. 'Giants' refers to the passion of fear in the naming individual. As such, its meaning is proper. But with reference to the individuals which it names, 'giants' has a figured meaning. Only after continued encounters will the proper word, 'man', be invented, leaving the metaphor of the gigantic in the place of the illusion of the passion.

This description of the figural basis of language provides a clear, if indirect answer to our question about what sort of passion causes its invention. Though fear is the passion which Rousseau's natural man names in the example, the process of this first stage of naming involves the same type of 'mistake' (in epistemological terms) which precipitated his love for Sophie d'Houdetot. The original referent in his affair with her was not the living woman, but the imaginary model through which he saw her. The process of linguistic figuration — 'lorsque la passion nous fascine les yeux' — affects the namer exactly as does the passion of *amour*. The transfer of Rousseau's passion from the fictive Julie to Sophie is figural in the same way that language creates the figured before the proper meaning. In both instances, the connection between a name and its referent is made through the passional force of the imagination, and involves a moment of fiction or illusion.

As with *amour*, the process of linguistic naming is meaningful because of the mistake. Values are created when the name 'giant' is given to a person who is really 'man'. For when the illusion has run its course, a proper concept replaces the initial trope, and the trope remains for metaphorical purposes. One is then left with a 'primary', proper name and a 'secondary' metaphor. Discourse then becomes less fascinated and fascinating (except in literary and imaginative texts, which play seriously with metaphor and demonstrate its fundamental importance), and can proceed calmly with an assured reference to the world of actual objects rather than to the illusions of passion.

But so long as it is alive and creative of meaning, language will not be rid of its basis in passion. The error of naming, which in Rousseau's example seems to stem from that uncontrolled use of the imagination which he wants to temper in *amitié*, subsists in all his linguistic acts. It undercuts his construction of a textual world even as it makes it a meaningful option. Like *amour*, Rousseau's linguistic world will be open-ended and valuable because his use of language can never attain a reciprocal, one-to-one correspondence with its referent. Any final referent, if we must name one ourselves, must result from the process of taking an illusory passion for an actual referent; in the case of Rousseau's autobiography, of taking the 'illusion' of reverie for the personal world of the self. His attempt to name himself in writing will proceed on the basis which he describes in the *Essai*. Rousseau mistakes himself to write the autobiography. The value and moral force of his work can be measured by his whole-hearted belief in his action, by the way belief makes it more than a mistake.

### *'La Langue des signes qui parlent a l'imagination'*

'La langue des signes qui parlent à l'imagination' (IV: 645) is alluded to in the *Essai* and considered in more developed fashion at a significant juncture in *Émile*. It corresponds broadly to language as action, to signs which convey their meaning immediately.

Rousseau needs a notion of language as action to validate his decision to confront the world through writing. In the *Essai*, he emphasizes the priority of spoken over written language, and contrasts the clarity and coldness of writing with the force and individualized accent of speech. This difference is unfortunate, in his view. The written word does not simply reflect and stabilize the spoken word, it modifies its effect. 'L'écriture, qui semble devoir fixer la langue, est précisément ce qui l'attère; elle n'en change pas les mots, mais le génie; elle substitue l'exactitude à l'expression' (p. 108). The two uses of language are qualitively different: 'L'art d'écrire ne tient point à celui de parler. Il tient à des besoins d'une autre nature' (p. 105). Rousseau does not specify exactly what these 'besoins' are. No doubt he intends here the needs of commerce and civil society, which require an 'acception commune' (p. 108). Speech is 'natural', whereas writing is 'corrupted'.

This view of writing presents some problems for the autobiography. If 'l'on rend ses sentiments quand on parle, et ses idées quand on écrit' (p. 108), the 'sentimens secrets' (I: 1148) which Rousseau wishes to convey to his reader would be rendered much better in spoken than in written language. As noted in Chapter I, he would probably prefer to sing the autobiography, in an extended 'récitatif' of natural conviction. Yet writing apparently extinguishes the melodic origins and the accent of speech. Somehow, the author must reconcile his theoretical views in the *Essai* with the practice of self-expression in this texts.

A version of language as action helps in this regard. It would allow Rousseau to bypass the long-winded 'circuit' of writing (IV: 647), and to express his textual world in an immediate, non-figural manner. The implications of this view of language are therefore far-reaching: it makes autobiographical writing a natural action, and undoes the negative consequences of the figural process of naming. What, more precisely, does Rousseau mean here?

'La langue des signes qui parlent à l'imagination' is present, unnamed, in the *Essai*. It surfaces as a digression in Rousseau's discussion in 'De l'écriture'. While commenting on the historical development of alphabetical script, he pauses to admire 'les inscriptions des ruines de Tchelminar', or cuneiform script.

Cette langue inconnue, et d'une antiquité presque effrayante, devait pourtant être alors bien formé, à en juger par la perfection des arts qu'annoncent la beauté des caractères, et les monuments admirables où se trouvent ces inscriptions. Je ne sais pourquoi l'on parle si peu de ces étonnantes ruines: quand j'en lis la description dans Chardin, je me crois transporté dans un autre monde. Il me semble que tout cela donne furieusement à penser. (p. 104–5)

Rousseau appears to repeat his Pont du Gard reverie here in a linguistic context. The 'monuments' associated with cuneiform script are startling emblems of a time which, though no longer extant, retains the force and energy which the author feels are lacking in written language. 'Il faudroit pour ce que j'ai à dire inventer un langage aussi nouveau que mon projet', he will write in the 'Préambule de Neufchâtel' (I: 1153). But here in the *Essai*, in a language which is so distant and monumental that it belongs to the 'autre monde', Rousseau already mentions his 'new language', and gives an oblique insight into his project. The inscriptions from 'Tchelminar' speak powerfully to his imagination because they do not say anything. Untranslatable, without any determinate or actual meaning, they do not denote. For this very reason, they show everything to Rousseau, in an act of sheer connotation.[31] And despite this diffusion of meaning, the signs do not cease to be unique. The author thus discovers a prototype for the language with which he will reveal his 'natural' self. It combines reverie and writing in an immediate self-display.

In *Émile*, 'cette langue inconnue' is reintroduced explicitly as 'la langue des signes qui parlent à l'imagination'. Rousseau invokes it at that crucial point in the education of Émile when the contract of *amitié* is established to guard the student from the illusions and dangers of *amour*. 'Il est des époques dans la vie humaine qui sont faites pour n'être jamais oubliées', the Mentor begins grandiosely. 'Telle est pour Émile celle de l'instruction dont je parle; elle doit inflüer sur le reste de ses jours' (IV: 645). The instruction in question is quite simply Émile's long delayed sexual education. Student and Mentor must discover together the mysteries of the opposite sex, and Rousseau wants to include the difference of *amour* within their identity of interest.

The key to this pivotal contract lies in the voluntary, rational and ultimately bizarre decision by Émile to place his freedom of choice in the hands of the Mentor. The 'législateur' of education then employs the authority of friendship to guide Émile into a relationship with a pre-selected Sophie. But the first step in the process is rhetorical and persuasive, and involves the language of signs which speak to the imagination. Explicitly distinguishing between 'raisonner' and 'persuader', the Mentor sets himself the task of persuading Émile of the rational value of a contract of *amitié*. The contradiction here would be amusing if *Émile* did not take its educational project so seriously. The Mentor suggests following the practice of antiquity. 'Les anciens', he states,

agissoient beaucoup plus par la persuasion, par les affections de l'ame, parce qu'ils ne négligeoient pas la langue des signes. Toutes les conventions se passoient avec solemnité pour les rendre plus inviolables; avant que la force fut établie les Dieux étoient les magistrats du genre humain: c'est par devant eux que les particuliers faisoient leur traittés, leurs alliances, prononçoient leurs promesses; la face de la terre étoit le livre où s'en conservoient les archives. (IV: 645–6)

Notice, in this wonderfully rhetorical passage, how 'la langue des signes qui parlent à l'imagination' has become simply 'la langue des signes'. Rousseau is paring language down to a bare minimum, until, like an untranslatable cuneiform script, it is hardly language at all. To found and to justify 'toutes les conventions' of language, both ends of the performative/constative distinction are used. On the one hand, we find objects – 'monumens grossiers mais augustes de la sainteté des contrats' (IV: 646) – which serve as signs. On the other, we find actions which, though non-linguistic, act performatively to effect a meaning:

Trasibule et Tarquin coupant des tetes de pavots, Alexandre appliquant son sceau sur la bouche de son favori, Diogéne marchant devant Zenon, ne parloient-ils mieux que s'ils avoient faits de longs discours? (IV:647)

In this section of *Émile*, Rousseau attempts to establish a level of discourse which will guarantee the promise which the student makes to his Mentor. To bind the contract of *amitié*, he must invoke a point of reference outside normal conventions, including the convention of language. Hence the borderline character of his examples: are these objects and actions really linguistic? 'Des marques de dignités, un trône, un sceptre, une robe de pourpre une courone . . .' (IV: 646). And why should there be an implicit appeal to a ceremonial, ritualistic hierarchy, if the Mentor is apparently only maintaining natural equality in his relationship with Émile?

The limited discussion here cannot do justice to these questions. But the quasi-linguistic, certainly rhetorical category of signs which Rousseau is describing points to some of the issues which will arise when he attempts to consolidate the move to autobiography we have followed throughout the present chapter. For the crucial concern at this juncture of *Émile* is authority. The Mentor must persuade the student to continue, willingly, unquestioningly, and from rational conviction, to accept his authority. To anticipate, Rousseau's project in the autobiography will involve him in a similar relationship with the reader. He will employ all his persuasive powers to transform the conventional, highly personal artifice of his textual world into a natural domain. A version of language like 'la langue des signes qui parlent à l'imagination' would allow Rousseau's text to be at once natural and conventional. 'Quel circuit de paroles eut aussi bien rendu les memes idées?' the Mentor asks in *Émile* (IV: 647). Indeed, the allegory of Julie's garden and of its prolonged 'circuit' of water, Rousseau's entire imaginative construction, will have to be justified in the eyes of the reader if the author is to make it real in the autbiography. In the next two chapters we shall see whether he succeeds in establishing his textual world on such easy terms as the Mentor enjoys with Émile.

# IV

## THE WRITING SELF

When Rousseau proposes to exemplify the truth of human nature in a personal account of his life, he begins a writing enterprise different from earlier texts – his autobiography. Several introductory declarations set its unequivocal tone:

1. Je forme une entreprise qui n'eut jamais d'exemple et don l'exécution n'aura point d'imitateur. Je veux montrer à mes semblable un homme dans toute la vérité de la nature; et cet homme, ce sera moi.
2. Moi seul. Je sens mon cœur et je connois les hommes. (1: 5)

Rousseau's uniqueness is meant to distinguish the work from that of any predecessor or disciple; the immediacy of his sentiment is to give it certainty; his knowledge of other men is to establish its validity. But although these provocative assertions help to generate and sustain the flow of narrative in *Les Confessions*, they do not remain unchallenged in autobiographical sequels. By the equally outspoken opening of *Rousseau Juge de Jean Jaques, Dialogues*, the author's voice has broken into multiple, contending perspectives. A strange reversal occurs:

R. Quelles incroyables choses je viens d'apprendre! Je n'en reviens pas non, je n'en reviendrai jamais. Juste ciel! quel abominable homme! qu'il m'a fait de mal! Que je le vais détester! (1: 667)

In the *Dialogues*, a monstrous, unnatural image challenges the image of 'a man in all the truth of nature'. Rousseau's earlier self affirmation gives way to self-accusation. The new strategy is designed to make the autobiographer his own mediator and advocate. Rousseau attempts to exorcize a spectre which his own project has brought into being.

*Les Rêveries du promeneur solitaire*, in a provisional manner, resolve the polarities of the autobiography. This unfinished yet final work effects a moving reconciliation between life and writing as Rousseau begins once again, now in a voice of isolation and resignation:

Me voici donc seul sur la terre, n'ayant plus de frere, de prochain d'ami, de societé que moi-même. (1: 995)

The three major autobiographical works are successive stages in Rousseau's attempt to identify himself within his imaginative universe, to bring his textual world back directly into the fabric of his life. This involves transforming the author's life into the act of writing, into a book so consubstantial with Rousseau that it *is* his life and can speak for him, even after death. 'Que la trompette du jugement dernier sonne quand elle voudra', he states at the start of *Les Confessions*; 'je viendrai *ce livre à la main* me présenter devant le souverain juge' (1: 5 – emphasis added). In principle at least, the autobiographical project makes the written work identical with its author.

As the opening lines demonstrate severally above, however, the practice of Rousseau's autobiography is neither direct nor stationary. The attempt to make life and text coincide moves through three very different works, written during the fifteen-year period from 1764–78. It occurs as a rhetorical process. By 'rhetorical', I mean in part the linguistic procedures of persuasion used by the author to convince himself and his reader of his project. Language is in this sense very much an act, and the rhetorical aspect of the autobiography is tied to the autobiographer's need to sustain the belief (primarily his own belief) that his textual world is real, not just an aesthetic creation.

But by 'rhetorical' I also understand the more general sense of how Rousseau structures his discourse, the changing manner in which he conveys his belief and writes about himself and his life, or the fact that *Les Confessions* take the form of a narrative text, the *Dialogues* an unusual, tormented conversation, and the *Rêveries* an elusive undefined prose. To examine a rhetorical development in this second sense is the major concern here. It requires direct attention to the author's *énonciation,* and to such notions as sentiment and allegory for *Les Confessions*, frames and framing for the *Dialogues*, and circumscription for the *Rêveries*.

I assume that these changes constitute in some way a logical development, that each stage has in common the intuition of indeterminate unity experienced in reverie and elaborated textually as an image of personal identity. Different autobiographical texts, as they convey this intuition and image in different ways, may shed light on some of the experiential structures analysed earlier. But the changes in the autobiography do not simply reflect changes in the author's life, particularly during the last fifteen years of it. Rousseau's project will transform his life as much as it reflects it.

## Les Confessions

> Surely happiness is what everyone wants, so much so
> that there can be no one who does not want it. But if
> they desire it so, where did they learn what it was?
>                    Augustine, *Confessions* (p. 226)

> Cet espoir du bonheur temporal qui meurt si difficilement
> dans le cœur de l'homme . . .
> La soif de bonheur ne s'éteint point dans le cœur de
> l'homme.            Rousseau, *Les Confessions* (I: 213, 413)

### Beginning

The best way to approach *Les Confessions* is to examine how this complex narrative gets underway. At a textual level, Rousseau's life could be said to begin with the phrase, 'Je suis né à Genève en 1712 . . . (I: 6). The point of departure belongs to narrative time; and once the narrative time of *Les Confessions* is set, the story seems to unfold like the life itself, of its own accord. But although this particular sentence begins the autobiography, the autobiography certainly does not originate in it. If we may distinguish, with E. Said, between two types of beginning, the first order of interpretation lies in the birth of the narrative rather than in the narrative itself.[1] Before Rousseau speaks of *his* birth, he must establish the textual time in which the tale may be told. What appears as an introduction is in fact the way the autobiographer launches himself and his text into time.

Two factors ought to be mentioned here. First, Rousseau does not bring his text to life alone – the reader is a full partner in its conception, as we shall see in the next chapter. And secondly, *Les Confessions* are introduced more than once. The first version of the introduction is the meditative 'Préambule de Neufchâtel', written in 1764. It offers an instructive and relatively undramatic entry to the text. Rousseau set it aside, however, when the narrative took its final shape. During the rapid composition and revision of Books VII-XII, probably in 1768, he drew from the 'Préambule' a short 'avant-propos' and three introductory paragraphs. These appear in the definitive 'Manuscrit de Genève'. As we shall see, the affective register of Rousseau's voice alters in the four years between the two versions, the latter being a shrill and shortened adaptation of the former.[2] Both are relevant here.

One phrase from the final 'avant-propos' to *Les Confessions* gives an indication of how the autobiography gets started. In support of a plea to the reader to preserve his text, Rousseau proposes it as:

un ouvrage unique et utile, lequel peut servir de prémiére piéce de comparaison pour l'étude des hommes, qui est certainement encore à commencer . . . (I: 3)

The anthropological overtones of 'l'étude des hommes' stand out in the phrase, but it is the juxtaposition of the two adjectives 'unique' and 'utile' which deserves attention. These reveal, in outline, the two divergent attitudes which are central to the introduction to *Les Confessions*. Inasmuch as the work is 'unique', it will be as different from other works as Rousseau is from other men, the 'first' of its kind. Inasmuch as it is 'utile', it can be a 'point of comparison' for other men, an example having much in common with them. The two propositions implicit in the two words are incompatible, yet persist side by side throughout the introduction to the work. Taken together, they help to generate the momentum for the text to get underway. One might say that Rousseau holds two contradictory positions in the unity of a paradox. The important result for *Les Confessions* is the narrative, the textual time, which the paradox, when held as a unity, sets in motion.

Paradoxes tend to be protean and dynamic, and the juxtaposition of 'unique et utile' is only one symptom of a more basic structure which underlies the start of *Les Confessions*, and which different versions of the introduction ramify in different ways. In the earlier 'Préambule de Neufchâtel', for instance, Rousseau cogently presents his intention in terms of an epistemological dialectic between knowledge of self and knowledge of other individuals. 'Chacun ne connoit guéres que soi', he states,

s'il est vrai que quelqu'un se connoisse; car comment bien déterminer un être par les seuls rapports qui sont en lui-même, et sans le comparer à rien? Cependant cette connoissance qu'on a de soi est le seul moyen qu'on emploie à connoitre les autres. (I: 1148)

To know others one must first know oneself; yet self-knowledge is acquired only by comparison with other men. According to Rousseau, this allows only for relative knowledge, both of oneself and of others. An epistemological impasse results. Rousseau then mentions one forced exit, that of raising self-knowledge to the level of a general rule. 'On se fait la régle de tout . . .' (I: 1148). But he quickly criticizes this move, 'non dans les jugemens que j'ai portés des autres . . . mais dans ceux que les autres ont portés de moi; jugemens presque toujours faux' (I: 1148).

*Les Confessions* set out to provide full clarification. One need only rectify, continues Rousseau,

cette régle unique et fautive de juger toujours du cœur d'autrui par le sien; tandis qu'au contraire il faudroit souvent pour connoitre le sien même commencer par lire dans celui d'autrui. (I: 1149)

He then takes the major and novel step of proposing *himself* as a model.

Je veux tacher que pour apprendre à s'apprecier, on puisse avoir du moins une piéce de comparaison; que chacun puisse connoitre soi et un autre, et cet autre ce sera moi. (I: 1149)

Here again Rousseau presents himself both as unique, 'autre' from other men, and as exemplary, a useful model. As an example, he appears to efface his individual person. Like an anthropological specimen, he becomes a mere 'piéce de comparaison', useful for didactic purposes. Autobiography in this sense is a highly indiscriminate type of discourse, which could be written by anyone. Since every human being carries within himself the model of humanity that Rousseau claims to advance in himself, anyone is entitled to the autobiographical project. As the author suggests in the 'Préambule', its profound subject is not any individual man, but 'l'être commun aux uns et aux autres, l'homme' (I: 1150).

In the mode of uniqueness, on the other hand, Rousseau's utilitarian modesty gives way to a new attitude. 'M'étant bientôt senti une espéce d'être à part . . .', as he also states in the 'Préambule', the author is irrevocably different from other men (I: 1148). He can write the autobiography precisely because it is *his*, and has nothing in common with that of another person. The attitude of uniqueness is therefore one of uncompromising individualism and subjectivity. It makes *Les Confessions* 'une entreprise qui n'eut jamais d'exemple et dont l'exécution n'aura point d'imitateur' (I: 5).

The logical polarities of the 'Préambule' take the form of an affective tension four years later, in Rousseau's final version of the introduction. Uniqueness becomes the self-glorification of 'Moi seul', a proclamation which inevitably rejects or insults the reader. Utility takes the opposite form of a heated plea for the preservation of the text. Rousseau oscillates between these two extremes without finding any middle ground. While the positions are incompatible, he will give

up neither.[3] Rousseau seems to expect us to believe that the usefulness
of his work lies in his uniqueness. Behind his apparently disinterested
offer of himself as a point of reference for others lies a very practical
personal gain. The autobiographer's role as representative 'autre' –
the value of his act for objective knowledge – must include a reference
to his individual person. The reader accepts the man with the model;
the result, eminently desirable for Rousseau, is that others see him as
he sees himself. Proposing himself as a model, he is also trying to free
himself from misunderstanding.

Furthermore, whereas Rousseau employs irreproachable logic in
asking the reader not to set up judgements of oneself as a norm for
judging others, he tends to exempt himself from this restriction when
he declares, 'Je sens mon cœur et je connois les hommes' (I: 5). Sensing
and knowing are quite different for Rousseau; he would never state,
'je connois mon cœur'. But does his capacity for sentiment exempt him
from the dialectic of relative knowledge? The defiance of 'Moi seul',
at any rate, indicates that Rousseau is transgressing the very limits he
sets for others.

Despite these difficulties, the start of the autobiographical narrative
does demonstrate a strong consistency with earlier works. Presenting
himself as a particular instance of 'un homme dans toute la vérité de
la nature' (I: 5), Rousseau forges a direct axis between the second
*Discours* and *Les Confessions*. The conceptual framework of the first
work, maintained in the Portrait/Tableau distinction in the Preface in
dialogue to *La Nouvelle Héloïse*, extends intact through the 'Préambule
de Neufchâtel'. Once again, the author intends to distinguish between
what is acquired and what comes from nature. Once again, he makes
the opposition between an 'image' of 'fantaisie' and 'ce modelle
intérieur' (I:1149). But Rousseau now proposes to present the 'modelle intérieur' of humanity in conjunction with his own, personal
'image'. In beginning the autobiography, he repeats at the level of an
individual life the strategy of the second *Discours*, and claims to
distinguish in himself between two terms which remained indistinguishable, in a state of suspension, in the Preface to *La Nouvelle Héloïse*.

The reasons or cause of this change are not really a concern here.
We shall follow instead the rhetorical stages of the autobiography which
are its effect. Since the works preceding *Les Confessions* prepare the wa
way for the step into autobiography, the paradox which his introduction involves is not entirely evident to him. The change appears an
obvious, 'natural' option. For our immediate purposes, it is mainly

significant that Rousseau does not begin his story until he has posed and assumed as his own, even if unconsciously, the paradox we have witnessed. Once he declares himself a unique example, he gains the momentary authority required to bring his imaginative universe to life, establishes the narrative time in which to recount his birth; and the autobiography gets underway. The narrative, far from explaining or resolving the incompatibility, instead enacts it. Like the life recounted, Rousseau's action must be its own justification.

### Narrative and Sentiment

With 'Je suis né à Genève en 1712 . . . ', the narrative proper begins. Rousseau's highly idealized, though generally faithful account of his life renders a personal vision of the past and of time. The narrative line of *Les Confessions*, as it conveys this vision, has two sources. The facts and events of Rousseau's life are a principal source, what one could call the raw material of the narrative. But the principle for selecting and ordering this material lies elsewhere, in the image of personal identity elaborated in the author's textual world, before the autobiography could begin. Although the image is aesthetic and fictional, it is whole and complete in a way which the actual auto-biographer is not: Rousseau interprets the past in its light, bringing fiction into contact with fact to produce the story of his life. To read *Les Confessions* is to follow a narrative line balanced, at the outset, between an elaborated image of identity and the time of the actual past. When he writes the first stage of the autobiography, Rousseau is therefore remaking his past by means of the text, transforming the objective time of his existence into a temporal order of his own construction. The process of elaboration in the pre-autobiographical works thus continues, but now as the appropriation rather than the construction of an image.

The key to Rousseau's temporal concerns is his notion of sentiment. What we first noticed in the pre-text of reverie reappears as the primary interest of the narrative. 'J'écris moins l'histoire de ces éve(ne)ments en eux-memes que celle de l'état de mon ame, à mesure qu'ils sont arrivés', he forewarns. 'Les faits ne sont ici que des causes occasionelles' (I: 1150). From the start, he construes his work as an account of 'ses sentimens secrets dans toutes les situations où il s'est trouvé' (I: 1148). Again, at the start of Book VII, he favours sentiment over fact:

Je n'ai qu'un guide fidelle sur lequel je puisse compter; c'est la chaîne

des sentimens qui ont marqué la succession de mon être, et par eux
celle des évenemens qui en ont été la cause ou l'effet. (I: 278)

Sentiment is the *referent* of the narrative rather than any specific
facts or events, and this should be no surprise. Since Rousseau defines
the unity of his personal identity in terms of his sentiments, to say
that sentiment is the referent of *Les Confessions* is not very different
from asserting that the author is their referent, or that the text is an
autobiography. The claim is close to a tautology. And *Les Confessions*,
as they 'refer' to Rousseau's sentiments, do not represent them, nor
even the personal identity comprised of them. Instead, the narrative
enacts sentiment. The narrative line would in this sense be a textual
embodiment of the various and even incompatible facets of his identity
as they inhere in a continuous development. Rousseau's remarks on
style in the 'Préambule' furnish perhaps the best gloss on this
connection. 'En me livrant à la fois au souvenir de l'impression receue
et au sentiment présent', he states there about his project,

je peindrai doublement l'état de mon ame, savoir au moment où
l'evenement m'est arrivé et au moment ou je l'ai décrit; mon style inégal
et naturel . . . fera lui-même partie de mon histoire. (I: 1154)

The style of *Les Confessions* is meant to span time in the same
manner as the referent of the text, meeting the simultaneous demands
of past and present in the autobiographer's life with a narrative that
functions 'doublement'. For Rousseau, the word 'doublement' indicates
a strong desire to maintain unity in duality, whether in an interpersonal
relationship, in relation to his textual world, or in his relation to the
childhood which he rediscovers in the writing of *Les Confessions*.
But in terms of the narrative itself, 'doublement' corresponds to the
past and present of the autobiographical discourse.[4] As he writes,
Rousseau alternates between the two, combining past and present in
a narrative line which performs the unity of his 'état d'ame'. The style
of *Les Confessions* recalls his comment in the *Essai* about music, which
articulates 'doubly the voice of nature' (*Essai*, p. 156). Narrative in the
first stage of the autobiography is meant to refer to sentiment by
conveying the same paradoxical state of unity in transition as is
expressed by the musician in melody.

The celebrated 'tout dire' of *Les Confessions* can also be understood
in terms of sentiment. 'Je serai vrai; je le serai sans réserve', Rousseau
states in the 'Préambule':

Je dirai tout; le bien, le mal, tout enfin . . . Car si je tais quelque chose on ne me connoitra sur rien, tant tout se tient, tant tout est un dans mon caractére. (I: 1153)

Rousseau will repeat this promise at the end of Book IV and deflect the burden of it on to the reader (I: 175).[5] But he utters it initially out of his belief that sentiment is a 'tout', an affective whole. The 'tout dire' of *Les Confessions* corresponds to the 'tout' of the referent. And both have a decided impact on the rhetorical mode of the text. For how can a 'tout' be named in language? As such, sentiments are unnameable, and must be carried in the form of a history. 'Le bonheur', for instance, the sentiment *par excellence* in Rousseau, cannot be contained within his narrative. It can only be repeated. 'Encore un coup le vrai bonheur ne se décrit pas', he states:

il se sent, et se sent d'autant mieux qu'il peut le moins se décrire, parce qu'il ne résulte pas d'un recueil de faits, mais qu'il est un état permanent. Je me repette souvent, mais je me répéterois bien davantage, si je disois la même chose autant de fois qu'il me vient dans l'esprit. (I: 236)

The narrative line of *Les Confessions* is a consequence of 'le bonheur', a textual time which repeats the time in which the sentiment was constituted. Rousseau goes so far as to describe narrative as the effect of sentiment, what follows from its unity, or its 'suite'. 'Ceci n'est pas clair,' he remarks at one point in a description, 'mais il le deviendra dans la suite; les sentimens ne se décrivent bien que par leurs effets' (I: 104).

Narrative conveys the moral significance of the autobiographer's life because Rousseau aspires to show the ground of his personal identity, what he would term his 'natural' self, in *Les Confessions*. In this sense 'doublement' signifies that the text alternates between the virtual and actual aspects of the writer's identity, in a rhetorical mode that we shall in due course analyse as allegory. The virtual self of *Les Confessions* belongs now to Rousseau's past, to the childhood about which he writes; the actual self, to the adult author. But the melody of the text delivers itself as a fine line between them, evoking the living present.

*Two Episodes: Sentimental and Narrative Development*

An instance of sentimental development described in the text puts these theoretical remarks into a practical perspective. In Book I,

Rousseau's narration of two episodes at Bossey when he was spanked constitutes a striking example both of how his moral and affective inclinations developed in childhood, and also of how this development is taken up within the autobiography. The very fact that he considers them worthy of attention is unusual, not for the superficial sordidness of the incidents (which shocked some contemporary readers), but because such concentration on childhood events was entirely new in the eighteenth century.

Each episode holds an archetypal status – the first because it initially arouses, and then confirms, his masochistic tendencies; the second because it awakens a strong sentiment of indignation against injustice. Both sentiments persist in influencing his adult actions, Rousseau emphasizes. In the development of the narrative, the two episodes are equally significant and complex. The author characterizes the first as 'le prémier pas et le plus pénible dans le labirinthe obscur et fangeux de mes confessions' (I: 18) – a rather grandiose description which suggests that what he narrates will reflect on the project of *Les Confessions*.[6]

Rousseau's notion of a 'cause occasionelle' is a helpful point of entry here. He uses the term (borrowed probably from Malebranche) to refer to a specific type of cause–effect relation between objective sensation and the sentiment which it provokes, such as in the phrase, 'les faits ne sont ici que des causes occasionelles'[7] Common-sense understanding is adequate here: a sensation, fact, or event, as occasional cause, simply gives rise to one or another sentiment; it 'occasions' the sentiment. But because the relation between cause and effect is not strictly necessary, a sentiment cannot be reduced to its factual cause. It attains a measure of autonomy, or takes on a life of its own. Such autonomy of sentimental effect is, in a sense, what authorizes Rousseau to narrate the facts of his life through his sentiments rather than vice versa. But it also leaves room for discrepancies, for an incommensurability between cause and effect.

In Book I, the first episode occurs at the hands of Mlle Lambercier, a woman whom, Rousseau says, he loved 'comme une mere, et peut être plus' (I: 22). The child discovers erotic pleasure with such force that he must withstand the temptation to misbehave deliberately in order to receive another such spanking.

Il falloit même toute la vérité de cette affection et toute ma douceur naturelle pour m'empêcher de chercher le retour du même traitement en le méritant: car j'avois trouvé dans la douleur, dans la honte même, un mélange de sensualité qui m'avoit laissé plus de desir que de crainte de l'éprouver derechef par la même main. (I: 15)

A second opportunity for pleasure arises after the child commits another, unspecified, but avowedly involuntary misdeed. Rousseau is then confirmed in his masochism, and aroused to such an extent that Mlle Lambercier notices. She immediately desists. The autobiographer's affective destiny, he tells us, is set for life.

Cette récidive que j'éloignois sans la craindre arriva sans qu'il y eut de ma faute, c'est à dire, de ma volonté, et j'en profitai, je puis dire, en sureté de conscience. Mais cette seconde fois fut aussi la derniére: car Mlle Lambercier s'étant sans doute apperçue à quelque signe que ce châtiment n'alloit pas à son but, déclara qu'elle y renonçoit, et qu'il la fatigoit trop . . .
Qui croiroit que ce châtiment d'enfant receu à huit ans par la main d'une fille de trente a décidé de mes gouts, de mes desirs, de mes passions, de moi pour le reste de ma vie, et cela, précisément dans le sens contraire à ce qui devoit s'ensuivre naturellement? (I: 15)[8]

Rousseau comments at some length on the significance of this 'gout bisarre' for his later life (I: 16–18). He asserts, rather paradoxically, that the perversion guarantees his 'mœurs honnetes' first his masochism insures an ignorance of accepted forms of erotic pleasure, and therefore makes him unprepared to indulge in them; and later it deprives him of the temerity necessary for success with women. 'Ce qui devoit me perdre me conserva', he argues. Untainted by direct contact with the opposite sex, Rousseau achieves satisfaction indirectly: 'J'ai donc fort peu possédé, mais je n'ai pas laissé de jouir à ma maniére; c'est à dire, par l'imagination.'

After a pause in the narrative, distinctly shown by a break in the numbering which accompanies the opening paragraphs of *Les Confessions* and by a transitional paragraph, the author begins to recount the second episode of spanking. It runs as follows. A comb of Mlle Lambercier is found broken. Despite appearances to the contrary, the child Rousseau denies that he is responsible. Once again, he undergoes a punishment – though with two differences from the first episode. In this instance his Uncle Bernard delivers the blows; and they are no longer pleasurable. Second, they are shared by the ideal childhood *ami,* something of a consolation. 'Mon pauvre Cousin étoit chargé d'un autre délit non moins grave: nous fumes enveloppés dans la même execution. Elle fut terrible' (I: 19).

In the second incident, Rousseau feels 'l'indignation, la rage, le desespoir' (I: 20) — emotions opposite to his earlier pleasure. But the later spanking, if different in its effects, provokes them in as far-reaching a manner as did the first episode. The author's first encounter with unbending injustice serves as a basis for a subsequent generaliz-ation of the event into a moral imperative to help others. After de-scribing his irrational reaction to what he as a child found an irrational punishment — the scream 'Carnifex', repeated in a unified chorus with his cousin — Rousseau states:

> Je sens en écrivant ceci que mon pouls s'èléve encore; ces momens me seront toujours présens quand je vivrois cent mille ans. Ce premier sentiment de la violence et de l'injustice est resté si profondément gravé dans mon ame, que toutes les idées qui s'y rapportent me rendent ma prémiére émotion; et ce sentiment, relatif à moi dans son origine, a pris une telle consistance en lui-même, et s'est tellement détaché de tout interest personnel, que mon cœur s'enflamme au spectacle ou au récit de toute action injuste . . . comme si l'effet en retomboit sur moi. (I: 20)

The discrepancy between cause and effect in these incidents could be seen to lie in the fact that two different and apparently unrelated sentiments are stirred by one type of 'cause occasionelle', a spanking. Moving from the first to the second episode, Rousseau employs a vocabulary which heightens the contrast we have followed so far.

> Qui croiroit, par exemple, qu'un des ressorts les plus vigoureux de mon ame fut trempé dans la même source d'où la luxure et la molesse ont coulé dans mon sang? (I: 18)

The hard, metallic 'ressort' would seem to have little in common with 'la luxure et la molesse', and the brusque transition of 'tremper' applies equally well to the shift from one sentiment to the other. Masochism and an indignant awareness of injustice are about as far apart on the affective scale as is a hot metal from the cold water into which it is plunged. Yet Rousseau, even as he sharpens our sensitivity to their difference, also emphasizes that both sentiments derive from 'the same source'. 'Sans quitter le sujet dont je parlois', he states as he moves to the second episode. Obviously, some sort of unity inheres across the two sections of narrative; and to find it requires careful, critical attention.

If one tries to understand the unity thematically, in terms of the act of spanking, then the disjunction between cause and effect does not truly reach the level of the sentiments themselves, and masochism and a sense of injustice remain unrelated. Rousseau is simply spanked once, with one effect; and he is spanked later, with another. But although the theme of spanking constitutes an undeniable narrative link in *Les Confessions,* the differing circumstances of the two incidents certainly help to determine the separate sentimental developments which they provoke. Mlle Lambercier is not Uncle Bernard, nor the individual privilege of the first punishment the same as the shared pain with the cousin. Rousseau himself underlines such basic differences when narrating the first episode. And he encourages an interpretation which would link the two episodes in a more profound manner, in a comment made just after the description of the final spanking. 'Quand, cherchant le reméde dans le mal même, on eut voulu pour jamais amortir mes sens dépravés, on n'auroit pu mieux s'y prendre. Aussi me laisserent-ils en repos pour longtems' (I: 19). Assuming for a moment that the common element in the episodes is not the act of spanking itself, how can we account for Rousseau's claim?

If we conceive of unity in a formal sense, a second avenue of interpretation opens. Let us consider again. The first episode begins with a fault on Rousseau's part. When Mlle Lambercier spanks the child, he experiences the punishment as pleasure. Here it is possible to notice a first disjunction in the cause/effect relation: a corrective punishment, intended to put an end to the fault which first led to the need for punishment, instead ensures its own repetition. The punishment of one specific fault adds to and reinforces the general fault of the child. Rousseau is strongly tempted to misbehave, solely in order to receive the same (non)punishment a second time. Because of this reversal of norms, his behaviour can be labelled a perversion, masochism.

According to the autobiographer, the child Rousseau is aware of his discrepancy, and only the involuntary nature of his next misdeed allows him to enjoy the pleasure of the consequent punishment 'en sureté de conscience'. For an involuntary misdeed is itself a mismatch of intention and action, and formally equivalent to the causal structure of the masochistic experience. Cause and effect have become dissociated in both instances, and the framework of intentionality, of intentions matching deeds, breaks down, at least at the level of the conscious, directed will. When Mlle Lambercier makes her own discovery of this fact, she has no choice but to discontinue the punishment altogether. 'Cette seconde fois fut aussi la derniére: car ce châtiment n'alloit pas à son but' (I: 15).

Several tentative conclusions can be drawn here. First, Rousseau's masochism demonstrates his peculiar ability to experience the punishment of faults as pleasure – in this instance, the act of atoning for a fault becomes interchangeable with the fault itself. And since the title of *Les Confessions* implicitly refers to this same process, inasmuch as Rousseau is 'confessing' past faults, we are authorized to make a further, speculative remark. The act of narrating the episode – which he has named 'le prémier pas et le plus pénible' in his autobiography – is ostensibly a cathartic self-exposure which will atone for the fault of masochism which has been revealed. In this sense, it is similar in intention to the original punishment of Mlle Lambercier. But in fact it perpetuates the same problem at a different level. Apparently confessing the development of a flaw in his character, and thereby amending it, the autobiographer indulges in this flaw once again in his text. Like the operatic Devin, Rousseau's self-exposure in the autobiography implies a simultaneous concealment. The concealment at the level of his narration concerns the pleasure which he receives from the act of writing itself, particularly from writing about episodes such as this. This process can only build upon itself as the autobiography progresses, since the fault of writing will itself require a further punishment – in writing – that generates yet further pleasure. Why writing autobiography should be a fault is not immediately evident, but as we follow the development of Rousseau's project, we shall find evidence for the present speculation. It is important at present to make the connection between the pattern of self-revelation and self-concealment, which we first noticed in the performance of *Le Devin du village,* and that of Rousseau's masochism. They both demonstrate what I have termed here a causal disjunction, making cause and effect reversible and indistinguishable, and generating a repetitive series of effects which seems to have no cause, no beginning, and no end. This is of course the very opposite of a narrative, a primary function of which is to establish a beginning, middle, and end, and thereby to create a coherent and understandable order between them which is the sense of the autobiographer's life.

Second, the equivalence between punishment and pleasure effectively places Rousseau outside the reach of any law decreeing that faults must be punished. It is not by chance that the circumstances in which the equivalence flourishes involve a maternal Mlle Lambercier. For the law which comes immediately to mind is the Oedipal injunction forbidding the fault of undivided pleasure between mother and son — or of an undivided relation between Rousseau and his text, as in the autobiography. Masochism makes Rousseau innocent by dint of excepting him from punishment and — indirectly — from the law. At the very least, the masochism which he describes in the first episode indicates his desire to be innocent and exempt from punishment. With these tentative conclusions in hand, we may reread the second episode.

The broken comb is an effect whose cause is missing. As long as there is dissociation, there can be no fault. Hence Rousseau's claim of innocence, that he did not break the comb. But the adults at Bossey, consistent with the appearances they observe, put cause and effect together. They name Rousseau the cause, and make him responsible for a misdeed which is not his. There *is* a sense in which he is responsible — the sense of the first episode: Rousseau's masochism has undermined the coherence of the causal order, and the law has lost its authority. In the underlying logic of *Les Confessions,* therefore, the spanking in the second episode punishes the child for his earlier subversion, not for the broken comb. Authority now asserts itself ruthlessly, gratuitously in the child's eyes, and in a punishment administered by a man and father figure. The overwhelming sense of injustice that Rousseau recalls in Book I derives not so much from the actual spanking as from the abrupt and merciless manner in which he has been made generally responsible for the breakdown of cause and effect stemming from the first episode.

The spanking for the broken comb in no way alters the basic problem, since the discrepancy begun in Rousseau's masochism persists through the second episode. A punishment intended to restore authority and justice instead perpetrates an injustice, and makes the child rebellious against authority. Structurally, the episodes are identical. But their sentimental results still seem diametrically opposed. The child who experiences the punishment of fault as pleasure in the first incident becomes aware in the second that he must bear the brunt of the paradox. Loss of intentionality cuts two ways. It makes an offender exempt from the law, since his actions and responsibility for them do not really belong to him. But it also justifies the presupposition of fault where none exists, and permits an application of the law which is as arbitrary, indiscriminate, and powerful as any means of making oneself an exception to it.

The formal correspondences between the two episodes suggest that masochism and a sense of injustice may be related in more than an anecdotal manner. Would it be possible to move from an analysis of structure to a definite connection between the sentiments? Their juxtaposition now has little to do with the actual spankings, which bring the episodes together in the conscious memory of the author, and which give them a point of contact at the surface of the narrative. It concerns instead an impasse between desire and the law. Book I of *Les Confessions* raises this only indirectly, at the level of the *énoncé*, in terms of incidents from the past, and through a complex set of feints and buffers in the narrative voice, which guard the reader (and probably Rousseau) from an awareness of what is at stake.[9] It is not until the imagined plot of the *Dialogues* that the connection between masochism and a sense of injustice is made explicit. Then it will occur primarily at the level of the *énonciation*, within the act of writing, and as a problem related to Rousseau's effort to make his textual world real. But although we are not yet in a position to understand it fully, the sentimental development described in Book I bears directly on the project of the autobiography, and several preliminary remarks might be made. Rousseau the autobiographer desires the wholeness of his image. He attempts in writing to effect the union that Rousseau the child attempts through masochism to achieve with Mlle Lambercier. To fulfil this desire is to transgress, and the apparently unwarranted punishment which the infringement provokes corresponds to the persecution and counter-image which later afflict the author. The implications of the impasse between desire and the law are thus not at all confined to the episodes which Rousseau narrates. Writing about the life, he is still living it. The fact that what he narrates implicitly reveals a knowledge which might turn the autobiographer from his project will in no way keep Rousseau from repeating the sort of development we have followed. Our analysis of the autobiography must effectively catch up with the insights indirectly offered by this early sequence in the narrative.

## Time – Fiction – Continuity

Rousseau's narration of the spanking episodes marks the onset of time in *Les Confessions*. 'Là fut le terme de la serenité de ma vie enfantine', he states directly afterwards. 'Dès ce moment je cessai de jouir d'un bonheur pur' (I: 20). His description of the past, suggesting that actual life at Bossey was a paradise which has somehow been lost, has a biblical ring to it. The preceding episodes function like variants of the Christian doctrine of the Fall into time, recast in Rousseau's personal mythology (I: 20, note 1). The child spanked by Mlle Lambercier discovers his former virtue in the same moment that he discovers his masochism. Despite Rousseau's rather remarkable claim that masochism preserves his virtue, the episode conveys primarily the sense of virtue lost. Similarly, the moment in which the child becomes aware of his fundamental innocence in the later spanking is also that in which innocence is unjustly denied him. The difficult pattern of a gift which is also a denial, of a discovery which is also a loss, is perhaps a truer indication of time than the author's straightforward evocation.

It is important to distinguish the onset of time in Book I from the beginning which we examined at the start of *Les Confessions.* Rousseau narrates the shattering of happiness at Bossey as part of his past experience; the introductory generation of the narrative established the textual time in which he may speak of this past. The two are as different as the levels of *énonciation* and *énoncé* in the work. But they are different in other ways as well. Rousseau recounts the Bossey experience as an expulsion, a veritable forced exit into time which he undergoes passively and involuntarily. The reconstruction of time begun at the start of *Les Confessions,* on the other hand, he actively creates and prolongs with both painstaking care and occasionally obvious pleasure.

This contrast is helpful when one considers Book I from the point of view of the narrative, rather than at the level of the life. It was suggested earlier that the narrative of *Les Confessions* is Rousseau's transformation of objective time — the order of facts and events in his past — into a temporal order of his own construction. In this sense, the narrative is a rhetorical equivalent to the transformation between sensation and sentiment in reverie, analysed in Chapter 1. But this very equivalence calls for a new step in our analysis. Was there not a necessary moment of fiction in reverie, which for Rousseau was the source of its unity? In the transitional paragraph between the two episodes, the narrator makes a remark which bears on this issue:

En remontant de cette sorte aux prémiéres traces de mon être sensible, je trouve des élémens qui, semblant quelquefois incompatibles, n'ont pas laissé de s'unir pour produire avec force un effet uniforme et simple. (I: 18)

This remark, referring to the development of the sentiment of virtue via the circuitous path of masochism, refers equally well to the development of the autobiographical narrative. The incompatible elements that unite to produce the 'effet uniforme et simple' of the narrative are however quite different from those which Rousseau has narrated. In *Les Confessions,* they are the self-image which the author has already constructed and the life which he continues to live. The one is an elaborated fiction, whole and closed; the other open and unfinished. In order to present the *story* of his life, Rousseau must be to a certain degree outside the life, seeing it as a whole with a beginning, a middle, and some end in sight. The autobiographer's image of himself, poised against the facts of his past, is an indispensable source of the sense and direction which he is able to convey in his narrative. The image is what makes the narrative and story *his.*

Within Rousseau's narrative, Bossey is a beginning, a place outside the disjunction of time, where the wholeness of fiction is visible in the text, and in the author's nostalgic tone. Bossey is of course an actual place, a factual part of Rousseau's past. But its significance in *Les Confessions* stems from the fictional attributes which he confers on it, making it a firm point of reference, a place from which continuity can begin, at the start of an otherwise ungrounded succession of events. In actual time, one could say, nothing is either lost or gained. The discovery and loss, gift and denial which Rousseau makes one feel at this point in the narrative are mere semblances, which show that he has fastened his affections and despairs of quitting them. But when we have said this, we have said a great deal. With the involvement of sentiment, semblances are not 'mere'; they become a profound human reality.

Bossey provides a myth of paradise lost. As an author, Rousseau narrates this beginning, but he does not create it in his life. *Les Confessions* need a paradise regained, where Rousseau recovers what he claims to have lost. This would be the central focus of the narrative, a ground for both the life and the text. It occurs in Book VI, in the account of 'les Charmettes'.

## Books II – V

The narrative between the end of Book I and the start of Book VI affords perhaps the most enjoyable reading of the autobiography. Dramatic and sentimental episodes occur at regular intervals, appealing to the reader's sympathy and sense of pleasure – Rousseau's abrupt departure from Geneva, his inevitable meeting with Mme de Warens, his experiences with Catholics and aristocrats in Turin, with young ladies in Annecy, and with a host of travelling adventurers in between. The author brings these and other episodes to life with deftness and delight. The tone of the picaresque novel, the closest literary forebear to Rousseau's presentation at this point, combines with all the elements and force of a *roman d'apprentissage,* the genre which Stendhal and Balzac will develop from it.

Two aspects of this long narrative segment are of particular interest here. The first concerns episodes of 'caprice' and 'étourderie', or what Rousseau describes as 'momens de délire inconcevable où je n'étois plus moi-même' (I: 86; 101; 129; 148). These are various and more widespread than one might at first think. Some are harmless and make for 'good' stories in the autobiography. The adolescent Rousseau, for instance, decides he wants to be a musician. He invents a name — Vaussore de Villeneuve — to make himself an immediate success, even writes a concerto to present to the bourgeois community of Lausanne. The project goes ahead energetically until the actual performance, when the audience discovers and laughs at the pretence.

As an autobiographer, Rousseau can confidently wring every ounce of shame from this episode. The eventual success of the Devin redeems it completely. A similar adolescent episode, his wilful treatment of the Gouvon household, in Turin, also has no untoward consequences. No matter that this aristocratic family takes a penniless runaway from Geneva under its wing and intends to make a diplomat of him. Rousseau has greater aspirations. His irrational attitude and abrupt departure are more than justified by the later diplomatic post in Venice, or by his eventual relationship with the Luxembourgs.

Other episodes of 'caprice' and 'étourderie' make for 'bad' stories within the autobiography; they can never be redeemed. The story of the 'ruban volé' is the primary example here. Rousseau steals a ribbon to give to a maid he fancies. The theft is discovered, the household convened. In public, shamed, Rousseau disavows his action and states that the maid stole the ribbon to give him. The young girl is let go. More shame ensues. Rousseau-the-autobiographer describes at length and with even a degree of pleasure the inforgivable consequences of his deed. A similar 'bad' story occurs when Rousseau abandons M. Le Maitre, while this travelling companion falls ill on the streets of Lyon. 'Il fut délaissé de seul ami sur lequel il eut dû compter,' he writes. 'Je pris l'instant où personne ne songeoit à moi, je tournai le coin de la rue et je disparus' (I: 129).

Incidents such as these occur with surprising frequency. In them,

Rousseau appears dissociated from himself and performs actions against his stated will. What is striking to the reader is the discrepancy between the event actually described and the act of describing it, or the narrator's controlled pleasure in recalling his loss of self-control.

The second aspect of the narrative concerns Rousseau's relationship with Mme de Warens. From Book II onwards, she provides a constant point of reference, steadying the young man through his schizophrenic tendencies and adolescent wanderings. Except for the author himself, Mme de Warens is the single unresolved figure of the first six books. Her place in his life is still open, puzzling to Rousseau as he writes. This uncertainty serves to reinforce the importance accorded her in *Les Confessions*. This woman, because of her presence to Rousseau as he writes, becomes the one element of certainty in the autobiographer's account of the past. The young Rousseau leaves her only to return to her. Around her life he orientates and defines his own. When 'Maman', on one of his returns, has herself left for Paris, he begins his most extended series of unstable episodes (Book IV). For Rousseau, the continuity both of personal identity and of his narrative are closely linked to the fate of this relationship.

In Book VI, at 'les Charmettes', the two aspects of Books II–V come into direct contact. By establishing a permanent relationship with Mme de Warens, Rousseau hopes to establish firmly his own identity. The impulsive, irrational episodes will end; he will finally 'become himself'. This goal of course pertains not only to the relationship with an actual woman in the author's life; it applies also to his relation to the autobiographical text, which repeats at a rhetorical level the same will for stability which Rousseau ascribes to this period of his past.

### 'Les Charmettes': Context

Several paragraphs at the start of Book VI form the small narrative section truly central to 'les Charmettes', but their immediate context is also of decided interest. Near the end of Book V, Rousseau sets the stage, as it were, and states, 'Je touche au moment qui commence à lier mon existence passée avec la présente' (I: 212).

The moment of conjunction between a past and a present existence is crucial for any autobiography. It suggests both that the author feels distinctly separate from his past, has changed enough to consider himself a different person from what he once was; and also that he is enough the same person to narrate and to make sense of the change.

Without the feeling of separation, a person might never become an autobiographer, since the impulse to pick up a pen and to write about oneself is generally linked in some way to uncertainty about where one has come from and why, to a desire to restore a connection which has been lost, or to a certainty that one has arrived in the right place and can therefore better understand the place left behind. The pattern in all of these instances is unity in transition, the general framework of 'les Charmettes'. 'Les Charmettes' occurs at a moment of fundamental personal change, through which Rousseau wishes to maintain the continuity implied in the verb 'lier'.

There are precedents for this moment. Rousseau's instant of personal change on the road to Vincennes is one extreme; his theory of natural man's transformation into cultural man in the second *Discours* is another. But whether it is conceived as individual or collective, instantaneous or historical, transition in Rousseau always occurs along the lines of the temporal paradox of reverie and involves the affective notion of sentiment. Both transition and sentiment function 'doublement', bridging two different times (whether this be the past and the present, or the present and the future), and forging a continuity between the two. This continuity is the unity of affection and identity. When we enter Rousseau's narration of 'les Charmettes', therefore, we enter a macrocosm of sentiment: in it, he is both past and present, connected with the childhood of Books I–V, yet already introduced to the adult world of the latter half of *Les Confessions*. The transition at stake in 'les Charmettes' occurs at the level of Rousseau's life as a whole, and the sentiment involved is nothing less than 'le bonheur'. Accordingly, it forms the turning point in the first stage of the autobiography, the centre of the narrative.

It is no accident that the author should place his 'séjour . . . de bonheur et de l'innocence' (I: 224) in the critical passage from boyhood to manhood. Within his œuvre, the second *Discours* is the strongest precedent. Although their points of reference are apparently quite different, *Les Confessions* emulates the structure of the earlier text with remarkable consistency. In Rousseau's life, 'les Charmettes' plays the role of the 'juste milieu', the middle ground, in his historical anthropology. It bridges the gap between the 'natural' first half of the text, and the avowed deterioration in the second half. This period of time – truly temporal in that it marks precisely a moment of change – 'dut être l'époque la plus heureuse, la plus durable' according to the second *Discours* (III: 171).[10] The same imperative holds for *Les Confessions*.

Rousseau places his 'bonheur', his one overriding sentiment, at the moment in his life where he is most explicitly 'doublement'. The autobiographical narrative will strain to elevate and to prolong the stay at 'les Charmettes' to the mythical, atemporal status of the 'juste milieu' described in the theoretical work. This comparison suggests that the continuity which Rousseau attains in the opening of Book VI is the continuity of fiction. Fiction is the important link in the formation of temporal duration, both at the level of the life (in reverie) and in the autobiographical narrative (in Book VI).

Two facts support this argument. The first comes from the second major precedent for the opening of Book VI – an autobiographical precedent, since it occurs in the *Lettres à Malesherbes*. There, the move to l'Ermitage plays the same role attributed in *Les Confessions* to 'les Charmettes' (I: 1138). This redundancy in no way detracts from the value of either of Rousseau's versions, as if they became thereby 'merely' fictions. There are clear reasons for the change, and even stronger reasons why the procedure of inventing a fiction and taking it to be real is valid and important. In early 1762, the date of the *Lettres*, Rousseau's perspective on his life probably extended back only to 1750 and to the beginning of his activity as a writer. For this particular period of time, the move to l'Ermitage indeed constitutes the crucial moment of transition in his existence, since it marks the retreat of the writer from the social world toward the creation of a textual world. Several years later, in the period of the drafting and writing of *Les Confessions*, Rousseau's perspective has changed. He has fled from Montmorency into exile; 'Maman' has died. These events help to encourage a visit to Savoy, and his childhood can begin to take on a new significance (I: xxii). The transitional period at twenty-six years of age is now more easily construed as central to the entire life of the author. It separates existence along lines more in keeping with the second *Discours*, into a natural 'before' of childhood and a corrupted 'after' as a writer in Paris. The most important new element is Mme de Warens, with whom Rousseau shares the experience of 'les Charmettes'. More than Thérèse, Mme d'Épinay, or Sophie d'Houdetot, she alone is eligible to participate in the myth of continuity which the author desires. The description of their reciprocal attachment, the interpersonal reverie of two persons in one, is accordingly placed at the end of Book V, just before the narration of 'les Charmettes' (I: 222).[11]

Rousseau focuses on 'les Charmettes' in much the same terms as he did l'Ermitage. He projects it into a fictive register, and takes it to be his one essential experience of continuity and happiness. *Which* experience is given the wholeness of fiction is not so important as the need to have *one* fiction, or as the need for unity which makes the fiction into a reality for the autobiographer. We touch here on an issue which may pertain to autobiography in general, not just to Rousseau, although he brings it to the fore more clearly than most. For him, the need for unity stems mainly from the threat to personal identity imposed by time — a threat which ensures that the fictional 'lieu privilégié' will be placed at a crucial point of transition in the auto-biographer's life. This is the basic point of my reading of *Les Confessions*. Personal identity is a choice — to invent, to believe, and to will a fiction *as* one's identity. The choice itself is a response to, and, in Rousseau's case, a barrier against the arbitrary — the fact that time may at any moment undo the invention, and show it and therefore its inventor to be a fiction. But the choice itself is not at all arbitrary; it is a necessity. The choice, not the fiction chosen, nor the time which makes one choose, is what makes identity personal in a life or a text. Rousseau will say about 'les Charmettes' that it gives him 'le droit de dire que j'ai vécu' (I: 225).

The second consideration supporting our argument concerns the actual inconsistencies and repetitions in *Les Confessions* at this particular stage of the narrative. They suggest that the author interrupts what must have been a confused and tortured period of his life in order to transform retrospectively the 'court et précieux intervalle' of 'les Charmettes' into a 'sentiment délicieux' (I: 222; 223). The signs of myth-making are primarily evident in the anomaly of Rousseau's happiness when it is contrasted with other events which, he tells us, occurred in the same period. His life with 'Maman' is possible only at the cost of an ongoing psychosomatic illness, induced largely to postpone the entry into manhood which she encourages him to make. The sombre tone employed to describe this dilemma does not just highlight the description of happiness, it is inconsistent with it. Rousseau tells us enough about his relationship with Mme de Warens to show that in reality she was hardly the person his fond remembrance would make her.

A second interruption is evident in the narration itself, which becomes disjointed in the shift from Book V to Book VI, and again partway into Book VI. The likely explanation for this unusual lack of coherence is that the actual process of Rousseau's composition was interrupted; he wrote Book VI at a later date and in a different place from Books I–V (I: xxvi–xxvii; 243–5; 1342). But it is also possible that the delay in composition and consequent overlappings are a reflection in the narration of tensions which belong to what is being narrated. In any event, the construction of the myth of 'les Charmettes' and its insertion into *Les Confessions* force a change in the narrative. Taking the narrative line itself as the textual version of time, we find confirmed from a different angle the earlier point about time. Rousseau's happiness must even fight against the temporal verisimilitude of his own autobiography.

## Narrative and Allegory

Book VI opens with a short quote in Latin, Rousseau's first epigraph since the start of Book I. After a brief comment on it, he writes:

Ici commence le court bonheur de ma vie; ici viennent les paisibles mais rapides momens qui m'ont donné le droit de dire que j'ai vécu. Momens précieux et si regrettés, ah recommencez pour moi vôtre aimable cours; coulez plus lentement dans mon souvenir s'il est possible, que vous ne fites reellement dans votre fugitive succession. Comment ferai-je pour prolonger à mon gré ce récit si touchant et si simple; pour redire toujours les mêmes choses, et n'ennuyer pas plus mes lecteurs en les répétant que je ne m'ennuyois moi-même en les recommençant sans cesse? Encore si tout cela consistoit en faits, en actions, en paroles, je pourrois le décrire et le rendre, en quelque façon: mais comment dire ce qui n'étoit ni dit, ni fait, ni pensé même, mais goûté, mais senti, sans que je puisse énoncer d'autre objet de mon bonheur que ce sentiment même. (I: 225)

Here, more than at any other point in *Les Confessions,* Rousseau faces directly the issue of narrative and its reference to sentiment. The passage eloquently displays the temporal problems involved. Rousseau begins with a strong affirmation of the 'court bonheur' in his life. 'Ici commence', he states, as though creating the sentiment by declarative fiat. But his happiness is so short-lived that the text immediately becomes a sort of invocation, a request for the grace of what he has just affirmed. 'Ici commence...' turns into 'ah recommencez pour moi', and the text quickly shifts to an elegiac tone.

The imagery of the passage expresses two different aspects of time. One involves the continuity of a liquid 'cours', flowing slowly in memory. It is obviously this sense of gentle unity which Rousseau desires to call forth and to 'prolong'. But the mention of time also describes it as a 'fugitive succession', its mode 'reellement'. The reader can only stand by, watching the author in a dialogue with these two aspects of time – the one affective and human, the other almost mechanical and inhuman. For the passage thereafter becomes a question, and demonstrates its inability to convey the sentiment of happiness except in repetition. A series of prefixes in 're' within the question – 'recommencez . . . redire . . . répétant . . . recommençant . . .' – then gives way to Rousseau's textual enactment of his sentiment, in the actual repetitions which continue the passage:

> Je me levois avec le soleil et j'étois heureux; je me promenois et j'étois heureux, je voyois maman et jétois heureux, je la quittois et j'étois heureux, je parcourois . . . j'errois . . . je lisois . . . et le bonheur me suivoit par tout; il n'étoit dans aucune chose assignable, il étoit tout en moi-même, il ne pouvoit me quitter un seul instant. (I: 225–6)

The sentiment of happiness narrated here is like time itself, continuous in repetition, like the regular pulsing of a heartbeat. Discursively, it presents the difficulties noticed in connection with the writing of reverie. The text cannot represent reverie or happiness, because they are self-sufficient wholes, without reference outside themselves. The repetition is not just a textual re-enactment, it is the only direct way the narrative of *Les Confessions* can express completeness and totality. For Rousseau, all of time focuses in the 'short interval' of 'les Charmettes', so short that it is really no more than an instant. His experience there is that of the necessary fiction in which one believes oneself to be outside time, and therefore outside the disintegrating succession of actual events. For this reason, the autobiographer takes it to be the cornerstone or ground of his personal identity, a place where he is truly himself. But when he tries to express and to prolong the totality in his narrative, Rousseau has recourse only to the repeated phrase, '. . . et j'étois heureux . . .', which indicates the pathos of inaccessibility as much as an affirmation, a refrain miming the succession of time, not its wholeness.

Why is Rousseau unable to give his happiness the duration it deserves? Why, at this particular point in the narrative, are his lyrical powers so entwined with a repetitive structure which seems their exact antithesis? As early as Book II, he has prophesied the coming of the happiness described above; and the account in Book VI serves as the standard against which all subsequent experiences will be judged (and found wanting). As the time and place where Rousseau was

Rousseau, no matter how much he has changed or might change, 'les Charmettes' is the point of convergence for the prospective and retro-spective movements in the text, constitutes the hinge on which the narrative turns, and the source of its unity. Why do we find simply the eloquent paragraph of repetitive invocation above, surrounded on either side by a mixed account which includes the descriptions of Rousseau's various illnesses and sorrows at the time?

The analysis of the last chapter may be of some assistance here, particularly our discussion of 'l'Élysée'. It is instructive to compare 'les Charmettes' with 'l'Élysée', since the two 'lieux privilégiés' function in a similar manner in the two texts where they are found. Both are versions of the traditional convention of the Utopian topos where existence is 'other' than, separate from, normal life. Readers are able to understand the two retreats from the actual world against this common background. But they are also quite different. 'L'Élysée' is a fairly static vision, rigorous as its configuration may be for an under-standing of Rousseau's imaginative universe. The intricate detail and beauty of the garden are in keeping with the author's ability to render the topos in spatial terms, and through allegorical references which are formal and purely literary (primarily to the *Roman de la rose*). A literary, intertextual mode of allegory is consistent with the framework of *La Nouvelle Héloïse,* which refers to the sentiments of fictive charac-ters, not to their author.

One could say that 'les Charmettes' is 'l'Élysée' in temporal form. In the autobiography, the topos cannot be purely fictional, or fully interpreted in Utopian terms, because it is meant to refer to the author's life. Like *La Nouvelle Héloïse, Les Confessions* have a strong allegorical element, but the allegory is not 'about' anything in particu-lar – it is the narrative line itself. This non-referential, temporal alle-gory articulates a double commitment of the autobiographer. Rousseau's first commitment is to the actual past, to the facts, events, and sensations which follow one another in the discontinuity of a 'fugitive succession'. His second, more positive commitment lies in the elaborated image in the fictive, pre-autobiographical writings, in the pre-writing of memory, and in the continuity of an 'aimable cours'.

In more basic terms, the two sides to the autobiographical allegory repeat at a rhetorical level the dual structure broached in our intro-ductory description of the autobiographical self. Without regard to what it is actually 'about', the narrative line of the text can be ab-stractly considered as the indeterminate, temporal boundary between two heterogeneous levels of the self, held together in the unity of a personal history. But what was once a potential identity, a virtual self, is now Rousseau's self-image in his textual world. Its consistency and strength suffuse and colour the autobiographer's account of the past, and give the narrative in *Les Confessions* its direction and force. This does not mean that the past is distorted – Rousseau is rarely unfaithful to it, and 'les Charmettes' is outstanding among the occasions when the need for coherence and fiction is more important to him than the facts. But the 'facts', in any event, do not of themselves make a narrative. It is the commitment to both fact and fiction, image and actual self, which engenders and sustains the narrative line of the autobiography, and which makes it a textual equivalent to the movement of time in the author's life.

'Les Charmettes' brings to the surface the allegorical structure of *Les Confessions* because Rousseau attempts there to establish, *within* the narrative, a firm point of reference for his story. He fastens his image of happiness to a specific episode from the past, holding to it, not as an image, but as himself. He does this in order to retain the innocence of childhood, the 'ce qui n'est plus' of the autobiography, within the adult world which he must begin to narrate. The episode thus links past and future in the narrative, in a present which Rousseau wants to make into the stable unity of a 'juste milieu'. But the narrative itself is incapable of expressing this unity except as a history. While Rousseau hesitates, to bring his fiction directly into the text, the text itself becomes structurally more like the succession of actual time, and less like a fiction, than at any other point in *Les Confessions*. In other words, as soon as Rousseau tries to bring the completeness of his textual world *into* the text of the autobiography, the text itself must stop momentarily, marking time with the repetitive diction of 'et j'étois heureux'. The autobiographical allegory is undone, shows its underside, and, by announcing the temporal opposition between the 'aimable cours' and the 'fugitive succession', goes outside its own limits in much the same way that 'l'Élysée' did in the spatial opposition between the gentle water-play within the garden and the disruptive 'jet d'eau' outside it.

*Transition to Dialogues*

'Cette seconde partie n'a que cette même vérité de commune avec la prémiére ... A cela près, elle ne peut que lui être inférieure en tout', Rousseau states, vaunting his continued veracity at the beginning of

Book VII (I: 279). The final six books of the narrative were revised and written rapidly as a second instalment to the work in late 1769 and early 1770, two years after the author had completed the first six (I: xxviii–xxxx). Although large portions of Books VII, VIII and IX preserve the discursive integrity of the earlier half, Rousseau's critical comment about the latter portion aptly characterizes the literary quality of the remaining narrative. The playful, generally unified voice in the autobiographical account of childhood and youth becomes increasingly strident. The rhetorical structure of *Les Confessions,* likened earlier to melody, begins to display a multiplicity of voice and contrapuntal organization which we shall find again in the *Dialogues.*

The shift from one rhetorical stage to the next is not abrupt, but occurs gradually in the second half of *Les Confessions,* accelerating as the remembered time of the narrative approaches the actual present of the writing author. Nor is the shift entirely unexpected. Although one might wish to consider the change in tone and tempo as a result of Rousseau's haste, it pertains instead to an internal logic in the auto-biography. The unity and fluid coherence of the author's voice lasts only as long as he remains distanced from the story he has to tell, and can narrate it with immediacy and pleasure. 'Les Charmettes' marks a watershed both in the life and in the autobiography: it brings Rousseau into his adulthood with the certainty that the naturalness of childhood comes with him; but it also brings his story out of a closed circuit and into the open-ended process of the life he is still living.

'Affreuse illusion des choses humaines!', Rousseau exclaims near the end of Book VI, noting the change (I: 270). Within the narrative, he has discovered that life will never live up to the wholeness of the image he has made of it, nor to the whole happiness which, he now feels, has been left behind. With this awareness, a fundamental un-happiness sets in. But he can now consider 'les Charmettes' a 'sémence' of goodness, which with adversity will develop into a mature virtue:

Ainsi commencérent à germer avec mes malheurs les vertus dont la sémence étoit au fond de mon ame, que l'étude avoit cultivées, et qui n'attendoient pour éclore que le ferment de l'adversité. (I: 264)

This sentence marks the first point in *Les Confessions* where the phrase 'ici commence le court bonheur de ma vie', is balanced by its inversion, 'ainsi commencérent . . . mes malheurs'. The happiness declared at the start of Book VI, though repeated in that limited section of narrative, is singular. Rousseau's unhappinesses, on the other hand, are plural. They are repeated at varying intervals throughout Books VII-XII with an insistence equalled only by the first refrain, 'et j'étois heureux'. 'J'ai dû faire une pause à la fin du précédent livre', he states at the beginning of Book VIII. 'Avec celui-ci commence dans sa prémiére origine la longue chaine de mes malheurs' (I: 349). In the midst of Book IX: 'Ici commence le long tissu de malheurs de ma vie, où l'on verra peu d'interruption' (I: 446). Or at the start of Book XII: 'Ici commence l'œuvre de tenebres dans lequel depuis huit ans je me trouve enseveli' (I: 589).[12] Obviously, Rousseau does not construct and take for real his image of happiness without simultaneously generating a counter-image along similar structural lines. One could say that the point in *Les Confessions* where the author attempts to ground the narrative is also the point at which the narrative begins to break apart at the seams. For the opposition between image and counter-image, indicated in the sentences above, is the basis of the *Dialogues*. It emerges even before Rousseau formalizes the new structure explicitly in the second stage of the autobiography.

In the transformation, *Les Confessions* gradually lose their interest as a narrative text. Rousseau's life in Paris and in Venice are well described, and the account of the move to l'Ermitage, early in Book IX, creates an interlude, like a secondary topos of temporary happiness within his adult existence. But the haste of the 1769–70 composition manifests itself regularly thereafter. Rousseau's insertion of justificatory letters makes his text patchy and stuttering. The squabbling voices of Mme d'Épinay, Diderot, the Luxembourgs, and of the author himself foreshadow the rigid argumentation of the *Dialogues. Les Confessions* split into two levels, that of the letters and that of the narrative, and it becomes increasingly difficult to discern which accompanies which.

In Book XI, Rousseau's stock of letters depleted, the text resumes a more straightforward course. His account of a stay on l'Isle de St. Pierre, in Book XII, affords a backward glimpse of the serenity and happiness ascribed to 'les Charmettes', and might have made a fitting conclusion to the work, linking with Bossey, 'les Charmettes', and to a certain extent l'Ermitage, as an end to a beginning and middle. But *Les Confessions* do not conclude. They are open-ended, and lead to a struggle with the counter-image that has arisen. Rousseau will discover the significance of his reveries by the shore of the Lac de Bienne only

in the last stage of the autobiography, in a rhetorical mode at one
remove from the narrative we have investigated here.

## Dialogues

> Voulant être ce qu'on n'est pas on parvient à
> se croire autre chose que ce qu'on est, et voilà
> comment on devient fou.
>
> Je me suis accusé d'avance plus fortement
> peut-être que personne ne m'accusera.
>
> > 'R' in the Preface in dialogue to
> > *La Nouvelle Héloïse* (II: 21; 27)

> It is precisely the most general expression for
> madness that the individual has an absolute
> relationship to what is relative. From the
> aesthetic point of view this condition is to be
> apprehended as comical, since the comical is
> always rooted in the contradictory.
>
> > Kierkegaard,
> > *Concluding Unscientific Postscript*
> > (pp. 377–8)

To the reader who thinks of Rousseau in the sunlight and seeming
spontaneity of earlier portions of *Les Confessions,* his *Dialogues* present
a strange, difficult contrast. One opens the second autobiographical
text as if one were entering a darkened sickroom of the imagination,
cautiously, on tiptoe, with discretion and sensibilities muffled against
the diseased insistence of its author. The work is tortured, repetitious,
and difficult to read. In the reading, it offers little enjoyment. Once
read, it hardly warrants recommendation to another reader. One would
like to be able to disregard the work, or to relegate it to a peripheral
corner of Rousseau's œuvre.

Yet the *Dialogues,* despite their literary failings, are essential to
understanding Rousseau, especially when read as the second stage in
the development of his autobiography. Begun in 1772 and written
regularly every day for fifteen minutes over the four-year period to
1776 (I: 837), the text bears a metaphorical resemblance to a box of
vitamin tablets, collected and administered daily to keep the author
healthy in his paranoia. Rousseau's illness, the affective correlate of
his mistake as an autobiographer of taking his fiction for reality (a
step which by implication makes the world around him fictional and

unreal), reaches its most acute point during the writing of the work. The author battles textually to ascertain and salvage for posterity his 'true' identity, against what he considers the 'false' image fabricated by a plot of unknown 'Messieurs'. He feels society to be active and unanimous in its misunderstanding of him. The *Dialogues* are his attempt to stage an imaginary tribunal. Judging between 'J.J.' and the social image of him, they are meant to exorcize the impostor and to justify the innocent party.

Questions about the validity or invalidity of Rousseau's long-winded argument, about the very real persecution in his life, or even about the mental disorder which the text reflects and perhaps sustains, will not be the concern of the present analysis. We shall work instead to demonstrate the extraordinary rigour with which the author pursues his mad aims, and how the *Dialogues* function consistently within the autobiographical project. As Gagnebin and Raymond state, 'le tragique se déclare le jour où Rousseau, réellement persécuté, ne peut plus se passer de persécuteurs, le jour ou il lui faut des méchants . . . afin que la certitude de son innocence ne puisse plus être mise en question' (I: xliv). The *Dialogues* hardly share a common boundary with the objective persecution; they occur within Rousseau's affective tragedy. As a result, they are slightly ludicrous, a living, static melodrama. They are perhaps best considered as a play, deserving to be witnessed in performance but condemned to a 'répétition perpétuelle'. They never reach the stage, nor their intended audience. The *Dialogues* are a document, a monument to useless, sustained passion.

## Three Characters

In a Preface, 'Du Sujet et de la forme de cet écrit', Rousseau introduces the work and its three characters, 'Rousseau', 'le Francois', and 'J.J.' Each is essential to the *Dialogues,* the first two as the participants and (initially) opposed interlocutors, the third as the distanced and excluded subject of their discourse. The text is constructed around their respective roles. Rousseau states in the Preface:

La forme du dialogue m'ayant paru la plus propre à discuter le pour et le contre, je l'ai choisie pour cette raison. J'ai pris la liberté de reprendre dans ces entretiens mon nom de famille que le public a jugé à propos de m'ôter, et je me suis designé en tiers à son exemple par celui de baptême auquel il lui a plu de me réduire. En prenant un François pour mon autre interlocuteur, je n'ai rien fait que d'obligeant et d'honnête pour le nom qu'il porte, puisque je me suis abstenu de le rendre complice d'une conduite que je désaprouve ... celui que j'ai mis en scene est tel qu'il seroit aussi heureux pour moi qu'honorable à son pays qu'il s'y en trouvât beaucoup qui l'imitassent. (I: 663)

A unified 'je' speaks here, similar to the narrative voice of *Les Confessions.* But it is describing a division in identity and voice which will permit the *Dialogues.* Taking his cue from the attacks of what is called simply, 'le public', Rousseau adopts a defensive, self-justificatory strategy. Two independent clauses mark the split: 'Rousseau', the family name which the author recovers from the public domain,[13] will argue on behalf of 'J.J.' The christian name denotes a different, apparently unrelated character.

The two characters of the *Dialogues* embodying separate but inseparable aspects of Rousseau are an extreme demonstration of the intimate impersonality of the autobiographical self. The split between 'Rousseau' and 'J.J.' makes one character superficially independent and impersonal for the purposes of investigating and defending the intimate beliefs of the other. We are at the outset of a sort of anthropological expedition into the self, where the distance and strange affinity between two alien cultures occurs at the level of an individual identity. As much as the earlier, autobiographical narrative assumes the unity of authorial identity, the *Dialogues* presuppose its duality. Both texts involve the same claim of totality. The perspective is subjective, internal, and sentimental in the first instance; in the second, it is objective, external, and rational. The *Dialogues* will defend in argument the sentiments initially expressed in *Les Confessions.* This change is visible in the introductions to the two texts.

*Les Confessions:*
Moi seul. Je sens mon cœur et je connois les hommes ... Si je ne vaux pas mieux, au moins je suis autre. (I: 5)

*Dialogues:*
Un silence fier et dédaigneux est en pareil cas plus à sa place, et eut été bien plus de mon gout; mais il n'auroit pas rempli mon objet, et pour le remplir il falloit que je disse de quel œil, si j'étois un autre, je verrois un homme tel que je suis. (I: 665)

Uniqueness and difference, which Rousseau assumed *vis-à-vis* other men at the start of the narrative, he now assumes from himself. 'Rousseau', the personified extension of the conditional clause, 'si j'étois un autre', now speaks for the author's right to say 'je suis autre'.

This opening strategy allows the inclusion of a second, opposing view in the *Dialogues*. 'Le François' stands in for the public, speaking 'against' in the imaginary space of the text. This character, though anonymous, is strictly qualified. Not only is he an explicitly theatrical figure, in a 'scene' set and directed in the vested interest of the author, but the role of 'le François' also does not correspond to those elements of the public which Rousseau's writing is designed to combat. Because 'le François' is not an accomplice to the plot which the author feels directed against him, his arguments must be limited ones. Rousseau effectively neutralizes the opponent of 'Rousseau'. Far from representing any one person or point of view, 'le François' resembles an uncast character at the disposal of the director. Uncast, he serves to be persuaded rather than to persuade. He does have one determining trait, however; he is a man. It is hard to imagine Rousseau deploying his rational capacities against a female character. A 'la Françoise' would be quite out of place.

Instead of considering this 'you' as a straw man for the public, we would do better to interpret 'le François' as an unformed, neutral, and to a certain extent purely virtual figure, which will gradually assume shape and character in the course of the text. The definition will be especially useful in the next chapter, where it applies also to the reader in the autobiography.

The position of 'J.J.' as a third party ('en tiers'), or as 'it', indicates his qualitative difference from the two interlocutors. Like characters in a play, their speech constitutes the text. 'J.J.' remains perpetually in the wings. In this sense his role is a negative one. He can enter the *Dialogues* only through quotations conveyed by one of the interlocutors. 'J.J.' seems condemned to the status of an object, a piece of petrified discourse. A further stigma is also visible in the fact that there must be two 'J.J.'s, one for each speaker and side of the argument. So long as he is considered one individual, 'J.J.' befuddles their discussion. 'Rousseau' and 'le François', in order to stabilize their conversation, quickly proceed to invent and to argue for a particular version of the character. 'Vous unissez des choses que je sépare', 'Rousseau' remarks about 'J.J.' early in the first dialogue. 'L'Auteur des Livres et celui des crimes vous paroit la même personne; je me crois fondé à en faire deux. Voila, Monsieur, le mot de l'énigme' (I: 674).

The various reductions of 'J.J.' indicate in another sense his unspeakable importance. Third party to the text, he stands outside its range, an indeterminate question mark animating the discussion.

Rousseau, of course, writes the text in order to eradicate the indeterminacy and to resolve the question according to his own fictive answer. But the rational arguments he employs in the *Dialogues* serve to highlight the fact that the sort of identity involved in the character 'J.J.' is not susceptible to discursive analysis. The investigation by 'Rousseau' and 'le François' can only exacerbate the problem they set out to resolve. Exasperated, 'Rousseau' states at one point, 'la même chose ne sauroit être et ne pas être' (I: 879). 'J.J.' defies this axiom of rational discourse, the law of contradiction. Every affirmation of his existence implies its negation, the affirmation of his non-being. The thematic oppositions of innocence and guilt, natural and monstrous, white and black, which attach to the two versions of 'J.J.' are no more than determinate extensions of the two interlocutors, who have as their ongoing task to bring the unsayable into speech. 'J.J.' is not two individuals, he is one. But when Rousseau attempts through arguments to grasp this impossible unity, his own most intimate self, it confuses and slips through the net of binary oppositions in the *Dialogues,* and surfaces in the impersonality of a monstrous double. As 'Rousseau' states it, rational argument about 'J.J.' must finally cede to a different type of discourse: 'J'en use dans mon jugement sur cet homme comme dans ma croyance en matiére de foi' (I: 879).

## Getting Started – Outline

As with *Les Confessions,* the most instructive approach to the *Dialogues* is to observe how they get underway. The start is fairly odd and awkward – Rousseau generates momentum through the fabrication of a misunderstanding, inventing a problem in order to be able to solve it. This arises through interference between statements made by 'Rousseau' or 'le François' and the attitudes they can be expected to hold toward 'J.J.' For no apparent reason, the interlocutors become reversible.

In any dialogue, the positions of interlocutors must be interchangeable, in the simple sense that they take turns speaking and listening. But here the reversibility of 'I' and 'you' roles extends to the positions 'for' and 'against', which causes significant disruption. 'Rousseau', whom one expects to praise 'J.J.', begins by expostulating, 'Que je le vais détester!' (I: 667). He seems to take the position 'against' and 'le François', whom one expects to criticize the man and his works, instead praises *Le Devin du village* in glowing terms, or provides 'Rousseau' with ample descriptions of 'la ligue', the plot against 'J.J.', which can only damage his argument (I: 685; 700–21).

The false start produced by such role shifts is not uncommon in fictional texts. It can be used as a strategy and embellished through plot and character conflict to a high degree of sophistication. A text establishes an expectation, or a set of expectations, which it purposely does not fulfil. The resulting delay and uncertainty generate a process of resolution. This is the movement of the text. The *Dialogues* are noteworthy in this regard mainly for the awkwardness with which Rousseau sets and manipulates expectations.

There are two possible explanations for the patent falseness of the start of the *Dialogues*. First, the process of creating and resolving textual uncertainties is an art of fiction, best served by plot constructions. One might speculate that Rousseau's autobiographical plot has run especially thin after *Les Confessions,* and that his capacities for fiction, now exercised largely in the paranoid invention of 'la ligue', are not brought to bear in a text straining so desperately to exorcize this projection.

A second explanation for the initial confusion may perhaps lie in the ambivalent identity of 'J.J.' Until 'Rousseau' and 'le François' succeed in establishing two versions of the character (which they have not yet done at the start of the first dialogue) – in other words, until the tripartite structure of the *Dialogues* becomes quadripartite – the text wavers and stutters. In a technical sense, the reversibility of the interlocutors indicates a displacement of the indeterminacy of 'J.J.' on to the level of discourse. Their seemingly unnecessary misunderstanding reflects an essential misunderstanding attaching to him. When conventions about 'J.J.' are established, the argument quickly gets underway and proceeds more smoothly. The phenomenon of reversibility will not reappear until the text has run its course, when 'Rousseau' and 'le François' are as united in understanding as they were in misunderstanding. They then speak in one voice, practically scrambling over one another to praise 'J.J.'

The basic organization of the work is not complicated. The first dialogue enters almost immediately into a description of 'monde idéal semblable au nôtre et néanmoins tout différent', which 'Rousseau' and quotations from 'J.J.' defend throughout the text (I: 668–72). This fictional place and time, which informed the narrative of *Les Confessions* and was finally given the brief duration of 'les Charmettes', takes a fully Utopian, imaginary form in the *Dialogues*. It is not developed through actual events from the author's life, nor invoked for continuity at a moment of transition, but instead resembles a humanized, static version of the state of Nature given in the first section of the second *Discours*. Rousseau has regressed from the 'juste milieu' to a naturalism altogether precluding the need or possibility of change.

The first 'Dialogue' makes its way through various levels of misunderstanding between interlocutors, provoked mainly by the issue of authorship imputed to or denied 'J.J.' The discussion slowly lays the ground for an eventual clarification: 'Rousseau' and 'le François' make a contract. The first knows the texts but not the man; the second knows the man (through the eyes of 'la ligue'), but not the texts. Each agrees to complete his knowledge, by reading or visiting 'J.J.' This contract establishes the rationale and structure for the second and third 'Dialogues', both of which occur after returns from visits to man or text. In the second, longest dialogue – which effectively becomes a monologue for extended stretches – 'Rousseau' delivers his report and observations of 'J.J.' the man; in the third, shortest dialogue, 'le François' reports on his reading of the texts. Within this general outline, the text develops in complex and occasionally fascinating detail.

## *Frames and Framing*

The metaphor of the *frame* provides the most succinct approach to the *Dialogues*. This concerns first of all the different levels of discourse operating in a text. 'Level' is itself a spatial metaphor, not a definite concept. Each level of discourse defines itself in relation or opposition to other levels in the text, and through oppositions internal to it. A quote within a narrative, for instance, occupies a different level from the main body of the text; the letters which Rousseau inserts in *Les Confessions* can be said to be framed by the surrounding narrative. In the *Dialogues,* the primary textual level is the discussion of 'Rousseau' and 'le François', each the personification of an individual and opposed point of view.

From this primary level, secondary levels may be distinguished, each of them framing, or framed by, the dialogue. The preface, postscript, and footnotes constitute one secondary level. They form a coherent 'hors-texte', a distanced and 'objective' perspective on the *Dialogues* as a whole. At one remove, the author speaks in a single, unified voice. Rousseau is not 'Rousseau', and does not encroach directly upon discussion.

At a corresponding distance from the primary level of dialogue, framed by it, we find 'J.J.' His voice must be transported into the text in the form of quotation. 'Rousseau' and 'le François' converse about him with the same degree of 'objectivity' that Rousseau enjoys in talking about *their* conversation. But to what degree, and with what sort of objectivity, are so far uncertain.

The variety of levels of *énonciation* in the *Dialogues* is quite different from the single, unified 'I' that one expects in a narrative voice. Alternately 'au delà' and 'en-deçà', on the far and near sides of the imaginary conversation, the framing and framed voices of 'Rousseau' and 'J.J.' seem curiously at its mercy, unable to control its incessant argumentation. This structure, although it excludes them, also affects them. For the voices 'inside' and 'outside' the *Dialogues* (to employ explicitly the prepositions implicit in the spatial terms 'level' and 'frame'), are in fact identical. A passage from the second dialogue demonstrates the repetition. When 'Rousseau' returns from his visit to 'J.J.', his report includes the following remark:

Il a fait encore un effort et s'occupant derechef malgré lui de sa destinée et de ses persécuteurs, il a écrit en forme de Dialogue une espéce de jugement d'eux et de lui assez semblable à celui qui pourra resulter de nos entretiens. (I: 836)

Here the *Dialogues* discuss a 'J.J.' who has written a dialogue discussing a 'J.J.' . . . What happens? The reflexive reference generates a *mise en abîme*, a proliferation in the frames and levels already described. The voice of 'J.J.', in quotes, surges forward at this point in the *Dialogues* to displace the report of 'Rousseau'.[14] This shift of level is certainly not coincidental and is somewhat disturbing. For if, with the emergence of 'J.J.', 'J.J.' replaces 'Rousseau', what becomes at this point of 'Rousseau'? Does he not displace the apparently unified 'I' of the preface, Rousseau? And what then happens to the controlling author? It is not enough to state that the 'I' of the preface, postscript, and footnotes is identical with the 'I' who speaks in quotation marks. The problem lies in a loss of control and disappearance of the author.

The frames in the text can be repeated *ad infinitum*. When this repetition occurs, the distinction between what is framing and what is framed breaks down. The *Dialogues,* with Rousseau's characteristic thoroughness, display the potential for infinite regression in sharp relief.

Without thematic reference, the metaphor of the frame concerns only the structure of *énonciation* in the *Dialogues,* and remains dry and neutral. But a frame, and activity of framing, do have an obvious non-structural meaning which suits the primary theme of Rousseau's text. The author feels that he has been 'framed', made to assume guilt for a crime which he did not commit. Can one move from a purely formal to a figural definition of frame? Admittedly, the step is at this point tenuously dependent on a coincidence of the English language. But as soon as one begins to think it through, the connection proves a plausible, useful device for understanding the text.

The *Dialogues* include several anecdotes, taken by Rousseau from contemporary news journals, and which demonstrate the connection between the structure of frames in the *énonciation* and the author's thematic concern about guilt and innocence, or the figural frame enclosing him in the dock. They occur in the opening 'Dialogue' and are recounted by 'Rousseau' to support his argument for the innocence of 'J.J.' I shall analyse the first anecdote, adapted from the *Gazette de Leyde.*

Un homme accusé dans un tribunal d'Angleterre d'un délit notoire attesté par un témoignage public et unanime se défendit par un *alibi* bien singulier. Il soutint et prouva que le même jour et à la même heure où on l'avoit vu commettre le crime il étoit en personne occupé à se défendre devant un autre tribunal et dans une autre ville d'une accusation toute semblable . . . A force de recherches et d'enquêtes . . . on découvrit enfin que les délits attribués à cet accusé avoient été commis par un autre homme moins connu mais si semblable au prémier de taille, de figure, et de traits qu'on avoit constamment pris l'un pour autre. (I: 735–6)

The story is presented to show a man unjustly accused and to draw sympathy for 'J.J.' in a similar predicament (even the mention of England must have struck an emotional chord in Rousseau). It underscores the judicial aspect of the *Dialogues.* Like two attorneys (one of whom happens also to be the judge), 'Rousseau' and 'le François' have convened to give 'J.J.' a hearing. The problem of 'J.J.'s dual identity is like that of having a double. To be haunted by a separate but identical individual means that one can never take full responsibility for one's actions, nor act fully, since one never wholly belongs to oneself. Personal identity becomes quite meaningless, as does the notion of authorship, whether of actions or of texts.

Because of the double, the accused individual in the newspaper story has been 'framed' by circumstances beyond his control, and made responsible for a crime which he did not commit. But while the story definitely conveys this figural sense of 'frame', it also generates the same *mise en abîme* noted in the levels of *énonciation* in the *Dialogues*. Where was the defendant when the crime was being committed? In another courtroom, defending himself against another crime. Where was he at the time of the second crime? . . . In yet another courtroom, one must assume, defending himself yet again.

The newspaper story conveys in a microcosm the sense of the *Dialogues*. At both structural and thematic levels, it demonstrates the infinite regression of Rousseau's self-justification and misdemeanour, the horror of a man who must spend his entire life in a sequence of courtrooms defending himself against a crime committed while he was in the preceding courtroom. He never acts, but is constrained to exist in perpetual reaction. Like a man who writes his life instead of living it, the process becomes the vicious circle of a 'procès', a trial with which one can never be finished.

The link between the two types of frame may now be strong enough to support the hypothesis that the 'levels' of theme and structure in the *Dialogues* are themselves mere repetitions in the infinite regress we have observed at each level individually. This is a new argument, and proposes that *énonciation* and *énoncé* in the text are fundamentally indistinguishable, or that each discursive act in defence of 'J.J.'s innocence is simultaneously an accusation reinforcing his guilt. The implications of this position are difficult to contend with, but the argument itself is fairly simple. In terms of the newspaper story, one has only to dispense with the double, who supposedly busies himself in a new crime during each courtroom defence, to understand that the act of self-defence *is* the crime. Since 'J.J.' is in fact one individual rather than two (albeit with the ontological qualifications mentioned earlier), the alibi of an external double is not valid. The very act of writing the *Dialogues,* an *énonciation* ostensibly structured to disculpate its author, strengthens the 'frame' which is figured as a theme in the *énoncé,* and from which he wants to escape.

The severity of this hypothesis is such that we shall presently be led to inquire whether Rousseau's quandary does not in fact mask an entirely different story, in which the *Dialogues* would have a different function. Is the cycle of repetition really so vicious as it appears? Have we not already encountered the same structure in the analysis of masochism and injustice in *Les Confessions?* It may be that

Rousseau does not want to escape the predicament he sets in the *Dialogues,* and has a very different unconscious aim.

Vicious or not, the circular predicament at least helps to explain why the text all too often resembles a revolving phonograph record on which a stuck needle continually catches on the same groove. If *énonciation* and *énoncé* repeat and reinforce one another, the content of the *Dialogues* is synonymous with its form. The multiplication of frames tends to become self-constituting, making the text at best an echo-play of a lost authorial voice, at worst an instrument or machine controlling the author. Of all Rousseau's texts, the *Dialogues* is the work most closely akin to the mindless activity of copying which begins with, and co-exists alongside, the creation of literary works.[15] Though they are ingenious in a way which only Rousseau could have conceived, the *Dialogues* are also somehow *not* his. The author has been put into brackets; the field of discourse belongs to imaginary characters who drone endlessly about him; and Rousseau, helpless, is left to garner and to reproduce snatches of their conversation in fifteen-minute stints of writing, repeated daily like a 'constitutional' walk.

This debilitating loss of control is one consequence of Rousseau's effort to achieve control over his own fate. It indicates the full measure of the breakdown in the distinction between imaginary and real orders of existence. We have not yet mentioned the commonplace definition of 'frame', that of the protective border around a painting, which both displays and separates the work of art in its environment. Normally, a frame marks the boundary between what is imaginary and what is real; it distinguishes an 'inside' and an 'outside'. The frame demarcates an enclosure within which the very particular reality of the aesthetic work, a reality which develops and has its validity within the life of the imagination, remains separate from the reality surrounding it. Painting is the art form best suited to this commonplace definition of 'frame', but the principle involved holds equally in other aesthetic forms. Textual space instead of pictorial space – the frame is the prologue, or preface, separating the fiction of the text from the reality outside, and establishing the author's ability to distinguish between them.

In the *Dialogues,* Rousseau no longer plays with the indeterminate line where fiction and reality meet, as he did in the Preface in dialogue to *La Nouvelle Héloïse.* The two texts of dialogue are uncannily similar; the discussion in the *Dialogues* simply centres on 'J.J.' rather than on the status of a novel. And the question of authorship, which at first he both coyly and honestly refused to answer, now torments Rousseau. In the second stage of the autobiography, what was once a boundary has become the sharp edge of paranoia.

This illness can be described in part as a confusion along the frame separating an imaginary 'inside' and a real 'outside'. The paranoid person takes his imaginings for reality, and so loses his grasp on the sense of the world surrounding him. This confusion, in turn, can be interpreted within the terms of Rousseau's autobiographical project. At the start of *Les Confessions,* when the author takes the step of identifying himself in a textual world, his 'autre monde' is no longer simply 'autre', an aesthetic creation. It is meant to become real, Rousseau's world. An identity between author and text is what defines the work as autobiography, what distinguishes it from *La Nouvelle Héloïse* despite the strong autobiographical elements of the novel. We have seen that personal identity is inextricably bound up with the process of constructing a text, whether this process be taken to the extreme of writing a book, or whether it remains implicit, in the elaborations of memory or other imaginings. A life can be what is here termed textual without directly involving the writing of texts, or the creation of a textual world. And its direction and meaning are directly linked to one's ability to make experience textual in this extended sense of the term. But even assuming a broad definition of the notion of textuality, can personal identity be justified within purely textual bounds? In the *Dialogues,* Rousseau's autobiography aims toward this end.

The question can be answered in the affirmative only if one takes the position that texts are in some sense indeterminate. In discussing *La Nouvelle Héloïse,* Rousseau suggests this; and it is a fairly radical thought. For a text usually involves some sort of specific structure, being an act which gives coherent form and meaning to intention. At present, it is perhaps better to state that texts articulate an indeterminacy, rather than that they are themselves indeterminate. Rousseau the autobiographer, at any rate, wants to hold a more secure position. His act of identifying himself in his textual world at the start of *Les Confessions* effectively equates his personal identity with human identity, the 'image' with the 'modelle intérieur' (I: 1149). With only the determinate structures of the texts to guide us, it is impossible to pin-point the intention motivating his act — is it the desire for ontological stability, a totalitarian need for control, or, given the background of reverie and the preceding rhetorical development, simply the 'natural' thing to do? But we are able to observe that his autobiographical project involves multiple stages and rhetorical forms, and that by the second of these, the author has lost his grip on the distinction between fiction and reality which was the mark of his earlier lucidity.

In the *Dialogues*, therefore, the 'autre monde' of fiction has not become real; 'J.J.' merely replaces *La Nouvelle Héloïse* in the debate on the question. The author is now at stake – this demonstrates the extent to which personal identity has become a textual phenomenon. But while Rousseau fears for the integrity of his authorship, struggling to effect the closure of the aesthetic order in his own life, the question itself remains open, no more resolveable than in the Preface in dialogue. And the longer it remains open in the autobiography, the more the world around the author becomes 'autre', foreign, hostile. Reality now reflects Rousseau's aesthetic image of himself in inverted, caricatural form.

The parallel development of Rousseau's paranoia and his autobiography is visible as early as 1762, when the *Lettres à Malesherbes* were composed during the crisis over the publication of *Émile*. It resurfaces in 1767, when the completion of major portions of *Les Confessions* probably contributed to Rousseau's sudden, frantic desire to leave England. And the illness, clearly present in the final sections of the narrative text, culminates during the writing of the *Dialogues*. A heightened personal sensibility (which any autobiographer must manifest) inevitably isolates the individual, magnetizing him, as it were, at an opposite, usually negative pole in relation to the positive mass of society. Prophets are the best example of this sort of willed paranoia in a religious sensibility – to divine the instructions of God and carry them to men is hardly short of madness. It is important to state the link between autobiography and paranoia in Rousseau, but difficult to infer more generally that all autobiographical writing implies paranoid tendencies. Rousseau is extreme not only in the degree of his identification with his textual world, but also because he creates this world largely on his own terms, in conscious opposition to the social world of mid-eighteenth-century France. The implicit models informing other autobiographies are not so exclusive, nor identification with them so far-reaching.

Examination of the plot which Rousseau conceives and combats in the *Dialogues* concludes this discussion of 'framing'. 'Le François' gives most of the details about 'la ligue', and his descriptions attribute to it almost unlimited knowledge and power over 'J.J.' Its extensive scope and comprehension is matched in the autobiography only by the intensive claim about self-understanding which Rousseau made at the start of *Les Confessions.*

The most consistent and revealing description of 'la ligue' occurs through the metaphor of sight. 'Rousseau', criticizing the judgement of 'le François', provides one example:

Pour faire ce calcul avec justesse, il faudroit auparavant savoir combien de gens dans cette affaire ne voyent comme vous que par les yeux d'autrui. Si du nombre de ces bruyantes voix on ôtoit les échos qui ne font que repeter celle des autres . . . il y auroit peut-etre moins de disproportion que vous pensez. (I: 698)

Each member of the plot, seeing through the eyes of other members, is unable to judge for himself. He repeats their opinions and condemns 'J.J.' Generalized, this repetitive structure of vision and judgement creates an endless, sequential or successive ordering of prejudice which figuratively binds 'J.J.' in chains. Rousseau gives various names to the 'fond' of the plot, 'ces Messieurs' and 'les Auteurs' among them (I: 662). But although the 'ligue' apparently organizes an entire society, it has no actual cause. Rousseau never succeeds in naming its author. For here his own sight and judgement fail. He is necessarily blind to the fact that the paranoid projection is the indirect manner by which he seeks to name himself. By externalizing that openness of identity which threatens the autobiographer in him, he is ridding himself of it, and effecting the desired closure.

In the next chapter we shall return to the metaphor of sight. The phrase 'voir par les yeux d'autrui' will reconnect to the analysis of *amour* with which it began in Chapter II, but in the new context of the author–reader dialogue. Here it confirms one earlier conclusion. The plot directed against 'J.J.', the most obvious of the 'frames' in the *Dialogues,* manifests a structure identical to that of the other 'frames' in the text. Its thematic presentation should be associated with Rousseau's *énonciation,* since the author defends himself only against what he has himself brought into existence. Paradoxically, the paranoid never exercises more control than when he fabricates the web of persecution which, he believes, robs him of all control over his destiny.

The metaphor of sight also provides the first hint that the *Dialogues* need not be interpreted purely in spatial terms such as 'frame'. 'La ligue' has a curious connection with the temporality of reverie, though obviously not in any thematic sense. For its structure is reminiscent of the 'fugitive succession' lamented at the start of Book VI, with each member in the unremitting network of persecution personifying an irreversible moment of loss in the march of time. Rousseau writes the text as a sort of reverie gone wrong, in which the omnipotence normally deployed by the *rêveur* is directed against him. A comparison with an earlier, social instance of reverie – the gratifying performance of *Le Devin du village* at Fontainebleau – is instructive.

Dès la prémiére scene, qui véritablement est d'une naiveté touchante j'entendis s'élever dans les loges un murmure de surprise et d'applaud-issement jusqu'alors inoui dans ce genre de piéces. La fermentation croissante alla bientot au point d'être sensible dans toute l'assemblée, et, pour parler à la Montesquieu, d'augmenter son effet par son effet même. (I: 378)

'Toute l'assemblée' can refer either to the public of the *Devin* performance or to the public in the *Dialogues:* the force of the 'fermentation croissante' and the pattern of the crowd's response are the same in each instance. Rousseau is the primary cause of both responses, but remains separate from them. They develop as an independent series of effects, in which each effect also functions as a cause, binding and strengthening the series. Hence Rousseau's exhilaration at Fontainebleau over creating a drama which has an independent life of its own. Participating in his creation from a position of withdrawal, he becomes equivalent to a god, involved yet absent. But although an identical structure obtains in the *Dialogues,* its significance is the reverse. Gratifying applause is now the repetitive sight of a malicious 'ligue', which Rousseau creates but which seems to persecute him against his will. Instead of a god, 'J.J.' is a monster, excluded from social life, and deprived of his authorship. These contrasting extremes are like two sides of one coin, reverie as ecstasy and reverie as nightmare.

*Transition to 'Rêveries'*

The notion of frame has helped to clarify the rhetorical structure of the *Dialogues,* and suggests that their major thematic concern, 'la ligue', is a figurative extension, or an effect in the *énoncé,* of a repetitive pattern in the *énonciation* of the text. But a different sort of question remains to be answered: How does Rousseau resolve the dilemma? According to the descriptive analysis followed thus far, the various frames of the text are self-perpetuating and mutually reinforcing. Theoretically, they defy resolution. What then occurs in the practice of the *Dialogues* to allow for the sudden shift to a new attitude and very different type of discourse in the *Rêveries?* What does Rousseau gain by the process we have described above in formal terms? If the second stage of the autobiography resolves a problem which it has itself helped to pose, it does so only by embodying some conscious or unconscious choice which the author has made.

Two perspectives may be helpful here. The first is the analysis of masochism and injustice in *Les Confessions.* Earlier, we established a formal equivalence between them, and left off inquiring whether they are so separate as the two episodes in which the author presented them in the narrative text. The *Dialogues* shed new light on this, linking the two sentiments together through the act of writing. The injustice which Rousseau suffers is evidently 'la ligue', against which he struggles with the same incomprehension and bewilderment as the child in Book I. But his masochism is visible in the fact that 'la ligue' does not simply represent a phantasm, but is instrumental in sustaining it. 'La ligue' and its injustice belong as themes to the *énoncé* of his discourse; his masochism to the *énonciation.* We have seen these to be indistinguishable.

Rousseau casts the *Dialogues* in the same involuntary framework as Book I, and writes, as it were, despite himself. His sense of injustice functions as an alibi, concealing even to him the pleasure which he takes in defending himself, and which (like the character in the *Gazette de Leyde*) triggers yet another repetition in a closed cycle. The pleasure received from writing is therefore not discernible at the surface of the *Dialogues,* nor so directly erotic as in the first childhood episode. It still pertains, however, to his effort to fulfil a desire for wholeness, in the undivided relation between self and text embodied in the 'natural' and 'innocent' version of 'J.J.' The image which made the autobiographer's story his own in the narrative allegory is now challenged by a counter-image which appears unjustly to deprive him of it. But both the image and the counter-image arise through writing, through Rousseau's desire to give to his life the closure of a text. The second stage of the autobiography is still a story about him and about the limits of personal identity, even though he has lost conscious control of it and no longer tells it directly.

The second perspective on the *Dialogues* is the markedly different possibility that the work is an unusual type of sacrifice. This would also be a story not directly visible in the text, nor present in Rousseau's awareness as he writes. Sacrifice is in general a social rite, directed toward God or the gods. It is a means of establishing indirect contact, through the intermediary of a sacrificial victim, with a divine source of authority. Since the participants in the ritual are taken up by it, they do not consider it a means to an end. It is a real drama. Indeed, in taking a sacrificial object for something which it is not, the participants could be said to misunderstand their actions. But a degree of misunderstanding is essential to the efficacy of the sacrifice, and to the redemption which follows from it.[16]

The *Dialogues* modify the direction of the sacrificial process while retaining its basic form. Rousseau's writing engages him in an individual rite, directed toward society rather than toward the gods, in which he attempts indirectly to establish the authority of his own self-image. The volatile identity of 'J.J.' is an indication of his role as the victim. 'J.J.'s duality allows Rousseau to benefit, through a reverse effect, from the values which seem to be denied him by his monstrous double. With two versions of the character, one can be put down, and the other redeemed.

In this perspective, the misunderstanding of the figurative 'frame' is an inherent part of a ritual in which the author has been taken up, and the various levels of repetition in the text (including Rousseau's daily fifteen-minute writing sessions) are not a stylistic defect, but positive aspects of an effort to make indirect and continuous contact with a source of authority outside the range of discourse in which 'Rousseau' and 'le François' operate. Even the account in the 'Histoire du Précédent Ecrit' of the steps taken to find readers after the *Dialogues* are completed, can be considered in the light of a deconsecration of the elements used in the sacrifice, or as what Hubert and Mauss term the 'exit' from the ritual.[17]

I make this quick comparison between the *Dialogues* and a sacrificial process not so much to provide an explanation of the work as to indicate that its significance arises almost without reference to the intention of its author. Any assessment of the second stage of the autobiography which concerns itself with the author's self-awareness, with whether or not Rousseau understands his actions, will tend to miss the point. Immersed in a modern version of an ancient ritual, he writes a paranoid prayer, a combination of passion and suffering that he actively inflicts upon himself. It is not relieved until Rousseau wakens from nightmare into the individual society of the *Rêveries*.

Rêveries

Et me trouvant enfin ramené par degrés à moi-même et à ce qui m'entouroit, je ne pouvois marquer le point de séparation des fictions aux réalités.

*Rêveries* (I: 1048)

Je tâchois de me mettre tout a fait dans l'état d'un homme qui commence à vivre. Je me disois qu'en effet nous ne faisons jamais que commencer, et qu'il n'y a point d'autre liaison dans notre existence qu'une succession de momens présens, dont le prémier est toujours celui qui est en acte. Nous mourons et nous naissons chaque instant de nôtre vie, et quel intérest la mort peut elle nous laisser?

*Émile et Sophie, ou les Solitaires* (IV: 905)

*Les Rêveries du promeneur solitaire,* begun in the autumn of 1776, and the third and final stage in the rhetorical development of Rousseau's autobiography, follow consistently from the two texts which precede them. In *Les Confessions,* Rousseau gave a narrative account of his past. In the *Dialogues,* he tried to assure an ideal view of his own innocence for the future. Past and future now cease to affect him. Although the author does look backward and forward in the *Rêveries,* he surveys himself from a stationary present, disengaged from society and linear time. When, in July 1778, death intervenes to break off the composition of the tenth 'Promenade', it does not disrupt any development within the final stage of the autobiography. The *Rêveries* in no sense develop. Each 'Promenade' begins, has an ostensible subject, discusses it, ends. Except for the Third (by itself a mini-autobiography), none unfolds according to a chronological or narrative order. This idiosyncratic organization also characterizes the work as a whole, in which little thematic or logical progression is discernible. Instead, Rousseau's designation of the text as 'un appendice de mes *Confessions*' (I: 1000) signals a return to the dream which he left unfinished in Book XII of the narrative work – his vision of permanent temporal happiness on l'Isle de St. Pierre. After the protracted labour and opacity of the *Dialogues,* the author abruptly begins again. A matter of months separates his new beginning from the ceremonial attempts to attract attention and readers to the *Dialogues.* But the change is final. Had Rousseau lived to produce more autobiography, it is difficult to conceive of his continuing to write in any rhetorical form other than that of the *Rêveries.*

The end-point of the autobiography coincides significantly with a late pre-autobiographical work, *Émile et Sophie, ou les Solitaires.*[18] The parallel between the positions of Émile in the unfinished fictional work and of Rousseau in the *Rêveries* is striking. Each entrusts himself to the present, 'délivré de l'inquiétude de l'espérance' (IV: 905; I: 986, 997), and considers 'le passé comme étranger' (IV: 899). The author reaches in 1776 an attitude depicted fictively in 1762. This confirms the idea that his life and autobiographical writing imitate his fiction. But it also suggests that Rousseau's long itinerary, the process of appropriating the personal image which he elaborated in earlier texts, is coming to an end. To realize this image has involved elaboration in its own right, namely the rhetorical development of the autobiography. The development stops during the sudden shift from the *Dialogues*. The author now exists in his textual world, and his textual world co-exists with his life, in a reversible stasis.

What is uncanny about the last stage of the autobiography is the fact that the *Rêveries* exist at all. According to our thesis, the elaboration is over; no process of appropriation remains. Yet the author starts again, continues to write, and produces a purely gratuitous text, resembling the notion of a gift which is perhaps its strongest thematic element. If the *Rêveries* go one step further than any of Rousseau's previous texts, it is because they create their sense while leading nowhere.

What is the rhetorical form of the *Rêveries*? Why is it an appropriate and necessary end-point for Rousseau's autobiography? The author's suggestion, that his text be considered an 'informe journal de mes rêveries' is both unhelpful and misleading (I: 1000). The adjective 'informe' well describes its digressive, unhurried character. One sentence leads to the next with a limpid rhythm. But, like clear water, it is difficult to gauge the depth of the *Rêveries* from the surface. Rousseau achieves this formless effect only by working and reworking the text. It is in fact highly shadowed and structured.

The word 'journal', similarly, helps to emphasize the presentness of the work. To the extent that Rousseau now writes for himself alone, his text resembles a journal. But are the *Rêveries* in any way a chronicle of the author's final years? They are indeed based temporally in the present, but in an atemporal present, the time of reverie. This experience Rousseau proposes as the referent of his final text, just as his sentiments were the referent of *Les Confessions*. Even this connection, however, is initially puzzling. Aside from the second, fifth,

and part of the seventh 'Promenades', the *Rêveries* discuss other subjects: quotations, botany, gifts, varied anecdotes. The few direct
instances of reverie, furthermore, tend to shift the text from its ram-
bling tone into a descriptive register closer to narrative. The relation
of text to referent in the last stage of the autobiography does not
lie in any specific reverie experiences which the author might recount
there, but in the fact that he recreates their ordered disorder in his
writing. The proper subject of reverie, which makes the text seem
indeterminate, is to have no subject in particular. The work is about
any and all subjects. It describes a solitude which is also a 'lieu commun'.

### *'Plein Calme'*

Rousseau begins the first 'Promenade' with a conclusion: 'Me voici
donc seul sur la terre, n'ayant plus de frere, de prochain, d'ami, de
societé que moi-même' (I: 995). Signifying with the force of the
missing main verb, the 'donc' resumes in one word all the author's
earlier work, and expresses the presiding sense of closure. Where can
he turn, what is left for him to write, if he starts by concluding? The
qualifying 'que moi-même' in this initial sentence opens on to an
answer. Rousseau now deliberates within the boundaries of an individual society, in a self-sufficient textual world. It replaces the
brother, neighbour, friend, and society from whose company he feels
irrevocably excluded.

The adequacy of the *Rêveries* in fulfilling a social function does not
depend entirely on Rousseau's dual role as both author and reader.
True, even as he writes, he promises himself the eventual pleasure of
conversing with himself through the text, as with 'un moins vieux
ami'. The internal reciprocity established in this manner recreates
the social exchange which the *Rêveries* so emphatically deny. But
such reciprocity must already exist, as he writes, for Rousseau to take
any comfort at the thought of reading his work. The new relation
between author and autobiographical text is not evident at a lexical
or syntactical level. Rousseau repeats the same complaints and lamen-
tations first uttered in the *Dialogues* and the second half of *Les
Confessions.* The repetition now has the effect of a litany, however,
expressing fidelity. It reverberates inside a world which Rousseau
himself has created, within limits where he is certain to recover a
feeling of 'plein calme' (I: 997).

The accident which Rousseau describes in the second 'Promenade' triggers a first instance of 'plein calme' in the *Rêveries*. Our introductory reading of this episode might be furthered here.

Rousseau's fall and subsequent awakening into the world are a reverie within a reverie, since he is returning from a long walk and 'herborisation' when surprised by the carriage and dog. The circumstances of the first reverie help one to understand why he will attach so much importance to the second. Rousseau evokes the pathos of shedding trees on the late October day, the completed harvest and almost deserted countryside. 'L'image de la solitude et des approches de l'hiver' surround him, reflecting his own solitary condition. 'Seul et dé laissé je sentois venir le froid des prémiéres glaces', he says, 'et mon imagination tarissante ne peuploit plus ma solitude d'êtres formés selon mon cœur'. This apparent pathos is balanced by a rather large self-satisfaction, as the mirrors of memory and writing augment the mirror of the countryside. 'Je revenois avec complaisance sur toutes les affections de mon cœur', the author continues, 'et je me préparois à les rappeller assez pour les décrire avec un plaisir presque égal à celui que j'avois pris à m'y livrer'. If the activity of writing the *Rêveries* is a 'rêverie seconde', Rousseau could now also be said to write mentally while in reverie (I: 1004).

The pleasurable equilibrium of this first reverie, however, goes hand-in-hand with a disquieting change from other texts and reveries – Rousseau's elaborative imagination, so constant earlier, has gone still. 'Je m'enivre moins du délire de la rêverie', he admits, 'et il y a plus de reminiscence que de création dans ce qu'elle produit desormais'. After the *Dialogues*, where the author's projective capacities served mainly to invent 'la ligue', this change may seem a good thing, the source of the 'plein calme'. Instead, it leaves Rousseau alone and impotent before his fate. 'Un tiéde allanguissement énerve toutes mes facultés, l'esprit de vie s'éteint en moi par degrés'. Without the imagination, his 'autre monde' is slowly emptied of force and reality. And without his 'autre monde', Rousseau is unable to will, feeling only worldly exclusion and approaching death. Such is the setting for the second, involuntary reverie.

'Au fort de ma reverie', Rousseau goes on, 'j'en fus tiré par l'évenement qui me reste à raconter' – the accident (I: 1004). He gives a short, precise account of his fall, and then describes the return to consciousness, 'lorsque je revins à moi. L'état auquel je me trouvois dans cet instant est trop singulier pour n'en pas faire ici la description' (I: 1005). His description is once again worthy of reproduction:

La nuit s'avançoit. J'apperçus le ciel, quelques étoiles, et un peu de verdure. Cette prémiére sensation fut un moment délicieux. Je ne me sentois encor que par là. Je naissois dans cet instant à la vie, et il me sembloit que je remplissois de ma legere existence tous les objets que j'appercevois. Tout entier au moment présent je ne me souvenois de rien; je n'avois nulle notion distincte de mon individu, pas la moindre idée de ce que venoit de m'arriver; je ne savois ni qui j'étois ni où j'étois; je ne sentois ni mal, ni crainte, ni inquietude. Je voyois couler mon sang comme j'aurois vu couler un ruisseau, sans songer seulement que ce sang m'appartint en aucune sorte. Je sentois dans tout mon être un calme ravissant auquel chaque fois que je me le rappelle je ne trouve rien de comparable dans toute l'activité des plaisirs connus. (I: 1995)

The sense of mortality pervading the first reverie has been concentrated in one arbitrary and brutal event, which brings Rousseau close to death, and certainly through a symbolic form of death. Like a physical equivalent to the jolt of a caesura, the accident marks a qualitative passage from one level of experience to another. It interrupts the complacent reflections of the *promeneur,* and deposits him rudely on the ground. Rousseau experiences the transition only as a blank – literally, as a loss of consciousness. But he 'comes to' on the far side of death, and very much in the world, with a feeling of birth. Solitary nostalgia has given way to an immediate, sensuous connection with objects; autumnal chill to a light but vivid sense of wholeness.

If the direction of the first reverie was inward and self-absorbed, here it is outward and releasing. Rousseau is either not yet himself or more than himself in the awakening, but the depersonalized state is in any event one with which he identifies most profoundly. In the instant of his emergence, orchestrated above in the unfolding rhythm of the first sentences, he discovers his 'autre monde' within *this* world. This is the major change from first to second reverie, the source of the 'calme ravissant'; and it is especially striking for the fact that the imagination plays no part in it. Rousseau is back where he started from, one could say – in the everyday world. But it is entirely new and wondrous to him. He enters it as though for the first time. He starts a life, at the end of his life, in which the imagination and the will have no more place than in a dream. This same discovery is also described in a late poem by the American poet Wallace Stevens almost two hundred years later. Writing in winter, at the end of his own imaginative enterprise, Stevens questions himself: 'I wonder, have I

lived a skeleton's life/ As a disbeliever in reality/ A countryman of
all the bones in the world?' — and then affirms:

Now, here, the snow I had forgotten becomes

Part of a major reality, part of
An appreciation of a reality

And thus an elevation, as if I left
With something I could touch, touch every way.

And yet nothing has been changed except what is
Unreal, as if nothing had been changed at all.[20]

### Circumscription: l'Isle de St. Pierre

The indeterminate tone of Rousseau's awakening continues throughout
the *Rêveries*, in the discursive freedom of the writer if not always in
the subject matter about which he writes. The casual yet precise manner in which he passes from one topic to the next, from one section
of argument to another, resembles the strange combination of sharpness
and woolliness with which he perceives 'le ciel, quelques étoiles, et un
peu de verdure'. His glance is both light-headed and deeply serious,
rigorous and giddy, and is embodied in a style which proceeds like a
camera running in slow motion, focused on the movement of an instant
of time.

When Rousseau returns to the topic of reverie again in the fifth
'Promenade', it is to give duration to this moment of birth through
the cradling motion of lake water around l'Isle de St. Pierre.[21] His
portrayal of happiness on the island places it in a sentimental lineage
with 'les Charmettes', at the start of Book VI in *Les Confessions*.
'Je compte ces deux mois pour le tems le plus heureux de ma vie',
he remarks in the *Rêveries*,

et tellement heureux qu'il m'eut suffi durant toute mon existence
sans laisser naitre un seul instant dans mon ame le desir d'un autre
état. (I: 1042)

In Book VI of *Les Confessions,* time had the same completeness.

Le bonheur me suivoit partout; il n'étoit dans aucune chose assignable,
il étoit tout en moi-même, il ne pouvoit me quitter un seul instant.
(I: 226)

It is necessary to distinguish here between the actual circumstances and events which the author recounts, and what he makes of them in the *Rêveries*.[22] But, as with 'les Charmettes', our major interest lies in Rousseau's ongoing act of writing autobiography. The description of happiness on l'Isle de St. Pierre, which is a myth of the present, is quite different from its sentimental equivalent, the myth of the past midway through the narrative in the first stage of the autobiography. 'Elle est très agréable et singuliérement située pour le bonheur d'un homme qui aime à se circonscrire', Rousseau states about l'Isle de St.Pierre. With its several permanent residents who see to everyday needs, he lives in a circular, self-sufficient world. He pursues his passion for botany (attempting to collect and classify all the plants in the island world), dreams by lakeside, and even claims to give up reading and writing. 'Un de mes plus grands délices étoit surtout de laisser mes livres bien encaissés et de n'avoir point d'écritoire' (I: 1042).

More than the island, the surrounding lake is the most prominent feature of Rousseau's physical setting, and an indirect explanation for his disregard for writing. Water is the constant element in his imaginative universe: streams flow regularly through the recollections of childhood in *Les Confessions;* the lake below Clarens functions like a silent character in *La Nouvelle Héloïse;* and our interpretation of 'l'Élysée' gave some indication of the symbolic importance of this recurring element. The description of l'Isle de St. Pierre, however, is the only major instance of insularity in Rousseau's work, and organizes the familiar feature of water in a new way. The Lac de Bienne is a fluid boundary separating island and world into 'inside' and 'outside'. In one sense it protects Rousseau, like a barrier or defensive moat, and establishes the necessary distance for his reverie. But it also acts as a conductor, in constant motion and materially corresponding to his imagination. 'Le flux et reflux' of the water draws him out of himself and into a borderline condition between the world around him and his 'autre monde'.

Like the reverie in the second 'Promenade', this borderline state demands little or no imaginative energy from Rousseau. 'Sans aucun concours actif de mon ame', as he states, he dreams through the lake. Its continuous physical presence sustains and gives duration to the reverie (I: 1045). Not unsurprisingly, he dreams best when he ventures from the island on to the lake itself, stretched out and drifting in a boat. The buoyancy and whim of the water then act physically upon him, suspending him in motion, in a continuous 'in-between'.

In early reveries and most notably in 'la promenade', Rousseau travels from one point to another, 'in-between' or in a state of 'déplacement'. This physical condition forms a parallel to the moment of passage within reverie itself. L'Isle de St. Pierre, a location 'naturellement circonscritte' (I: 1048), places this 'state' of transition in a stationary physical framework. It gives reverie permanence without making it in any way static, or changing its basic terms.

At a temporal level, the circumscription of l'Isle de St. Pierre is more difficult to visualize, but no less present. The notion of 'in-between' corresponds in a temporal context to the instant — the no-man's-land between past and future — and the fluid permanence embodied in the lake to the paradoxical sense of duration which Rousseau discovers there. How is it possible, the 'bonheur suffisant, parfait et plein' which he cautiously delineates? In the brodest sense, time means change, and ensures inconstancy of sentiment:

Tout est dans un flux continuel sur la terre: rien n'y garde une forme constante et arrêtée, et nos affections qui s'attachent aux choses extérieures passent et changent comme elles. (I: 1046)

Since human sentiments develop and derive whatever force they possess from attachments to external, temporally determined things, continuity of time is required to enjoy continuity of sentiment. In the fifth 'Promenade', as elsewhere, Rousseau's regret of temporal change is therefore directed first and foremost to its effect on the affections of the heart. 'Il n'y a rien là de solide à quoi le cœur puisse s'attacher', he states. 'Ces courts momens de délire et de passion' are in his view all that man can hope to experience. Yet the very presence of the word 'hope' suggests an incompleteness. Rousseau contrasts such fleeting happiness with happiness of a different sort, in an 'état ... permanent'.

Le bonheur que mon cœur regrette n'est point composé d'instans fugitifs mais un état simple et permanent, qui n'a rien de vif en lui-même, mais dont la durée accroit le charme au point d'y trouver enfin la supreme felicité ...

A peine est-il dans nos plus vives jouissances un instant où le cœur puisse véritablement nous dire: *Je voudrois que cet instant durât toujours.* (I: 1046)

Sentimental instability is linked closely to the word 'instant'. The adjective 'fugitif' accompanies it with the regularity of an epithet.

The instant marks the successive, irreversible ordering of time: one instant follows another, loss upon loss. Time never accumulates, it simply passes. For sentiment, this movement is a deterioration.

Rousseau finds permanence within such impermanence by what one could call a temporal circumscription. He draws himself together within a circular present, within a moment which does not follow on and is not followed by other moments, but which nonetheless persists and endures through time. As though astride a boundary between time and the atemporal, he attains a sense of duration which does not change, a sentiment in time but not subject to it — a continuous instant. The horror of being perpetually 'in-between', 'always ahead or behind ourselves' then turns into what Rousseau understands as 'le bonheur'. In a carefully qualified, precise sentence, he describes it.

Mais s'il est un état où l'ame trouve une assiete assez solide pour s'y reposer tout entiére et rassembler là tout son être, sans avoir besoin de rappeler le passé ni d'enjamber sur l'avenir; où le tems ne soit rien pour elle, où le présent dure sans neanmoins marquer sa durée et sans aucune trace de succession, sans aucun sentiment de privation ni de jouissance, de plaisir ni de peine, de desir ni de crainte que celui seul de notre existence, et que ce sentiment seul puisse la remplir tout entier(e); tant que cet état dure celui qui s'y trouve peut s'appeller heureux. (I: 1046)

The desire for happiness speaks so strongly in these lines that one easily overlooks the hypothetical mode in which the sentence unfolds; the very innocuous 'celui qui s'y trouve', which depersonalizes the individual involved; the 'notre existence', which opens the experience on to an interpersonal plane. Rousseau does remark more forcefully, one sentence later, 'tel est l'état où je me suis trouvé souvent à l'Isle de St. Pierre dans mes rêveries solitaires', but the 'desir' speaking here is muted in tone, barely personal and bracketed within a prepositional clause headed by 'sans'. If one compares this passage to the description of 'les Charmettes', the muted tone stands out in clear relief. 'Et j'étois heureux', Rousseau affirmed there, over and over again. His personal stake in that critical moment of transition in his life required a constant repetition of the phrase, as if he had to keep happiness abreast the 'succession' of time in the narrative *Confessions*. No such urgency impels the *Reveries*. They circulate in a present moment, to which the demands of continuity from past to future do not pertain. The 'durée' above does not extend across instants in the normal sense of a duration through time, for which we saw fiction to be an integral part. The 'durée' above is confined to one instant, where the personal stake in continuity and in fiction drops to a minimum. This temporal withdrawal involves a definite movement of limitation and closure: when time has been reduced to 'le présent', particularized, relative sentiments can no longer be differentiated. They become one, the 'sentiment de l'existence', or happiness. 'Commençons par redevenir nous, par nous concentrer en nous, par circonscrire notre ame des mêmes bornes que la nature a données à notre être', Rousseau has stated in the *Lettres morales* (IV: 1112). At the limit of such concentration, when the insubstantial and indeterminate instant of time has been transformed into an 'assiete assez solide', he uncurls in it, as it were, filled by the 'sentiment de l'existence'. One can no more speak of 'Rousseau' at this point than in the moment of awakening in the second 'Promenade'. The fact that the author does not speak in the first-person singular is confirmation that his personal identity is not at stake. But he nonetheless identifies himself in this state:

De quoi jouit-on dans une pareille situation? De rien d'extérieur à soi, de rien sinon de soi-même et de sa propre existence, tant que cet état dure on se suffit à soi-même comme Dieu. (I: 1047)

Etymologically, the word 'circonscrire' contains 'circon', meaning 'around' or 'in a circle', and 'scrire', to write. If one takes the verbal root in a literal sense, the circumscriptions of space and time which Rousseau describes may also be associated with the *Rêveries* as a text, and with the act of writing in the final stage of the autobiography. Since he does not write in circles (as might a concrete poet), and since the rhetorical structure of a text does not translate easily into descriptive metaphor (as when one says that an instant becomes an 'assiete assez solide'), this third mode of circumscription does not lend itself readily to direct examination. We might instead here call upon a notion of Michel Beaujour, concerning a type of text and writing which he calls 'autoportrait'.[23]

In the *Rêveries,* the lack of chronological development, of a beginning and an end, of a story to tell, is tied to the fact that the text is not, properly speaking, an autobiography. The writing self at this stage is hardly a personal identity. Instead, the author circumnavigates his imaginative universe in the way Rousseau floats on the Lac de Bienne, picking up the small currents of discourse, following them where they lead, and then drifting on. In Beaujour's terminology, the *Rêveries* are an 'autoportrait', a text which is self-addressed but not restricted to one voice or individual personality. It speaks of 'le vide', of everything and anything, with equal facility, taking its subject matter from the clichés and 'lieux communs' of a given cultural period and structuring them in the idiosyncratic manner of a given author. (In the case of the *Rêveries*, one might amend this criterion by suggesting that the clichés and 'lieux communs' worked by Rousseau belong as much to his own textual world as to the cultural period in which he lives.) Upon this subject-matter, the 'autoportraitist' works in an analogical and poetic rather than narrative mode. The text proceeds by association and chance, not in a linear or directed manner.

These general criteria for distinguishing an 'autoportrait' fit the *Rêveries* well. The notion of circumscription in the fifth 'Promenade', taken in this sense, could be called an active principle throughout the text. A final aspect of Beaujour's definition is perhaps the most important, however; he states that the 'autoportrait' is a mode of discourse centred in the present, 'où l'énonciation . . . tente de dire qu'il est maintenant ce qu'il écrit'.[24] The *Rêveries* are very definitely this manner of present text, no more so than when Rousseau describes the 'bonheur' on l'Isle de St. Pierre, and repeats it in the process of writing about it. Near the end of the fifth 'Promenade', after first expressing a desire to return to his 'azyle', he claims the possibility to enjoy, several hours each day,

le même plaisir que si je l'habitois encor. Ce que j'y ferois de plus doux seroit d'y rêver à mon aise. En rêvant que j'y suis, ne fais-je pas la même chose? (I: 1049)

*Gifts*

Gifts are an increasingly prominent theme in the *Rêveries* from the fifth 'Promenade' onward (particularly in the sixth and ninth 'Promenades'), and constitute, after reverie itself, their most important topic. The theme develops according to a simple logic out of the author's relation to the 'sentiment de l'existence'. Once he participates fully in the sentiment, he becomes identified with life itself – in religious terms, with God; in ontological terms, with Being. He then sustains this identity through a self-dispersal, through the act of giving. As seen in the earlier context of the performance of *Le Devin du village,* the world becomes an extension of Rousseau, of the donor of a particular type of gift, the 'bienfait purement gratuit' (I: 1053).

Within this simple schema, sensitive issues of time, social recognition, and social exchange cluster around the topic of gifts. Their interconnections can be seen in a second form of donation, which Rousseau distinguishes from his own, and which he attempts to circumvent in the *Rêveries* — the gift as a contract.

One example of contractual gift-giving occurs at the start of the sixth 'Promenade', when Rousseau reflects on the significance of a detour that he has become accustomed to take in his walks. He determines that the cause behind the apparently arbitrary change lies in his relationship with a 'petit garçon fort gentil mais boiteux' with whom he had earlier made 'une espéce de connoissance'.

Il ne manquoit chaque fois que je passois de venir me faire son petit compliment toujours suivi de ma petite offrande. Les premiéres fois je fus charmé de le voir, donnois de très bon cœur . . . Ce plaisir devenu par degrés habitude se trouva je ne sais comment transformé dans une espéce de devoir . . . Dès lors je passois par là moins volontiers, et enfin je pris machinalement l'habitude de faire le plus souvent un détour. (I: 1050–1)

Rousseau's gift to the boy engages both in a small contract — a penny for a compliment. Gratified by the arrangement at first, he soon finds it a burden. For the connection established between himself and the boy is not restricted to the gift as an object. Little things become the symbol of larger concerns; Rousseau's money recognizes the complimenter with the compliment; and the compliment constitutes a recognition of the passing *promeneur.* The gift creates a social and interpersonal bond, with all its implications. 'Il ne manquoit jamais de m'appeller souvent M. Rousseau', the author comments, 'pour montrer qu'il me connoissoit bien, ce qui m'apprenoit assez au contraire qu'il ne me connoissoit pas plus que ceux qui l'avoient instruit' (I: 1050–1). For Rousseau, any social recognition is at this stage misrecognition (though his paranoia is doubly pathetic in this instance, when applied to a young boy).

The interpersonal exchange which the gift sets in motion is not in itself unpleasant; it becomes so only because of the repetitive, temporal dimension built into the process of recognition. Contractual gift-giving articulates and helps to establish this as well as the social dimension. Like a promise, the gift creates an expectation in the boy, a hope that

Rousseau will continue the exchange whenever he passes. The present is linked to the future, a temporal sequence created – the exact opposite of the circumscription which the author practises in the *Rêveries*. Since the gift commits him both to time and to the boy, it is not surprising to find that the adjectival form of the word 'succession' appears directly afterwards in the text. 'De ces premiers bienfaits versés avec effusion de cœur naissoient des chaines d'engagements successifs' (I: 1051).

In the digression sparked by this opening anecdote, Rousseau demonstrates his acute awareness of the ramifications of gift-giving. 'Je sais qu'il y a une espéce de contrat et même le plus saint de tous entre le bienfaiteur et l'obligé', he states.

C'est une sorte de societé qu'ils forment l'un avec l'autre, plus étroite que celle qui unit les hommes en général, et si l'obligé s'engage tacitement à la reconnoissance, le bienfaiteur s'engage à conserver à l'autre ... la bonne volonté qu'il vient de lui témoigner, et à lui renouveller les actes toutes les fois qu'il le pourra et qu'il en sera requis. (I:1053–4)

For Rousseau, gifts are 'interested', both an indication of the connections and hierarchies between individuals, and an important means of sustaining these connections through time. His practical experience with aristocratic patrons and well-wishers, no less than the contradictory tendencies in his theory of *amitié,* are in part responsible for this view. The 'interest' of gifts, what makes them the symbol of a moral transaction, is also what makes them a focus for the agonistic, violent character of human relations. Aware that the process of recognition is a struggle, Rousseau refuses to consider gifts as inherently benign. 'Un don fait par force ou par ruse, et qui n'est pas accepté, est un vol', he states in a late autobiographical fragment (I: 1190). Gifts not only articulate social and temporal connections, they can also impose them as a 'devoir'.

Given more exegetical scope and ingenuity, it would be possible to show that Rousseau's scattered remarks of contractual gift-giving significantly anticipate the more deliberate analyses of the sociologist M. Mauss, on the function of gifts in 'primitive' societies, and also to elucidate more fully the link between gifts and time.[25] But in the context of the *Rêveries,* where the author feels himself excluded from society, and attempts to overstep the constraints of time, this mode of giving is of secondary importance. It serves mainly as a background and contrast to his notion of the gift as a 'bienfait purement gratuit'. Rousseau's founding of the small rabbit colony on l'Isle de St. Pierre, the initial example of this notion, is followed by similar 'fêtes' in the ninth 'Promenade': the encounter with the young girls and the 'oublieur' in the Bois de Boulogne, or with the group of peasants and the apple-seller at a party of the Épinays, near l'Ermitage.[26] In each of these episodes, Rousseau's gift-giving takes the form of distribution among a group. The gift — whether small animals, pastries, or apples — creates a bond and places its recipients into a miniature society, held together by what it has received. Its unity derives from Rousseau. As the giver, he remains outside the group, able to survey and to enjoy its pleasure in a small epiphany of existence, of which he feels himself to be the source. 'Pour jouir moi-même de ces aimables fêtes', he states, 'je n'ai pas besoin d'en être, il me suffit de les voir, en les voyant je les partage' (I: 1093–4).

In that Rousseau's conferral delineates a social order, the basic structure of contractual gift-giving continues intact in the non-contractual gift. But Rousseau places himself outside the temporary societies which he creates, in a position of interested disinterest. This type of gift commits him neither to 'autrui' nor to time. His 'interest' in it, as the gift moves between individuals, is like his stake in the instant, the 'in-between' of a perpetual present — he is in the gift yet not bound by it.

The episode of the young girls and the 'oublieur' provides an apt summation here, illustrating the 'bienfait purement gratuit'. The 'oublieur' is a mobile vendor of pastry, an eighteenth-century figure who combined his selling with a game of chance. One pays to spin a lottery wheel, a 'tourniquet', and receives pastry according to the result of the spin. Rousseau recounts that one such vendor, in the Bois de Boulogne, attracts the attention of a group of young girls playing near him. 'Je vis que les petites filles convoitoient fort les oublies', he recalls,

et que deux ou trois d'entre elles qui apparemment possedoient quelques liards demanderent la permission de jouer. Tandis que la gouvernante hesitoit et disputoit, j'appelai l'oublieur et je lui dis: faites tirer toutes ces Demoiselles chacune à son tour et je vous payerai le tout. Ce mot répandit dans toute la troupe une joye. (I: 1090)

Several recognizable themes of Rousseau surface directly in his description of the event. He organizes the 'fête', setting the girls in a

row to pass, one by one, before the 'oublieur'. Ensuring that each
gets one turn, no less, no more, he is 'inexorable'. When he resolves
the small problems that arise during the general excitement, the scene
is a 'tribunal'. Rousseau presides like a judge over the proceedings
(I: 1091, note 1). But the episode also has less obvious, more extended
connotations. The presence of the 'gouvernante', 'une maniére de
Religieuse', adds a religious element to the story. Rousseau takes the
situation in hand during her indecision, and the 'oublies' which he
indirectly distributes are a gift in the fullest, most sacramental sense
of the word. The word 'oublie' derives from 'oblatus', like 'oblation',
meaning an offering. Its primary sense, subsequently displaced on to
pastries such as the girls receive, is that of unleavened bread intended
for consecration and communion. Rousseau's choice of anecdote,
whether or not he is aware of it as he writes it in the *Rêveries,* makes
him very much the God mentioned at the end of the fifth 'Promenade'.
His Table is based on chance; as each girl approaches it, she receives
her gift according to the 'lot' drawn. But Rousseau is beneficent. 'Afin
de rendre la fête encor plus gaye', he states,

je dis en secret à l'oublieur d'user de son adresse ordinaire en sens
contraire en faisant tomber autant de bons lots qu'il pourroit et que
je lui en tiendrois compte. (I: 1091)

Those inside the game continue to play without knowing that it has
been 'rigged'. They are children and feel their rewards more powerfully
for the uncertainty. Rousseau alone remains outside this game, not
subject to its rules because he has arranged them. He knows that all
will win in the end. By the end of the ceremony, he is even able to
invite the nun, initially so recalcitrant, to join in. 'Je priai la Religieuse
de tirer à son tour', he recalls; and she accepts (I: 1091).

# V

## THE AUTHOR – READER DIALOGUE

Je me répéte, on le sait; il le faut. Le prémier de mes besoins ...
c'étoit le besoin d'une societé intime et aussi intime qu'elle pouvoit
l'être ... Ce besoin singulier etoit tel, que la plus étroite union des
corps ne pouvoit encore y suffire: il m'auroit fallu deux ames dans
le même corps; sans cela je sentois toujours du vide. (I: 414)

Rousseau's work as an author, especially after his move from Paris
to the countryside, in 1756, transposes his life into an imaginative
space held open and elaborated through the act of writing. The presentation in Chapter III sketched several perspectives on his construction
of a textual world. The last chapter followed his effort to bring this
imaginative universe into time. But the subject of his 'societé intime'
remains to be explored. Rousseau desires this so strongly that he
deflects his social involvement from everyday life to the life of his
text. The 'corps' of the autobiographer is now fairly synonymous
with the *corpus* of his written work, and 'deux ames' are inscribed
there – author and reader.

The present chapter looks at the autobiography from the perspective of the author–reader dialogue, examining *Les Confessions,* the
*Dialogues,* and, briefly, the *Rêveries.* The discussion here will recall
the examination of *amour* and *amitié* in Chapter II, where Rousseau's
choice to engage 'autrui' through the writing activity first became
apparent. But a textual setting places the topic of dialogue in a new
register, and complicates the terms of discussion about it.

### Introductory Distinctions – Recent Criticism

An author–reader dialogue involves two interlocutors and a text.
In linguistic terms, these correspond to the personal pronouns 'I',
'you' and 'it' – a basic tripartite structure, with elements that can
develop and change in Rousseau's autobiography or in any written
work.

The critical reader makes subdivisions within this threesome. Each
of the interlocutors, for instance, functions at several different levels.

The author of a text is distinguished from its narrator (assuming the text is a narrative), and also from the characters narrated. Even when one individual appears to be speaking at all three levels, it is necessary to keep them separate in order to locate and to appreciate discriminations or shifts of voice, the modulations of ironic distance or of identification. In and through the interplay between author, narrator, and character develops what Wayne Booth has named the 'implied author'.[1] This second sort of author, implied by the text, is not the same as its actual author. One is normally careful not to equate them.

Parallel distinctions apply to the reader. Milord Bomston in *La Nouvelle Héloïse,* or the recipients of the letters which Rousseau includes in the second half of *Les Confessions* exemplify one type of reader, the reader who is also a character. To the narrator of a text corresponds what Genette has termed its 'narrataire'. The 'narrataire' is a purely textual presence, quite separate from the person actually reading.[2] The interplay between these three levels – the character who reads within the text, the 'narrataire' whom it addresses in the voice of the narrator, and the actual reader – creates what one might name the 'implied reader'.

Such subdivisions help in analysis of the variety and range of voice deployed between author and reader in literary practice. But how do they affect autobiography? 'Pour qu'il y ait autobiographie (et plus généralement littérature intime), il faut qu'il y ait identité de *l'auteur,* du *narrateur* et du *personnage',*[3] states Philippe Lejeune. An identity requirement is necessary to define autobiography as a genre. It establishes autobiography's non-fictional status and separates it from drama or from the novel. But crucial as the criterion may be, the manner in which it is posited is equally important. If identity must be absolute, the distinction between implied author and actual author collapses, as does the distinction between implied and actual readers. The criterion which, in theory, defines autobiography, may greatly restrict the different levels of dialogue and interplay of voice which are so important to its literary quality.

Lejeune fulfils the identity requirements through the proper name of the autobiographer, 'seule marque dans le texte d'un indubitable hors-texte, renvoyant à une personne réelle'. Invoked to link the author implied by the text with the individual who actually writes it, the proper name is meant to bridge inside and outside, functioning constatively like a natural sign.[4] 'Il y a presque autant de noms propres que d'individus', Lejeune remarks, somewhat optimistically. He goes on to argue that the proof of identity finally lies in the name printed on the cover of an autobiography, in the equivalent of an author's signature.

In practical criticism of autobiography, the three levels of the author–reader dialogue continue to be distinguished, and attention shifts from the question of identity to what Lejeune has termed the 'pacte autobiographique'. The problem of defining autobiography is now raised in the context of the author–reader dialogue itself, and takes on a dynamic, historical dimension. Not only does a 'pacte' establish a convention between author and reader, authorizing in a sense a wide range of possible voices within the text, but the critic is also able to delineate the development of autobiography by examining changes and transformations in specific 'pactes'.[5] In two different ways, literary history becomes possible. Either one analyses the roles assigned implicitly or explicitly to the reader in the 'pactes' of different autobiographies, or one examines the varying responses of actual readers in different periods to a particular text. These two approaches go under the broad name of *Rezeptionsgeschichte,* an historical criticism which takes the reader to be as important as an author in constituting the meaning of a literary work.

What is the connection between the two criteria defining autobiography? Lejeune and E. Bruss, in their analyses of the *concept* of the 'pacte autobiographique' (as opposed to examinations of 'pactes' in given texts), simultaneously invoke the more troublesome concept of authorial identity. But they are hard put to specify how the two are related. Lejeune's most explicit statement on the issue tends to reduce the notion of an autobiographical pact to the author's proper name: 'on dispose d'un critère textuel général, l'identité du nom (auteur–narrateur–personnage). Le pacte autobiographique, c'est l'affirmation dans le texte de cette identité'.[6] No indication is given of the problems which may arise when an author takes it upon himself to affirm the proper name which he bears. Is the identity of this name a personal identity? Or does the proper name not have to be made personal, appropriated, and filled? How does this affirmation affect the reader? Bruss takes a position similar to Lejeune's, though she employs the conceptual terminology of speech act theory. For her, the autobiographical text is an illocutionary act, structured according to variable formal aspects. What she terms the 'illocutionary center', the identity of the writing or speaking individual, is in her view not susceptible to change. Since the personal identity of an autobiographer very definitely does change, his major task in the text being to show the unity and coherence within this change, one is left with the conclusion that the identity criterion has no connection with specific dialogues between an autobiographer and a reader. The proper name or 'illocutionary center' succeed primarily in providing a logical (or very individualistic) basis for dialogue, and a normative genre definition. They do not lead to any insight into the dialogues of given texts.

The difficulty of finding an adequate identity criterion is not limited to autobiography. It affects all genres, and raises the much wider issue of conventional and natural forms of definition. In autobiography, the identity criterion is simply tied to the narrower, more noticeable issue of authorial identity. The notion of an autobiographical pact, on the other hand, has all the merits and demerits of Rousseau's version of *amitié*. It is a contract, established by two or more parties on the basis of identity. Yet a contract, like the concept of a literary genre, is conventional, not natural in origin. Its authority derives from the linguistic act or acts by which it is concluded. And in Rousseau's autobiography, this linguistic act is the text whose bounds the author is attempting to establish as the bounds of his world. The reader can be privy to Rousseau's pact only to the extent that he exists inside the text. Though certainly a potential 'ami', he exists initially outside it.

Unusual historical factors further complicate the author–reader dialogue in Rousseau's case. To the extent that it is a genre, autobiography certainly involves a set of contractual, conventional rules — textual codes which distinguish it from other genres and make it a specific, identifiable form of discourse. Once the rules have been established, writers and readers may implicitly accept or explicitly flout them, remaining all the while positively or negatively within a network of acquired expectations. We cannot assume them in the present instance. Rousseau's work is in large measure a departure from established codes, and a prevailing influence on the pacts of many subsequent autobiographies. His novelty undoubtedly pleases him, but it also complicates his relationship with the reader. Witness the contradictory extremes at the start of Les Confessions. On the one hand, Rousseau attempts to validate his textual world by gaining recognition from an independent reference. He unsubtly pleads the reader for this recognition. On the other hand, he wants recognition on terms internal to his textual world, his *own* terms. Here he defies the reader with equal vehemence. The attempt both to include and to exclude the reader is hardly a basis for an autobiographical pact.

It is impossible to explain or resolve these difficulties without reference to the third party in an author–reader dialogue, the text. Does a text not impose unusual conditions on the two interlocutors? What sort of dialogue do author and reader in fact engage in? Each person is alone, separate from the other interlocutor, yet also bound to him through the written work. So long as we construe the auto-biographical pact solely in terms of 'I' and 'you', the author and reader, we must conceive it either in terms of writing *or* in terms of reading. The result is two separate, internal dialogues. From the author's point of view, the reader is an empty possibility, an absence which allows the author to converse with himself while writing. From the reader's point of view, the writer is equally distant. An author is present in the reading process only to the extent that the reader re-enacts his intention while reading.

From the perspective of the text, the relation between the identity criterion and the pact of autobiography becomes clearer. Each of the two separate dialogues above involves a virtual entity, either a virtual author or a virtual reader. When one examines them by way of the text – which is truly the concern of the critic, and through which both dialogues must pass – it is apparent that virtual author and virtual reader are one and the same.[7] The text disjoins author and reader, placing them in remote, individual spheres. But it also joins them together. The text functions as both a barrier and a link. It connects the interlocutors across a distance which it enforces *and* bridges.

These basic points about dialogue apply in principle to any literary work. But a textual perspective is especially appropriate in the case of autobiography, where an identity criterion is so crucial and so hard to come by. It is not necessary to posit this criterion in a normative way. If, as we suggested in the Introduction, the autobiographical self is a heterogeneous combination of virtual and actual elements, and if author and reader display the same heterogeneity, then identity in autobiography is fundamentally between self and text. Self and text both function between two domains which are qualitatively different. Both effect a communication across this difference.

Neither the text nor the autobiographical self, abstractly considered, constitutes an entity or state of events which is identical to itself. It may seem gratuitous to propose an identity between concepts which are indeterminate and therefore not really concepts at all. But this difficulty has not hindered our work thus far. Though it binds self and text to a repetitive, non-progressive mode of existence, indeterminacy also calls forth definite structures which can be properly analysed, and which do change and develop in time. Such are the specific rhetorical stages in Rousseau's autobiography. We must simply be very careful to distinguish the notion of text in general from the particular, determinate texts which are its empirical instances.

This last point is especially important, given our argument that Rousseau develops his sense of personal identity through a constructive, textual process. For although specific texts may be personal, as they are written by a given individual, there is nothing intrinsically personal about the general notion of text, nor about what we have termed the autobiographical self. Strictly speaking, these notions designate the boundary between virtual and actual aspects of identity. They disjoin a person from himself, and thereby link him to 'autrui'. In the abstract, it matters little whether this 'autrui' is another person or the otherness which exists within one individual. Rousseau, living and writing, is no less distant from 'his' virtual self than are the author and reader in their dialogue.

Admittedly, when we move from the general notion of text to the specific rhetorical stages and texts of Rousseau's autobiography, it is impossible to maintain the identity between virtual author and virtual reader. For the indeterminate boundary then takes determinate form, and one must specify two very different types of reader – a reader 'outside' the bounds of the text (either the transcendental reader or a given individual who buys and reads the text); and the reader 'inside' the text, whom the autobiographer constructs in the course of his self-presentation as a sort of 'personne interposée' between himself and possible readings of him.

We shall examine primarily the constructed reader here, but these two types of reader imply a double viewpoint on the author–reader dialogue. Its general lines are already visible from the two different sentiments of *amour* and *amitié*. The reader 'inside' Rousseau's autobiography is his 'ami', an extension or projection of his own identity within the bounds of the text. The reader 'outside' is an unusual object of *amour,* whose recognition the author fears, but who he requires as an external reference to give value to his textual world.

The personal identity, proper name, or 'illocutionary center' of a writer in no way form the corner-stone or defining criterion of autobiography. An identity between self and text is both the start and the end-point of Rousseau's project, and makes it adequate to the process whereby personal identity itself comes to be constituted. There is no self-made individual. Every person is a patchwork quilt, more or less well designed and sewn, of identifications and appropriations of roles offered by other individuals. When an author comes to write about himself, he inevitably finds his 'personal identity' through images received from others. Just as inevitably, he presents himself through a constructed image of the reader. The most individualistic and subjective mode of discourse therefore has a fundamental structure of dialogue – not only when a reader opens an autobiography and begins to read (possibly finding 'himself' in the text), but also when the autobiographer works to set down his life in writing. The *Lettres à Malesherbes,* Rousseau's first major personal statement, well indicate the importance of an interlocutor. We shall see that in the most self-enclosed, apparently solipsistic moments of the autobiography, he is as entangled with 'autrui' as he ever was in his life.

## Les Confessions

By the uniformity of the narrative I converted the fable into truth in the minds of my hearers.

Goethe, *Dichtung und Wahrheit* (p. 63)

At the start of *Les Confessions,* when Rousseau announces the immediate unity of 'je sens mon cœur' and claims to have dispensed with the need to read into the heart of others to understand his own, he posits the identity between self and text which marks the beginning of the autobiography (I: 5; 1149). The reader seems to have no part in the proclamation. Rousseau's 'moi seul' relegates him to the sidelines, one among 'l'innombrable foule de mes semblables' convened in the third person plural to witness the author's self-revelation. If there is a 'pacte' at the opening of Book I, Rousseau concludes it with himself alone. Following Augustine, whose title he has borrowed, he does address himself to God, and calls upon the image of the Last Judgement as a gage of his veracity. But the autobiographer follows the tradition of confessional literature only in form. He quickly leaves God for Rousseau, in whom he is far more interested.

Rousseau's conviction that he can write everything (the closure of self-understanding pronounced at the start of *Les Confessions)* displaces the openness of his identity on to the role of the reader. The phrase, 'je sens mon cœur', does not make a monologue of either self or text; it simply means that the apparently insignificant reader now becomes the

virtual self with which Rousseau (following our general thesis) desires
to coincide. We are far removed from the range of authorial intention
when we make this claim, since in the autobiography Rousseau never
consciously accepts the thought that identity cannot be made fully
personal and stated in a determinate text. The inexorable process
whereby the reader in his text slowly comes to resemble and then
finally becomes a second Rousseau includes a built-in diversion, the
paranoia which makes all other individuals non-readers. This negative
development fills the author's awareness, making him oblivious of many
of the issues we shall discuss.

Where does one look for the reader in the first stage of the autobiography? The question is not so straightforward for *Les Confessions*
as it will be for the *Dialogues* and *Rêveries*. There 'le François', and
then Rousseau himself, occupy the position of the reader, which,
as a result, is relatively easy to locate and analyse. This situation is
in keeping with our hypothesis of displacement. A virtual entity can
hardly be outstanding; and the reader develops into a discernible
character only as Rousseau's process of identification in his textual
world increasingly leads him to body forth a new fiction, the reader
who will recognize him for what he feels himself to be. In *Les
Confessions*, this reader is still implicit — the 'narrataire', or the reader
parallel to the narrator. Several narrated episodes, where Rousseau the
character acts as a reader (particularly in his role as an amateur diplomat), shed light on this diffuse yet omnipresent figure.

### Childhood Reading

Reading for Rousseau is primarily a process of identification. He states
in Book I that the library left by his mother and her relatives was an
important part of his childhood, and he includes an anecdote about the
circumstances surrounding his reading of a preferred volume, the *Lives*
of Plutarch:

. . . et fils d'un pere dont l'amour de la patrie étoit la plus forte passion,
je m'enflammois à son exemple; je me croyois Grec ou Romain; je
devenois le personnage dont je lisois le vie: le recit des traits de constance et d'intrépidité qui m'avoient frappé me rendoit les yeux
étincellans et la voix forte. Un jour je racontois à table l'aventure de
Scevola, on fut effrayé de me voir avancer et tenir la main sur un
réchaud pour representer son action. (I: 9)

Rousseau undergoes an identification in a variety of ways here, not all of which have to do directly with reading. His father (with whom the child apparently pored over books until dawn) is one 'exemple'. Patriotism, which Rousseau attributes to the father, implies a further identification between citizen and country. But the young reader's connection with the character of a book is the strongest and most immediate in the anecdote. 'Je devenois le personnage dont je lisois la vie', Rousseau states; such that he even disregards physical harm to himself when retelling the story that he has read.

This anecdote from childhood resonates widely with later, more significant actions. The same 'constance' and 'intrépidité' characterize Rousseau's enactment of a role he has himself created, in the 'réforme personnelle', and even his effort to identify himself with his text, in the autobiography. The connection between an imaginative leap into the 'récit' and physical suffering of another person, furthermore, is highly reminiscent of the initial 'transport' of *amitié*. Taken in context with an earlier remark in Book I – 'j'ignore ce que je fis jusqu'à cinq ou six ans . . . je ne me souviens que de mes prémiéres lectures et de leur effect sur moi; c'est le tems d'où je date sans interruption la conscience de moi-même' (I: 8) – the present episode suggests that Rousseau's sense of personal identity is composed of identifications such as he describes here. But the description is short, and leads only to very tenuous conclusions. One can best affirm that Rousseau's own experience as a reader probably influences his demands on the reader of his text, from whom he will come to expect a response as strong and complete as that described above.

## Diplomacy

In descriptions of several forays into diplomacy, Rousseau provides a more extensive opportunity to observe the terms of the author–reader interaction in his autobiography. Diplomacy is his 'carrière manquée', the important but unfortunate job in Venice as secretary to M. de Montaigu being but the final employment of a talent also noticeable in Turin, at the household of the Comte de Gouvon, and, more unofficially, in Rousseau's role of interpreter for a travelling Greek Archimandrite. Even as a highly successful author, fêted by the Luxembourgs, he is tempted by the offhand offer of a post from Choiseul, the minister of state. No doubt eager to set right what he considers the injustice of his Venetian experience, Rousseau is plainly fascinated by the process of diplomacy. His predilections are not fortuitous. As one early diplomatic episode demonstrates, this 'carrière manquée' in fact functions obliquely as a sort of John the Baptist for his role as an autobiographer.

In the narrative sequence in Book IV of *Les Confessions,* Rousseau's encounter with the Greek Archimandrite follows closely on his musical projects as Vaussore de Villeneuve in Lausanne. In disgrace after the concert there, the young man ekes out a living as a music teacher, until his meeting with this stranger sparks a new adventure. 'Un jour', Rousseau recounts,

j'entrai pour diner dans un cabaret : j'y vis un homme . . . qui souvent avoit peine à se faire entendre, ne parlant qu'un jargon presque indéchiffrable, mais plus ressemblant à l'italien qu'à nulle autre langue. J'entendis presque tout ce qu'il disoit et j'étois le seul; il ne pouvoit s'énoncer que par signes avec l'hôte et les gens du pays. Je lui dis quelques mots en italien qu'il entendit parfaitement; il se leva et vint m'embrasser avec transport. La liaison fut bientôt faite, et dès ce moment je lui servis de truchement. (I: 154)

Rousseau's ability to speak two languages causes his initial acquaintance with the Archimandrite. Among those present at the tavern, he alone can translate for the traveller. As soon as he bridges the linguistic distance, an immediate 'liaison' occurs. The Archimandrite invites his new-found companion to dinner; the impoverished musician accepts; and the language of *amitié* quickly surfaces in the text.

Son diné étoit bon, le mien étoit moins que médiocre. En buvant et baragouinant nous achevames de nous familiariser, et dès la fin du repas nous devinmes inséparables. (I: 154)

As Rousseau recounts the story, it is only after this preliminary, unquestioning acceptance that a formal relationship begins. 'Il me conta qu'il étoit Prelat grec et Archimandrite de Jerusalem . . . il me montra de belles patentes . . .' The stranger discloses his identity and project, and proposes that the young man accompany him as interpreter in his appeal for support and funds. At this point, the episode moves to a new level. 'Notre accord fut bientôt fait', the author states. The phrase seems to repeat 'la liaison fut bientôt faite'. But between the 'accord' and the 'liaison' is the difference between spontaneous friendship and a contractual agreement, a distinction to which Rousseau clings later in life. Now, however, he enters into the agreement on easy terms.

Je ne demandois rien, et il promettoit beaucoup. Sans caution, sans sureté, sans connoissance, je me livre à sa conduite, et dès le lendemain me voila parti pour Jerusalem. (I: 154)

A promise from the Archimandrite forms the basis of a commitment between the two men, not dissimilar in nature from what one might call, in a different context, an autobiographical pact. On his way to the promised land ('Jerusalem'), the young Rousseau resembles a reader who has taken on trust the author's declaration of identity, and who agrees to read his text on these terms.

But the opening pact is only the beginning of the diplomatic episode, and Rousseau does not remain for long in the position of a reader. At their first stop, before the Senate of Berne, the interpreter is asked to speak on behalf of the Archimandrite, to represent his case for consideration. 'Je ne m'attendois à rien moins', he states. 'Qu'on juge de mon embarras!' (I: 155). The author emphasizes in retrospect the difficulty of the request, only to recall glowingly the gist of his speech in *Les Confessions*. For the young interpreter finds a facility of address and such self-assurance that he concludes his presentation by repeating, in grandiose terms, the promise made earlier by the Archimandrite. The Senators need only join and contribute to his cause. 'Je finis par promettre les bénédictions du ciel à ceux qui voudroient y prendre part' (I: 155). Such hyperbole reflects Rousseau's exhilaration at discovering himself able to speak well on his feet. As he remarks elsewhere, 'Je trouvois bien beau de prêcher' (I: 25). But the adult author, as if better to distinguish the speech, reflects more soberly: 'Voila la seule fois de ma vie que j'aye parlé en public et devant un souverain, et la seule fois aussi, peutêtre, que j'ai parlé hardiment et bien' (I: 156).

The nature and success of Rousseau's representation of the Archimandrite's case, and especially the insouciant promise which ends it, are material for critical reflection. In one sense, the young interpreter resembles the childhood reader of Plutarch, and identifies himself so effectively with another individual (in this instance, the Archimandrite) that he enacts his story as though it were his own. But what happens to Rousseau's own story and identity at Berne? Do they dissolve into those of the Archimandrite?

A quick comparison with the earlier concert at Lausanne is instructive here. There also, Rousseau stands before the public without adequate preparation. In both episodes, he makes or has made a promise which it is not in his power to fulfil. The respective outcomes of the two incidents, however, are diametrically opposed. Where the musician disgraced himself, the interpreter now receives 'des complimens dont j'eus l'agréable emploi d'être le truchement' (I: 155–6). Rousseau's sudden change of fortune requires some sort of explanation.

In fact, it is only because the project of the Archimandrite stands between him and his audience that Rousseau succeeds so well in his second public appearance. The interpreter does not totally lose himself at Berne; the identity of the Greek Prelate functions instead like a pseudonym, which he slips into when he begins to speak. Paradoxically, he discovers the gift of self-possession in the act of representing someone *other* than himself. At Lausanne, the would-be musician lacks this external protection. The anagram of Vaussore de Villeneuve, though intended to spark applause, succeeds only in involving him in a promise for which he is held responsible.

In a second sense, therefore, identification with another individual serves primarily as a pretext for Rousseau's self-glorification. He effaces himself in order to manifest himself all the more convincingly. At the same time he frees himself of responsibility for his action. We have noticed this dialectic of self-revelation and self-concealment before, and soon we shall trace its effects in the context of the author–reader dialogue. But the present diplomatic episode is useful preparation. Although we are not yet in a position fully to appreciate the distinction, one might, on the basis of the interpreter's speech, put forward the two notions of 'dégagement' and 'engagement' to account for Rousseau's mode of promising. Speaking in the name of another person, he lets himself go ('se dégage'), as it were, and is able to promise without regard for the consequences of his word. The beginnings of a more serious 'engagement' do not become visible until the next stage of the diplomatic itinerary.

At Soleurre, the evangelical mendicants meet a rather different reception. There the French Ambassador, able to communicate with the Archimandrite directly, hears them individually. Rousseau is deprived of his role as an intermediary, and must speak for himself. 'A la sortie de mon Grec', he states

je voulus le suivre; on me retint; ce fut mon tour. M'étant donné pour Parisien, j'étois comme tel sous la jurisdiction de son Excellence. Elle me demanda qui j'étois, m'exhorta de lui dire la vérité; je le lui promis en lui demandant une audience particuliére qui me fut accordée. (I: 156)

The French Ambassador evidently suspects the Archimandrite to be a fraud; and the phrase, 'm'étant donné pour Parisien' indicates that Rousseau's role as interpreter is only one of several pseudonymous elements in the tale – he has also misrepresented himself directly. No doubt the Parisien identity is one which the young man would like to possess, but it places him momentarily at the mercy of the Ambassador. 'La vérité' is demanded; the story threatens to turn sour. It develops benignly when Rousseau is granted the private hearing he requires to speak for himself. He is as incapable of speaking as another in private conversation as he is of speaking as himself in a large gathering. But given the intimacy of a one-to-one hearing, he rises to the same degree of eloquence and conviction marshalled earlier on behalf of the Archimandrite at Berne. A similar success ensues.

M. l'Ambassadeur m'emmena dans son cabinet dont il ferma sur nous la porte, et là, me jettant à ses pieds, je lui tins parole. Je n'aurois pas moins dit quand je n'aurois rien promis; car un continuel besoin d'épanchement met à tout moment mon cœur sur mes levres . . . Il fut si content de ma petite histoire et de l'effusion de cœur avec laquelle il vit que je l'avois contée, qu'il me prit par la main, entra chez Madame l'Ambassadrice, et me présenta à elle en lui faisant un abrégé de mon recit. Made de Bonac m'accueillit avec bonté et dit qu'il ne falloit pas me laisser aller avec ce Moine grec. (I: 156–7)

When Rousseau fulfils his promise (which seems superfluous *after* it has been fulfilled), he again leads his audience to contribute to the cause presented. But the interpreter is no longer in a position resembling that of a reader; he now recounts his own 'petite histoire', in his own name. In other words, he is now in the position held earlier by the Archimandrite, like that of an autobiographer. In recounting his story, moreover, he inspires the Ambassador to repeat the 'récit' to his wife. It is interesting to note that the act of promising, both in the tavern and in the present incident, is the initial stage in the establishment of a form of text, which is itself then relayed from one individual to another. The Archimandrite promises Rousseau, who promises to the Senators, who contribute to the project put before them. The movement of the text is like that of a chain letter, forwarded from one individual to another. At Soleurre, Rousseau's promise generates a short autobiographical narrative, which the Ambassador, as he accepts it, immediately relays to Mme de Bonac. She then becomes involved in the young man's fate. In the end, he is separated from the Archimandrite, and taken under the care of the Embassy.

If there is a 'moral' to be drawn from this sequence of events, it is Rousseau's well-tried lesson from his subsequent 'réforme personnelle' – that he can be what he wants to be, simply by being himself. A short while later he departs for Paris with a pocketful of money and recommendations from the Ambassador. The origin of the pseudonym becomes his actual destination, and the transformation from one to the other occurs when the young Rousseau makes the small but significant shift from representing another person (the Archimandrite) to representing himself. The way in which diplomacy thus turns into autobiography is confirmed by a singular coincidence which occurs before his departure.

M. de la Martiniére Secretaire d'Ambassade fut en quelque façon chargé de moi. En me conduisant dans la chambre qui m'étoit destinée, il me dit: cette chambre a été occupé sous le Comte de Luc par un homme celébre, du même nom que vous. Il ne tient qu'à vous de le remplacer de toutes maniéres et de faire dire un jour Rousseau premier, Rousseau second. (I: 157)

'Rousseau premier' is the poet Jean-Baptiste, whom 'Rousseau second' quickly sets out to imitate, composing his first verse at Soleurre. The poetic impulse of course does not last, and 'cette conformité', as he describes the occurrence, leads to a rather different 'destinée'. But the coincidence of proper names adds an unusual twist to the entire episode. The discovery of an appropriate model reinforces Rousseau's descision to speak 'la vérité'; in other words, for himself. In one consistent development, he becomes a namesake and enjoys a benefactor. There now seems no need to present himself as Parisian, or to become an interpreter for a con-artist of an Archimandrite. 'Rousseau' as pseudonym is a much more 'natural' combination, permitting the young man actually to become what was previously mere act. That his model should be a literary figure is part of its force, and leads directly to our present concern. For at the end of the episode Rousseau makes his initial attempt at writing autobiography.

M. de Martiniére voulut voir de mon style et me demanda par écrit le même détail que j'avois fait à M. l'Ambassadeur. Je lui écrivis une

longue lettre que j'apprends avoir été conservée par M. de Marianne . . .
Si je puis l'avoir par lui ou par d'autres, on la trouvera dans le recueil
qui doit accompagner mes confessions. (I: 157–8)

## Diplomacy in 'Les Confessions'

The autobiographical letter is unfortunately lost, and any curiosity
about how Rousseau saw and wrote of his life at the age of nineteen
must go unsatisfied. But the mention of it, in the narrative sequence
we have followed in *Les Confessions,* encourages some thoughts about
how this small venture in diplomacy sheds light on Rousseau's more
important venture in autobiography.

In a text, the diplomatic skills exercised by an author are directed
toward the reader. (We speak now of the reader 'outside' the text.)
Before he begins to write autobiography, Rousseau has no obligation
to speak for himself, in his own name, and finds his best voice speaking
in the name of another. The characters of the early dramatic works
and of many later texts stand between him and the reader. Like
'personnes interposées', they allow the author a textual analogue of the
'dégagement' which the young interpreter enjoys while speaking for the
Archimandrite at Berne. One could say that Rousseau both reveals
and conceals himself in many of his pre-autobiographical works; but
since his personal identity and role as an author are not directly at
stake in them, this quasi-pseudonymous mode of expression is the
real interest of the texts, and what makes them classifiable as fictional
works. Such freedom is a positive part of Rousseau's elaboration of
a textual world. And at this stage of his writing career, it is ultimately
the text itself, rather than specific characters in it, which functions
as a 'personne interposée' between the author and the reader.

In the autobiography, a major change occurs. The text, formerly
the third party to the author–reader dialogue, is now identified with
its author, who speaks in his own name. But does he speak only in his
own name? Is Rousseau assured of the private hearing accorded him
at Soleurre? The reader 'outside' the autobiography resembles just
as well the faceless Senators at Berne, and Rousseau's need for a protective 'personne interposée' does not diminish. Furthermore, the
glorification of 'moi seul' and the reference to the Last Judgement
at the beginning of *Les Confessions* strike a note closer to his decla-
mation of the Archimandrite's cause than to the repentant confession
to the Ambassador.

In *Les Confessions* Rousseau addresses himself to the reader 'outside' the text through a different sort of reader, the 'narrataire' within it. This reader takes varied forms. God is the 'narrataire' at the start of the narrative, even though 'l'innombrable foule de mes semblables' is undoubtedly the major audience. The invocation of divinity is a highly useful device: apart from momentarily placing the text in a recognizable tradition, it provides Rousseau with a warrant for the self-revelation he desires to make. Before God, he has nothing to hide; and since in principle He already knows all there is to know, the autobiographical narrator has an obligation to tell all.

Rousseau ceases to address himself to God after *Les Confessions* get underway, and the interlocutor within the text tends to be an implicit figure, accompanying the narrator as an invisible presence. He surfaces occasionally, as either 'vous', 'il', or 'on', in the singular or in the plural. Rousseau seems to alternate between these different modes of address in an indiscriminate manner.[8] But in the main, these explicit references reveal little of what the 'narrataire's' role might be, and how it is important to the autobiography.

In Books II and IV, two exceptions to this vagueness in the reader's position may be found, in passages where Rousseau reflects directly (if with some hyperbole) on what he expects of himself and his interlocutor. In Book II he states:

Avant que d'aller plus loin je dois au lecteur mon excuse ou ma justification tant sur les menus détails où je viens d'entrer que sur ceux où j'entrerai dans la suite, et qui n'ont rien d'interessant à ses yeux. Dans l'entreprise que j'ai faite de me montrer tout entier au public, il faut que rien ne lui reste obscur ou caché; il faut que je me tienne incessament sous ses yeux, qu'il me suive dans tous les égaremens de mon cœur, dans tous les recoins de ma vie; qu'il ne me perde pas de vue un seul instant, de peur que, trouvant dans mon recit la moindre lacune, le moindre vide, et se demandant, qu'a-t-il fait durant ce tems-là, il ne m'accuse de n'avoir pas voulu tout dire. (I: 59–60)

The 'narrataire' in this passage, although there is nothing divine about him, is expected to maintain the same omniscient regard towards Rousseau as was invoked at the beginning of *Les Confessions.* Between man and God there is a great gap fixed, and the omniscience of this human reader goes hand-in-hand with the injunction to tell all which the author places on himself. But once again, the requirement to tell all is precisely what Rousseau wishes. By presenting it through this version of the reader, he casts an absolute freedom of expression in the guise of external necessity.

Who in fact is the 'narrataire', the reader 'in' the text? Rousseau embodies the ideal of human omniscience in several characters of the pre-autobiographical texts, developing it most fully in Wolmar and the Mentor. And of the many traits shared by these two individuals, a common concern for *amitié* is perhaps the most important. Each presides, with clear vision and lucid judgement, over the reinstatement or preservation of innocence and friendship, before or after the ravages and 'crime' of Rousseau's version of *amour*. The 'narrataire' of *Les Confessions* is meant to be Rousseau's *ami*.

Rousseau gives some indication of the resulting author–reader dialogue when trying to play a similar role, after his love for Sophie d'Houdetot has run its course. The *Lettres morales,* part of his effort to salvage the relationship by transmuting it into *amitié*, include a passage in many ways similar to that in Book II. He writes:

Parmi tous ces dons que le Ciel vous a départis oserai-je compter celui d'un ami fidelle? Il en est un, vous le savez, qui non content de vous chérir telle que vous étes, se pénetre d'un vif et pur enthousiasme pour tout ce qu'on doit espérer de vous. Il vous contemple d'un œil avide dans tous les états où vous pouvez être; il vous voit à chaque instant de sa vie, dans le passé, dans le présent, dans l'avenir; il voudroit rassembler à la fois tout votre être au fond de son ame. (IV: 1083)

As an *ami* of Sophie and reader of her character, Rousseau follows her throughout her life with an omniscience like that of 'le Ciel' (from which his friendship apparently comes). In this way, he fulfils the role assigned to the 'narrataire' of *Les Confessions*. But the *ami* of the *Lettres morales* is more active than he has as yet become in the auto-biography. Rousseau observes Sophie not only as she is, but also as all that she could be. Furthermore, he sees her in the entirety of his own life, as well as of hers, and expresses the desire to embrace her existence within his own.

Why should Rousseau want a reader of *Les Confessions* to be like the *ami* he describes here? We cannot rightly affirm that the 'narrataire' acts as he does towards Sophie; strictly speaking, the 'narrataire' is not a real reader, and exists only as the narrator postulates, and in a sense constructs his identity in the course of the narrative. But it is plausible to suggest that Rousseau needs this sort of reader exactly as 'Rousseau second' needs 'Rousseau premier' at Soleurre. The auto-biographical author is no longer the young interpreter, but he is cer-tainly not all that he could and hopes to be, not fully himself. He requires a model which is not external to him, and in whose name he can speak, even when speaking in his own name. The 'narrataire' of the text, to whom Rousseau speaks as another individual, but who as *ami* shares a fundamental identity with the author, plays this important role.

There are obvious differences between the model at Soleurre and the 'narrataire' of *Les Confessions*. The 'Rousseau premier' in the diplomatic episode served to link Rousseau to the future, to an identity meant for him but which is not yet his. In the autobiography, the reader in the text (rightfully, 'Rousseau second') now helps to link the author ('Rousseau premier') to his past, that which he was, but is no more. 'J'écris la vie d'un homme qui n'est plus', Rousseau states in one of the 'Ébauches'. 'Cet homme c'est moi-même' (I: 1159). The narrator of *Les Confessions* is just as separate from his childhood, and the wholeness which he believes he experienced there, as the young man was from the wholeness which the future seemed at one time to contain.

Though the 'narrataire' in the first stage of the autobiography is largely an implicit figure, his role in the text is nonetheless crucial to Rousseau's project of 'tout dire'. One could say that he accompanies the author's return to childhood, and enables him to enagage the past and to make it live once again, in the light of all that the past could and should have been, as well as of all that it actually was. Or, more correctly, one could say that Rousseau makes this return only by simultaneously positing a reader who is willing to accompany him in it and capable of seeing the past in its entirety. Inasmuch as the author contstructs him, this 'narrataire' has nothing in common with the reader 'outside' the text. The narrator speaks about him as though he were, and, as we shall see later, Rousseau has difficulty in accepting the difference between the two. But although the *ami* implied by the text may be only an imaginary interlocutor, an extension or projection of the author's identity, he is an integral part in the production of *Les Confessions*.

If a 'narrataire-ami' helps the autobiographer to engage his past at a profound level, he also has certain demands placed upon him. A passage at the end of Book IV continues the basic thought from Rousseau's address to the reader in Book II, but with important qualifications. 'Je n'ai pas promis d'offrir au public un grand personnage', he now states:

J'ai promis de me peindre tel que je suis et pour me connoitre dans mon age avancé, il faut m'avoir bien connu dans ma jeunesse ... Je voudrois pouvoir en quelque façon rendre mon ame transparente aux yeux du lecteur, et pour cela je cherche à la lui montrer sous tous les points de vue ... afin qu'il puisse juger par lui-meme du principe qui les produit.

Si je me chargeois du résultat et que je lui disse; tel est mon caractére, il pourroit croire, sinon que je le trompe, au moins que je me trompe. Mais en lui détaillant avec simplicité tout ... tout ... tout ... je ne puis l'induire en erreur à moins que je ne le veuille, encore même en le voulant n'y parviendrois-je pas aisément de cette façon. C'est à lui d'assembler ces élémens et de déterminer l'être qu'ils composent; le résultat doit être son ouvrage, et s'il se trompe alors, toute l'erreur sera de son fait. (I: 174–5)

The general sense of this quotation (drawn from a long passage of considerable complexity) is fairly clear. Rousseau once again resolves to place his entire life before the eyes of the reader, and to make it a transparent 'tout'. But he now takes responsibility only for the facts of his life, and expects the reader to take an active role in determining what they mean. According to a constative ideal, he will provide the multiple, unconnected elements of his 'être', and the reader's judgement will make them into a coherent, meaningful 'ouvrage'. The autobiography thus becomes like a jigsaw puzzle, with the author supplying all the pieces, and the reader putting them together. Rousseau cannot lose at this game. Since the reader must discern the unifying principle in the text, any error will be his doing.

Before one dismisses this stance as the ploy of an irresponsible author, it is useful to recognize the logical value of Rousseau's position here. If we recall that in the autobiography he displaces the virtual aspect of identity on to the reader, the notion that the unity of his 'être' must derive or be determined from this source is a consistent one. Rousseau is thus neither far wrong in his remarks, nor remiss in holding up his side of the bargain by providing the necessary elements for a coherent reading.

But Rousseau would certainly never admit this theoretical insight, and while he disclaims any grandeur and importance for himself in the autobiography, he also benefits very definitely from his self-effacement. The 'narrataire' addressed at the end of Book IV fulfils much the same role as the Archimandrite at Berne. He permits the author to present himself in a state of 'dégagement', in the etymological sense that the constituent elements of identity are dispersed and unconnected, and in the sense that Rousseau can write without regard for the meaning or consequence of his text. This may seem an odd benefit, but it is also consistent with a basic desire of Rousseau. For the 'narrataire' extends the freedom of reverie ('tout cela me dégage mon ame') into the autobiographer's relationship with the reader. As an *ami* and a 'personne interposée', the reader in the text gives Rousseau scope for a total self-revelation, while also relieving him of responsibility for what he actually writes.

## Conclusions

The identity between self and text in autobiography sets off a complex author–reader interaction. Rousseau's first affirmation of this identity, in *Les Confessions,* brings him to a pact with his interlocutor. A contractual agreement is visible at various stages and levels throughout the text – it occurs in the promise of the Archimandrite, in Rousseau's promise to the Ambassador, and in the phrase from Book IV, 'J'ai promis de me peindre tel que je suis'. These instances of the linguistic act of promising (a performative, or illocutionary use of language) are directed toward the future, and toward the reader as the future of the author's work. One could say that the pact sets a basis for the development of the autobiographical text, the way Rousseau's promise at Soleurre allows him to narrate his short history there, or the way the Archimandrite's promise causes the young interpreter to accept him and his project.

But how, and to what sort of reader, does Rousseau promise? He concludes a pact with the 'narrataire' of the text, and since this reader remains within the bounds of his own imaginative universe the author's promise is directed primarily toward himself. Rousseau uses the contractual mode of autobiography (as he uses the convention of *amitié)* to advance an individual fiction – his view of his own, personal identity. In this sense, the pact of *Les Confessions* is similar to that which occurs between the interpreter and the Archimandrite in the 'cabaret'; it presupposes an initial, unquestioning acceptance of one interlocutor by the other, and the inseparability and reversibility of interest which characterizes interpersonal relations between friends in Rousseau's textual world. This type of 'narrataire' allows the autobiographer to promise in two, seemingly incompatible modes, and to combine the 'dégagement' and self-possession of speaking in the name of another with the 'engagement' of speaking in one's own name.

The reader 'outside' the autobiography enters Rousseau's pact only indirectly, reading and interpreting him through the image of the reader which the author has constructed in the text.[9] The actual reader may accept this 'personne interposée', just as the Senators at Berne and Mme de Bonac are invited to take up the cause put before them. But the 'narrataire' of course influences, and to a certain extent predetermines, the possible readings which the actual reader may make of Rousseau. If he refuses to enter the pact, the reader 'outside' is not simply rejecting the proper name of the autobiographer. He is refusing to recognize that version of Rousseau which is implicit in the author's image of the reader; he is refusing to become *Rousseau's* reader. But if he should identify with the 'narrataire', the reader 'outside' the text is no longer 'outside' it; he has stepped into the reader's role which the text has offered him, has become the author's advocate, and is already another 'personne interposée' for Rousseau, ready to pass him on to another reader. The curious relay network which we noticed in the diplomatic episode is a good illustration of the exchange which may occur between 'narrataire' and actual reader. The work quite literally *lives* in this exchange, and in its passage from one reader to another. One final point: the subtlety and underlying outrageousness of Rousseau's image of the reader, like his image of himself, is a major reason why readers and even critics of him have either been so rebuffed or so enamoured, willing or unwilling to take up his case; why his text continues to live.

*Transition to Dialogues*

Two shifts in the author–reader dialogue during the second half of *Les Confessions* are indications of the major change which will occur in the *Dialogues*. One is the insertion of letters into the narrative of Books IX and X. These create a new textual level, with its own set of readers. The recipients of the letters – Mme d'Épinay, Diderot, the Luxembourgs, even Rousseau himself – do not correspond to the 'narrataire'. They pertain to an historical sequence of events which is independent of the narrative order and interrupts it. The addition inevitably hinders the involvement and appreciation of an actual reader. Already responding to the 'narrataire', he must now accommodate a second reader in the text, whose explicit presence there makes it little more than a document. The growing disunity of the narrator's voice, which we noticed in the last chapter, is therefore paralleled by a fragmentation in the reader to whom he speaks. This change prefigures the rhetorical structure of the *Dialogues,* where 'Rousseau' and 'le François' effectively assume the places held by the author and the recipient of the letters in *Les Confessions.* The conversation between these two characters is imaginary rather than historical, but it succeeds no less in displacing the primary level of narrative in the first stage of the autobiography, and in turning the text into a document.

The three paragraphs appended to the end of *Les Confessions* mark a second step in a changing author—reader dialogue. There Rousseau refers to his live reading of the work to one among the several audiences who heard it in 1770 and 1771. He includes a defiant declaration, made at the conclusion of the reading and apparently intended to provoke a direct response from his listeners. None is forthcoming.

Rousseau's expectation that a live audience might respond immediately and favourably to *Les Confessions* is evidence of his confusion about the difference between 'his' reader (the 'narrataire' within the text) and the reader 'outside' it. Although his listeners may take him at his word, and hear the work as autobiography, they certainly do not enter the author's pact and understand him as he wishes to be understood. The failure is all the more striking when contrasted with the live readings of *La Nouvelle Héloïse* which so enchanted Mme de Luxembourg (I: 522–3). In that instance, the text itself served as a 'personne interposée' between Rousseau and his listener. Mme de Luxembourg could identify with it without identifying directly with him, and showered attention on him as a result. The silence which greets Rousseau after the reading in 1771 may largely disappoint him, or may indirectly confirm him in his role as an outcast. But it is in either event consistent with the new and uncompromising terms of his autobiography. Presenting his text as himself, Rousseau hopes to dispense with the 'inside'/'outside' distinction, the discrepancy between the 'narrataire' and the actual reader, and the need for any form of 'personne interposée'. Of course, no actual reader can fully match the image of the reader in *Les Confessions*; to do so, he would have to become a 'Rousseau second'.

Unaware of the objective reasons for the non-response, Rousseau persists in his autobiographical design, and puts the author—reader dialogue through a sharp change of tack in his next text. The public readings create a momentary stasis, in that they conjoin the narrative time of *Les Confessions* to the historical time of the author's present.

It is possible to consider the conception of the *Dialogues* as a fictional rendering of this present, as Rousseau's effort to find the response which he did not receive there. He substitutes 'le François' for the auditors of *Les Confessions,* 'Rousseau' for himself as the public reader, and 'J.J.' for himself as the author of the narrative text, as the voice which was established but not justified in it. In short, Rousseau becomes his own 'personne interposée' in the *Dialogues.* 'Rousseau' is an active version of the 'narrataire' implicit in the first stage of the autobiography, now quite visibly an extension or projection of the identity of the autobiographer. 'Le François' is the reader 'outside' the text, but now brought into it. The strategy is plainly paradoxical, since the author becomes an advocate for himself only in order to abolish the very notion of a 'personne interposée', and divides himself into two individuals in order to name himself directly. Rousseau is so anxious to insure that his image will reach posterity intact that he takes the role of the reader into his own hands, reverses his position in Book IV, and attempts by himself to state the principle of his being. 'J.J.' is placed 'on hold', as it were, made to wait out the duration of 'Rousseau's' argumentation, while the connection with 'autrui' goes through the imaginary circuitry of the *Dialogues.* By the time they are over, of course, the problem to which they are a response will have changed complexion. Rousseau will never return to the actual reader he tried to engage in *Les Confessions.* But even as they lead finally to a different type of resolution, the *Dialogues* definitely presuppose this prior stage in the autobiography.

*Venetian Diplomacy*

Before examining the author—reader dialogue in the *Dialogues,* we might cast a lingering glance at a final episode in diplomacy in *Les Confessions.* It occurs in Venice, and is the first incident which Rousseau chooses to recount in Book VII after he has described his duties there as Secretary to the Ambassador. Several actors, paid in advance to appear before the King of France, have reneged on their commitment, and are appearing on stage in Venice. Ambassador Montaigu charges Rousseau with the task of making the proper authorities take action, and, when a first attempt through regular channels fails, suggests a more unusual strategy. Rousseau recalls:

J'étois piqué; l'on étoit en Carnaval. Ayant pris la Bahute et le masque je me fis mener au Palais Zustiniani. Tous ceux que virent entrer ma

Gondole avec la livrée de l'Ambassadeur furent frappés: Venise n'avoit jamais vû pareille chose. J'entre, je me fais annoncer sous le nom d'"una Siora Maschera'. *Sitot que je fus introduit, j'ôte mon masque et je me nomme.* Le Senateur pâlit et reste stupefait. Monsieur, lui dis-je en Venitien . . . vous avez à votre theatre de St. Luc un homme nommé Veronese qui est engagé au service du Roi . . . je viens le réclamer au nom de S.M. Ma courte harangue fit effet. (I: 302 – emphasis added)

This passage circumstantially resembles the general tenor of much of the second half of *Les Confessions,* and of the whole of the *Dialogues.* In a Venice dominated by 'paraitre', during the 'Carnaval' when everyone is masked, Rousseau's job is to restore the justice and sense of obligation which actors have not respected.[10] (Certainly the 'pique' in the narrative here is helped by Rousseau's having written the *Lettre à d'Alembert.*) Normal channels of diplomacy do not suffice. Like 'Rousseau' in the *Dialogues,* the diplomatic secretary must fulfill his duty by separating himself from his normal identity; he puts on a mask, and enters the spectacle. According to the narrator the strategy attracts attention. Those who witness the mark of the French Ambassador are surprised to find this authorized diplomatic role appearing in an unexpected mask. But the greater surprise occurs when Rousseau casts aside the mask and performs the deed for the sake of which the story has undoubtedly been selected in *Les Confessions:* 'je me nomme'.

The act of naming oneself is the overriding concern of the autobiographer, and as the anecdote above reaches this central moment (underlined by the use of the present tense), we can notice both the affinity between autobiography and diplomacy, and how they diverge in Rousseau. For the true diplomat has no identity of his own, and he never names himself. His profession is to stand between two parties, presenting the interests of one to the other. Rousseau remains bound to this impersonal structure in the present episode, despite its autobiographical overtones, since the phrase, 'je me nomme', refers, not to 'J.J. Rousseau' but to the 'Secretaire de l'Ambassade de France', who speaks 'au nom de S.M.' Like the young interpreter, whose primary function was to translate Italian into French, Rousseau's job as diplomatic secretary places him at the intersection of two discontinuous domains, across which he effects a communication. The parallel between this description of his role and our initial remarks on the identity between self and text in autobiography is not fortuitous; it is what has allowed us to use diplomacy to shed light on the author—reader dialogue in *Les Confessions*. It is also what gives diplomacy, like any true translation and interpersonal or intrapersonal exchange, an aesthetic, artful, and pseudonymous character.

For Rousseau, however, what makes diplomacy an art is what makes him a poor diplomat, and a persistent autobiographer. In Venice, he is much more interested in displaying himself than in serving the Ambassador. 'J'avoue que je ne fuyois pas l'occasion de me faire connoitre', he admits in Book VII (I: 307); and one can hardly place all the blame for his eventual dismissal on the hapless M. de Montaigu. As we proceed into the *Dialogues,* moreover, where Rousseau strives to expel any form of impersonality from his text and to name himself with the éclat of the Venice episode, it will become evident that his first priority as an autobiographer — to make the two discontinuous domains of identity converge into unity — will lead to an extremely undiplomatic and strained author—reader dialogue.

## Dialogues

I only put on a mask at masked balls, I don't wear one
in public every day . . . I am not an intriguer, I am
proud to say. I should never have made a diplomat.
They say that the bird flies of its own accord to the
fowler. Quite true, I am prepared to agree: but
which is the fowler here and which is the bird? That's
another question, gentlemen.
    Dostoevsky, *The Double* (pp. 137; 147—8)

The *Dialogues* are a struggle for authority between two very different types of reading. The first reading Rousseau gives himself, 'Rousseau's' presentation of 'J.J.' The second reading Rousseau feels is made of him by other individuals, 'autrui' being embodied in 'le François' and, more importantly, in the 'ligue' which 'le François' is meant to represent. By bringing the reader normally 'outside' the text into the *Dialogues,* Rousseau dramatizes the struggle between the two interpretations, and attempts to resolve it in favour of his reading of himself.

This strategy leads in two opposite directions. On the one hand, Rousseau includes the reader only because he is willing to exclude himself, to remove 'J.J.' to third-party status. 'J.J.' both constitutes a pretext for discussion between 'Rousseau' and 'le François' and holds the 'it' position of a text, between an author—'I' and a reader— 'you'. When 'Rousseau' and 'le François' discuss his genre (is he monstrous or innocent?), they are by implication deciding the status and genre of the autobiographical text.

Here the *Dialogues* make explicit the identity between self and text which we posited earlier. They are a text about texts and how to read them, a sort of meta-text, allowing an apparently objective perspective on the author—reader dialogue. With 'le François' engaged within the *Dialogues,* the actual reader is not a member of the pact which the two interlocutors conclude at the end of the opening 'Dialogue' (I: 772), nor affected by the confusion and role reversals which precede this pact. As if in a laboratory, we are freed from any commitment or involvement in reading the text.

In a second sense, the strategy of substituting 'le François' for the actual reader thoroughly prejudices the dialogue we are able to observe so directly. The terms of the reading pact are designed by and for Rousseau. When the text finally moves forward in the middle 'Dialogue' it comprises only a report of the interview between 'Rousseau' and 'J.J.', an internal dialogue, the author's reading of himself. Rousseau therefore excludes 'J.J.' only to manifest his identity more convincingly, and to conjure away the threat of 'la ligue' (which, via 'le François', he has himself advanced). 'Le François' functions as a proxy reader. Like Émile before the instruction of the Mentor, he is an unformed character, whose purpose is to be educated. Since 'le François' is never an individual in his own right, his 'education' is not so much a process of manipulation as one of construction. Rousseau is slowly cornering and controlling the terms of his identity, by bringing the dialogue with the reader within the boundaries of the autobiography.

The interest of the *Dialogues* lies in the tension between these extremes, in the struggle between the two types of reading which 'Rousseau' and 'le François' make of 'J.J.' The thematic oppositions arising from their different interpretations are plainly evident in the text; they fit into the familiar pattern of innocence and guilt, natural and unnatural, virtuous and monstrous. To analyse *how* the two characters read and what the principle generating the string of binary oppositions might be, one must examine how 'Rousseau' and 'le François' *see.* The sense of sight is the primary metaphor in the *Dialogues* for the process of reading. At its best, reading conveys the force and presence of vision: as Rousseau remarks in another context, praising the works of Thucydides, 'on ne croit pas lire, on croit voir' (IV: 529). The verb 'voir' designates an activity no less complex than reading, and serves as the focal point of the conflict of interpretation in the *Dialogues.*

## Seeing and Reading

Rousseau first draws attention to the complexity of sight in *Émile,* during a discussion of the five senses and how to educate them. He describes sight as the most extended and recalcitrant sense: 'La vüe est de tous les sens le plus fautif, précisement parce qu'il est le plus étendu' (IV: 391). The difficulty of ensuring proper vision is linked to the fact that it is not a simple sense, in the way that taste or touch seem to be. Sight interprets as well as perceives. It is thus an act of judgement, a different order of behaviour from passive sensation. Sight is 'de tous les sens celui dont on peut le moins séparer les jugemens de l'espirit', we are told. 'Il faut beaucoup de tems pour apprendre à voir' (IV: 396).

In *Émile,* Rousseau keeps vision tied to the direct, 'natural' evidence of perception by adding a corrective second sense, touch. The problem resurfaces later, however, in the predictable context of a discussion of judgement, and he goes to great lengths to eradicate the illusion involved in seeing. 'Toutes nos erreurs viennent de nos jugemens', he states (IV: 483). To prove that Nature never deceives, he proffers the example of a stick half-immersed in water. Due to light refraction, the stick gives the appearance of being broken, a 'baton brisé'. In Rousseau's view (which Émile must be taught to follow), the stick is straight, like Nature. Only sight and judgement are faulty.

The example which Rousseau chooses to demonstrate his point is the most revealing aspect of his argument here. For the discussion occurs at the onset of Émile's adolescence, when the stick, arguably, can be interpreted as a symbol of broken manhood. This threat Rousseau dispels by correcting the optical illusion at play in the example. In several not entirely coherent steps (which require draining the water in which the stick is immersed), he shows how the senses alone enable one to achieve conformity between judgement and Nature. Sight is then as whole and unbroken as the stick: 'il n'est donc pas vrai que la vüe nous trompe' (IV: 485).

In the *Dialogues,* optical illusion involves the drama of reading instead of vision, and the authority of the author rather than the incipient manhood of Émile. These distinctions, at any rate, are not as strict as one might think. The breadth of the problem is evident from a quick survey of the places in the text where sight is an issue. Occasionally used alone, the verb 'voir' more often introduces another verb or series of verbs. 'Connoitre', 'croire', 'montrer', in that order, tend to follow and to depend on an initial act of sight. For example, the preliminary to knowing 'J.J.' is to see him: 'J'ai besoin de vous voir, de vous connoitre', 'Rousseau' writes in his letter of introduction (I: 776). When one knows 'J.J.', one is in a position to believe him: 'il a besoin d'être vu pour être cru', 'Rousseau' remarks later (I: 797). And belief leads directly to the possibility of acting on one's knowledge: 'tous les gens de parti . . . ne lui pardonneroient jamais de les avoir vus et montrés tels qu'ils sont', 'Rousseau' concludes (I: 926). Since sight is the opening step in this sequence of knowledge, belief, and action, an error of vision or reading can have protracted and severe consequences.

The struggle of the *Dialogues* results from two ways of seeing by 'Rousseau' and 'le François'. This is really no different from stating that the struggle arises from the opposite ways in which these two characters interpret 'J.J.', but it opens an unusual perspective on the text. For the main attribute of 'le François' is the fact that he sees through the eyes of others ('voir par les yeux d'autrui'). 'Rousseau', by contrast, sees through his own eyes ('voir par ses propres yeux'). 'Comptez-vous pour rien le calcul des voix, quand vous étes seul à voir autrement que tout le monde?' 'le François' asks in the first dialogue. 'Rousseau' replies:

Pour faire ce calcul avec justesse, il faudroit auparavant savoir combien de gens dans cette affaire ne voyent comme vous que par les yeux d'autrui. Si du nombre de ces bruyantes voix on ôtoit les échos qui ne font que repeter celle des autres . . . il y auroit peut-être moins de disproportion que vous ne pensez . . . En un mot je juge ici par moi-même. (I: 698)

'Rousseau' returns to the same point when he compares former judgements of 'J.J.' with those which people make of him at the time of the *Dialogues.*

Ils le voyoient alors par leurs propres yeux, ils l'ont vu depuis par ceux des autres . . . Voila pourquoi les jugemens qu'on portoit jadis sur cet homme font autorité pour moi, et pourquoi ceux que les mêmes gens en peuvent porter aujourdhui n'en font plus. (I: 775)[11]

The phrase 'voir par les yeux d'autrui' is not new. We observed in the last chapter that it serves as the generating principle for Rousseau's construction of the image of 'la ligue'. Each member of the supposed plot against 'J.J.' receives his opinion from a neighbour in the chain of persecution. The resulting, groundless succession of glances figuratively locks 'J.J.' into the frame from which 'Rousseau' is meant to free him. It is consistent that 'le François', the ostensible spokesman for 'la ligue', should see and interpret 'J.J.' as it does.

This way of seeing and reading gains in interest when we recall that the same phrase occurs in *Narcisse* as a metaphor for *amour.* The concatenation seems odd at first. Why should 'la ligue' be associated with *amour,* paranoia with this particular passion? How does this juxtaposition shed light on the author–reader interchange in the *Dialogues?*

### 'Amour' and Reading

The connection between *amour* and the imagined plot against Rousseau can be made in several ways. An editor of the correspondence seems to sense it intuitively, in his introduction to Rousseau's letters from the 1756–7 stay at l'Ermitage. 'Chez Jean-Jacques, la méfiance ressemble un peu à l'amour', R.A. Leigh writes: 'elle "cristallise" et se nourrit de tout' (*C.C.* IX: xxv). This insight is confirmed at the level of literary style. Consider the comments at the beginning of *La Nouvelle Héloïse,* where Rousseau justifies the novel's unusual style and diction in terms of the sentiments which it expresses. 'Une lettre que l'amour a réellement dicté', 'R' states in the Preface in dialogue,

une lettre d'un Amant vraiment passioné, sera lâche, diffuse, toute en longueurs, en désordre, en répétitions. Son cœur, plein d'un sentiment qui déborde, redit toujours la même chose, et n'a jamais achevé de dire . . . (II: 15)

Compare the style of love with the style of paranoia, described in 'Du Sujet et de la forme de cet écrit', the preface to the *Dialogues.*

Ce que j'avois à dire étoit si clair et j'en étois si pénétré que je ne puis assez m'étonner des longueurs, des redites, du verbiage et du desordre de cet écrit. (I: 664)

At a structural level, furthermore, additional similarities underline the affinity between Rousseau's conceptions of *amour* and 'la ligue'. Each manifests a successive structure of non-reciprocation, whether this be the pattern of unrequited love which we noticed in the author's love for Sophie d'Houdetot, or his chain-like configuration of malevolent individuals linked together ('ligare') in the imagined plot. Exteriority, singularity, and difference characterize both passions. Both isolate a person – Rousseau at l'Ermitage, 'J.J.' in the *Dialogues* – and separate him from any conventional, contractual relationship with others.

The basic connection between love and paranoia in Rousseau stems from the way in which the two passions depend on the imagination for their development and force. 'L'amour n'est qu'illusion', Rousseau has stated in *La Nouvelle Héloïse;* 'il se fait . . . un autre Univers; il s'entoure d'objets qui ne sont point, ou auxquels lui seul a donné l'être' (II: 15). If one substituted the author's feeling of paranoia for 'l'amour', the description would fit equally well. Although the respective passions develop in opposite directions, they are mirror images of one another. *Amour* and 'la ligue' have mainly in common the fact that each confers a positive or negative value. This value has its source in the process whereby the attributes of an imagined model are transferred on to the actual person who is the object of the passion.

The juxtaposition of *amour* and 'la ligue' opens on to a major aspect of the autobiography. At the start of this project Rousseau makes a 'mistake' similar to the transfer of *amour;* he sees himself through the eyes of another, or '*se* voit par les yeux d'autrui'. 'Autrui' in this instance is not another person; it is the model of identity in the author's imaginative universe, which he takes personally, as his own. In terms of the analysis in Chapter II, one could say that Rousseau effects an intrapersonal version of the exchange between the elaborated image of Julie and the actual person, Sophie. In the present act of writing autobiography, he sees his past life in the light, through the eyes, of his textual world. This process involves a high degree of optical illusion. The autobiographer's 'mistake' is the source of his sense of personal value, and he is necessarily blind to it.

What is the effect of Rousseau's 'mistake' on the author–reader dialogue? The process whereby the autobiographer recognizes and names himself must pass through a process of recognition which does include other individuals. Although Rousseau succeeds in balancing image and actual self in the narrative of *Les Confessions,* where the approach to the reader alternates diplomatically between the two attitudes analysed earlier, the dialogue hardens perceptibly as the autobiography moves from the past toward the present. Increasingly,

Rousseau strains to coincide with his image. His failure, in the two live readings of *Les Confessions,* to gain the audiences' recognition of what is effectively his own misrecognition of himself, leads him to displace the problem of misrecognition on to the reader.

The *Dialogues,* therefore, enact the drama of mistaken identity in the context of the author–reader interchange. They establish Rousseau's sense of himself through the strategy of negating the worst possible reading which could be made of him. 'La ligue', a plural representation of the reader 'outside' the text, is made responsible for propagating a monstrous, unnatural version of 'J.J.', the mirror image of his conception of a natural self. Both versions of 'J.J.' are products of Rousseau's imagination. The battle joined on their account remains purely internal to the logic of the autobiography. He invents the monster solely to reject it, and thereby to legitimate his appropriation of the 'natural' image.

Rousseau, who has committed his life to that of his text, undergoes this struggle with an intensity equal to his belief in his sight, and to his unwillingness to admit that it involves any illusion. He resembles Valère, the protagonist in *Narcisse,* doting on an altered image of himself. Rousseau's altered image is of the monstrous rather than the beautiful variety, but he dotes all the same. His fascination with himself also has a peculiar effect on the actual reader.

In contrast to other works of Rousseau, the *Dialogues* are not often read. Only with the surge in modern critical interest in autobiography does this unusual text receive the attention of interpreters. It is easy, while working to achieve that 'objective', meta-textual interpretation which the *Dialogues* invite, to borrow a page from Rousseau's strategy in them. We observe the paranoid illusion of the author, analyse it just as he has analysed what he takes to be the illusion of 'la ligue', and thereby assure ourselves that our sight, our interpretation, is free of error.

Uncommitted to the text, temporarily endowed with clear vision, we can call it a 'strategy'. But if this approach helps one to understand Rousseau, and the place of the *Dialogues* within his autobiographical project, it is only one type of reading, and strikingly dependent on Rousseau's reading, which in its own way frees him from what *he* thinks is an error. Fundamentally, our reading of the text is no more justified by its coherence and apparent rationality than Rousseau's self-reading by the coherence of his paranoia.

This realization sets limits on the validity and importance of the present interpretation. For there are other possible readings of Rousseau, more prone to illusion perhaps, but no less valuable for that. They occur when a reader 'outside' the text involves himself in an identification with it, and effects the same transfer between imaginative universe and actual existence which Rousseau makes in 'seeing himself through the eyes of another'. This type of reading may transform the text, since it brings it back into contact with the open reality from which it first arose. But it is more likely to transform the life of the reader, in which the text has been taken up. Although such a transformation presupposes or requires a degree of optical illusion, the reader's mistake and act of belief is a measure of a work's inherently dialogic structure. A text in this sense is like a promise. It engages the reader and provokes an open exchange, through the sort of relay network which we noticed in the first diplomatic episode from *Les Confessions.* The text lives through this connection, joining and contributing to an historical process outside its own circumscribed boundaries.[12]

To recognize the contrast between these two types of reading – the one 'objective' and unmystified, which explains Rousseau's work without identifying with it, the other an interpretative version of *amour,* in which the reader identifies with the text and tries to bring it into the circuit of life – calls for a clarification on our own part. How, through what eyes, do we see? Rousseau's determination to fix his reading of himself has effectively freed us from this task, and should rightly cause a reflection on the nature of our own reading. Is it in any way comparable to the two interpretative stances presented within the *Dialogues?*

The option of identifying with the work is not really open to us. This is to become a 'Rousseau second', like 'le François' in the final 'Dialogue'. He returns from his reading with a bundle of quotations, parroting the author. Rousseau's extraordinary passion for himself, in the second stage of the autobiography, calls instead for a cool, dispassionate response, the reception which Condillac gives it when Rousseau asks him to read and to respond (I: 981–2). There are good grounds for such coolness – the need to separate the life from the work, or the desire to avoid the spectacle of Rousseau's suffering. Tied to an indirect economy of masochistic pleasure, this suffering hardly seems genuine. A discreet withdrawal from the struggle of interpretation waged in the *Dialogues* seems the best route.

It is easy to disregard the *Dialogues,* to say that the author's 'problem' is his own, and simply to observe how he withdraws further and further from the actual world into what he believes is the reality of his world of the text. If the reader judges Rousseau's withdrawal in this manner, however, he avoids his suffering only at the expense of losing contact with the work (the critic's reality), and emulates the author's loss of contact with the world around him. Objective non-identification is in this sense little better than sentimental sympathy for Rousseau's predicament; it is like *amitié* and 'la pitié' in their superficial aspect, acknowledging suffering in another individual in order to dissociate oneself from it, to feel free and superior to it.

Rousseau often indulges this tendency, especially in the *Dialogues.* He works to avoid and to rid himself of responsibility for his own suffering by projecting its cause on to an external 'complot'. But the *Dialogues* themselves do not authorize the reader to repeat Rousseau's mistake or to avoid his pathos. More than any of his other works, they demonstrate the fundamental impossibility of giving an image full reality, of making personal identity sufficient unto itself, of appropriating the process of dialogue. Rousseau tries to effect a personal version of grace. He pushes himself and his autobiographical text to the limits of comprehension. But these limits do not constrain him alone. The reader shares them also. The *Dialogues* here point to the necessity of compassion – a finite grace, proper to man, and akin to *amitié* in its profound sense.

Stating this does not alter the basic problem, since it is through the work that one has compassion for its author, and Rousseau certainly does not write this work out of compassion. One becomes aware of limitations only as they are broken. Indirectly, however, the *Dialogues* demonstrate the hard truth, that what separates a person from himself is what links him to others.

Rousseau acknowledges the predicament lucidly at several points in the *Dialogues.* 'La solution de ces difficultés', he has 'Rousseau' say near the end of the initial 'Dialogue', 'doit se chercher selon moi dans quelque intermédiaire' (I:760). The conciliatory tone of this statement departs from the general stridency of the text. Several other comments are equally accommodating. For instance, before beginning the report of his visit to 'J.J.', 'Rousseau' states:

Ce que j'ai vu est meilleur à voir qu'à dire. Ce que j'ai vu me suffit, à moi qui l'ai vu, pour déterminer mon jugement, mais non pas pour déterminer le vôtre . . . Ce sont des récits qui d'ailleurs conviendroient mal dans ma bouche, et pour les faire avec bienseance, il faudroit être un autre que moi. (I: 797)

This admission tends to undermine the overall strategy of the *Dialogues*, as does a remark from the middle of 'Rousseau's' report:

Notre plus douce existence est relative et collective, et notre vrai *moi* n'est pas tout entier en nous. Enfin telle est la constitution de l'homme en cette vie qu'on n'y parvient jamais à bien jouir de soi sans le concours d'autrui. (I: 813)

But Rousseau ultimately resolves the conflict in a manner which asks little compassion of the reader. The *Dialogues* serve mainly to confirm him in what he takes to be a more fundamental necessity. 'Non, Monsieur, après nos discussions précédentes, je ne vois plus de milieu possible entre tout admettre et tout rejetter', 'Rousseau' declares at the end of his report about 'J.J.' (I: 898). The open-ended exchange of dialogue implied in 'voir par les yeux d'autrui' is replaced by a 'natural' vision. This is the interchange between 'Rousseau' and 'J.J.', in which each individual 'sees through his own eyes', and is the basis of the middle 'Dialogue'.

Aside from occasional interruptions by 'le François', the middle 'Dialogue' dispenses altogether with the reader. Observing Rousseau's feat of self-analysis, we are spectators of an internal, enclosed relay of vision. Who is seeing and who is being seen remains unclear, since 'Rousseau' and 'J.J.' are one *and* two individuals, both identical and different. So long as their 'visit' lasts, the oppositions of inside and outside, innocence and guilt, white and black cease to affect the author. Like the eye in the midst of a storm, the visit is an unexpected interlude in the struggle of interpretation. Rousseau perhaps conceived the *Dialogues* around this central calm. More likely, it emerges only through the heavy weather of debate. But the storm passes, and the enclosed yet all-embracing vision which informs the report of 'Rousseau' then radiates outwards. We have entered the uncanny tranquillity of the *Rêveries*.

### 'Rousseau' and 'J.J.' – Rêveries

What is the sort of sight which 'Rousseau' and 'J.J.' share? One description occurs among the many quotations in which 'J.J.' enters the discourse of 'Rousseau'. It concerns Rousseau's musical ability. (The questions about authorship in the *Dialogues* focus on the *Devin* more than on any of the written works.) To prove that 'J.J.' knows music is a prerequisite for proving that he is author of the opera; this proof, in turn, is meant to dispel doubts about his authorship generally, and to help to establish his 'innocence'. After duly expressing his reservations, therefore, 'J.J.' proceeds to produce a short song, 'aussi fraiche, aussi chantante, aussi bien traitée que celle du *Devin*', according to 'Rousseau' (I: 869). In the imaginary world of the *Dialogues,* the test has been passed. But 'J.J.'s' remark after the event, describing the reason for his success, is the most revealing part of the episode. 'Rousseau' recalls:

Le desir, me dit-il, que je vous ai vu de me voir réussir m'a fait réussir davantage. (I: 869)

The enfolded construction of this sentence articulates well the interplay of vision between 'Rousseau' and 'J.J.' Grammatically, its subject is the word 'desir', and the main clause reads: 'Le desir ... m'a fait réussir davantage'. But desire originates in the complex qualifying clause: 'que je vous ai vu de me voir réussir'. A rough translation may help to untangle the meaning of the phrase: 'The desire', 'J.J.' says, 'which you had to see me succeed, and which I saw you as having, made me succeed all the more'. This rendering captures the intuitive sense that the desire seems to belong initially to 'Rousseau', and that, being seen, it is taken up and increased by 'J.J.' It misses the important ambiguity of the sentence, however. Desire floats freely here; neither individual 'has' it. It pertains instead to the immanent activity of sight, in which they are equally involved. Within the qualifying clause, vision is perfectly symmetrical: 'je vous ai vu'; 'de me voir'. 'Rousseau' sees 'J.J.' and vice versa. Moreover, each sees the other seeing himself, and himself reflected in the sight of the other.

This sentence from the *Dialogues* brings us to the author–reader interchange of the *Rêveries,* where the two separate characters above have quite literally become the 'Rousseau premier' and 'Rousseau second' of the first diplomatic episode. Their sight is now the process whereby the autobiographer regards himself, reading, in the mirror of the text.

To reach the final stage in the autobiography, Rousseau requires external, public corroboration of the rejection and persecution which 'le François' describes within the *Dialogues.* The 'Histoire du précédent écrit', an appendix to the text, contains the narrative of this procedure. Rousseau first attempts to deposit his manuscript on the altar of

Notre-Dame, in a symbolic offering designed to instigate a judgement and reading by God and, secondarily, to attract the attention of the highest secular authority, the King. One is reminded by this strategy of the statement at the start of *Les Confessions,* 'Que la trompette du jugement dernier sonne quand elle voudra, je viendrai ce livre à la main me présenter devant le souverain juge' (I: 5). By the end of the *Dialogues,* the author's need for justification drives him to sound the trumpet himself, and to 'stage' the encounter with God within his life. Rousseau's effort to control the terms of recognition and judgement is nowhere more evident than in this gesture. He is impeded by an obstacle which conforms entirely with the sense of his manuscript. 'En entrant (dans Notre-Dame), mes yeux furent frappés d'une grille que je n'avois jamais remarquée', Rousseau writes. 'Au moment où j'apperçus cette grille je fus saisi d'un vertige . . . et ce vertige fut suivi d'un bouleversement dans tout mon être' (I: 980).

The grill is a concrete image for the interlocking network of 'la ligue'. It blocks the way to the altar, preventing the deposition. The world of isolation and persecution depicted within the *Dialogues* thus rejoins the world outside the text. Inside and outside coincide once again. Rousseau consciously is shaken, but unconsciously reassured in his project. The failure to achieve public recognition supports his growing certainty that recognition can come only from within himself.

Human readers provide a similar corroboration. When Rousseau gives a copy of the work to Condillac, he receives comments that bear primarily on its literary quality. When he entrusts another copy to an English acquaintance, Brooke Boothby, who happens to be passing through Paris, he worries whether the young man might not be a member of the 'complot'. It is possible to discern a movement of relaxation from control to chance in these successive depositions. The tight grip and struggle within the *Dialogues* loosen and abate as Rousseau enacts their drama in his life. He completes this process by writing a short letter, a sort of extract from his work, which he then distributes randomly, as a handbill, to passers-by in the streets of Paris. According to Rousseau's account, not one is accepted.

The ritual at the end of the *Dialogues* shows clearly a first inherent necessity in Rousseau's autobiographical project, that his self-presentation there is tied to recognition from an independent source. The appropriation of his image of personal identity remains weightless and unwarranted until the author has 'authorized' it through a reader 'outside' the text, even if negatively so. The public readings of *Les*

*Confessions* demonstrate this as much as the series of rejections narrated in the 'Histoire du précédent écrit'. Rousseau *must* have a reader who is not himself. But the author–reader dialogue in the autobiography also obeys a second necessity, in that Rousseau, mistaking his image for himself, cannot allow for any recognition other than that which his text already provides. We have therefore watched him create his own reader, elaborating a new image as he appropriates his own. By the end of the *Dialogues,* this elaboration has become so complete that the two images correspond, and the author can quite calmly ask himself, referring to other people generally, 'l'essence de mon être est-elle dans leurs regards?' (I: 995). For the reader in the final stage of the autobiography is the author himself, as he has been created by his project. The *Rêveries* come full circle in the process which began with the outspoken 'Moi seul' at the start of *Les Confessions.* Recognition from without now equals recognition from within; reading is indistinguishable from writing; and one may well wonder which is image and which Rousseau, as the autobiographer envisages his readership in the *Rêveries:*

Leur lecture me rappellera la douceur que je goute à les écrire, et faisant renaitre ainsi pour moi le tems passé doublera pour ainsi dire mon existence. En depit des hommes je saurai gouter encore le charme de la societé et je vivrai decrepit avec moi dans un autre age, comme je vivrois avec un moins vieux ami. (I: 1001)

# CONCLUSION

The critic appreciates his relation to the text only when he must conclude. Since the start of this reading, several unassuming phrases have
accompanied each step along the way. 'In Rousseau's view', 'for
Rousseau', 'Rousseau states' — these indicate the ambivalence of the
critical reader, engaged by yet distanced from the work at hand. We
remain engaged to ensure contact with the work, distanced in order
to understand it. The paradoxical combination of contact and separation, when brought to its best intensity, enables a critical repetition
of what the author first sensed in producing the work itself.

A good reading, like a good translation, exercises a diplomatic
tact. It effaces itself in the interpreted text. It is wholly un-autobio-
graphical and unlike Rousseau's project. But at the end of his work,
the support that Rousseau has provided suddenly disappears, leaving
us still standing and with a need to conclude. Any new step must be
in some way autobiographical, even if only the confessions of a critic.

This book has followed a logical story. Its narrative-like development
is not unduly complicated. The story began in the individual and
imaginative experience of reverie. It passed through *amour* and *amitié*,
Rousseau's basic interactions with other individuals, and followed the
elaboration in writing of his image of personal identity. Within the
textual world of the autobiographer, the three rhetorical stages of
Rousseau's project then intensified and reflected back upon the experiential delineations of the first chapters. The movement of my
reading has been both progressive and circular. I have attempted to
trace an interaction between life and text, Rousseau's autobiographical
development, in a sequence of interpretation which stays within his
writings.

Instead of the story (which belongs to Rousseau, and which has
come to an end), let us consider for a moment what has been necessary
to tell it. Here Rousseau's autobiographical project begins to shed
light on the effort of the critic.

In my introductory remarks, I characterized the autobiographical
project as the exegesis of a life. Rousseau performs this exegesis
through the intermediary of fiction. He constructs an image of personal
identity, a model of self. The image is a point of reference for the
autobiographer, and it gains consistency and strength through its

elaboration in writing. This fosters in the author the belief that he can understand and recount his life. Like Scripture for Augustine, Rousseau's pre-autobiographical writings provide a structure and frame in which he can interpret and make sense of past actions.

Yet the very act of becoming an autobiographer, of telling the story of his life and claiming to understand it, leads Rousseau to want his personal image to be real, to be himself. This closes down the distance that was necessary to make the claim of understanding in the first place. Rousseau's story, even though it apparently belongs to him alone, then slips out of his grasp, becoming a saga of misunderstanding and incomprehension.

The critic of autobiography analyses not a life, but a text or texts about a life. This involves many of the same opportunities and constraints evident in Rousseau's project. A central concept — the notion of a textual world — has functioned as a sort of equivalent to the autobiographer's image of personal identity. There is a double mirroring process here: first, in the specular image through which the autobiographer makes sense of himself, writing about his own life; second, also in the way this image corresponds for the critic to the central construct of a textual world, through which he attempts to make sense of the autobiography.

The fiction of a textual world has been as indispensable to my reading as Rousseau's fiction of personal identity is to his autobiography. It provides a measure of unity in the shift from experiential to rhetorical structure, permits the illusion that one can go 'outside' the text into the life of the author, while remaining within his writings. It permits an immanent criticism, in which one explains a text without relying on external points of reference — whether these be facts from the author's life, a static, essential identity of the writer, God, or other convenient hitching posts that help to secure works for the duration of a reading. Not unlike the direction of Rousseau's thought generally, this sort of criticism has something appealing yet suspicious about it. It allows one to present a closed reading as though it were open and 'natural'.

Whatever critical value my own reading may possess derives from the extent to which it re-enacts the value which Rousseau gains in the process of writing. In constructing his text and his image, he actively gives sense and direction to his existence. The corollary of this is that we exercise freedom most fully and most visibly in the elaboration of an aesthetic order, re-creating life in the creation of a work (though this work need not necessarily be literary). The artist epitomizes the human effort to become a second God, and to find in an imaginative space the value and wholeness implicit in life.

But is the notion of a textual world, however indispensable for critical understanding, fully believable? For Rousseau it seems to be. In the final two chapters we followed the ramifications of his belief. He acts upon it so vigorously and consistently that the autobiographical project transforms his life into a text. To him the text becomes real, while the actual world around him becomes progressively unreal and fictional. By the end of the process (the *Rêveries*), what is real and what is fictional have become indistinguishable. Rousseau's own conclusion is to hover between god-like self-sufficiency and an abysmal solitude.

In stepping out of Rousseau's text (and effectively ceasing to exercise a critical understanding), I want to indicate my hesitation about his autobiographical project. This is to risk the misunderstanding that occurs when the critic (or anyone) assumes a concluding, autobiographical stance.

My hesitation does not concern one superficial aspect of Rousseau's autobiography – that it involves him in an apparently self-indulgent and hermetic mode of existence, for instance. The individual aspect of the autobiographical project is entirely consonant with the religious tradition of confessional literature which Rousseau transforms. Grace and salvation are not primarily communal concepts. If Rousseau differs from Augustine by attempting to achieve a non-Christian salvation,[1] through the means of his own text rather than through the Word of God (and he succeeds in this effort, to a large extent, with the self-imposed necessity of the *Rêveries*), he cannot be faulted for the individualistic nature of this process. In any event, it is not at all certain that the power struggle in the autobiographical project is altered in any fundamental way when one moves away from an apparently solitary form of discourse. Rousseau's political writings suggest strongly that social units are composed as collective identities, along the same structural lines as personal identities. They may repeat at a different level – in ideologies, and in the power struggles and values which they generate – the same story we have followed in the autobiography.

Nor does my hesitation concern one of the more profound, potentially troubling aspects of Rousseau's work, the manner in which language seems to overwhelm the life of the author, as this is taken up within the autobiographical project. There is something inexcusable and irreversible here: once Rousseau begins to establish his existence within his textual world, his life becomes subject to, and determined by, linguistic structures which are independent from and which dominate the sense of self that the author is trying to make his own. After the analysis of Rousseau's account of figural naming, the autobiographer's fate was writ large with misunderstanding. His account effectively made personal identity an effect of a metaphorical, accidental process of denotation. It condemned to certain failure, before it even began, his own effort to give himself the stability which appears to belong to his proper name.

But the deep-seated, constitutive role of language in the autobiography is in itself no cause for concern. A sub-thesis in the Introduction was that we exist in language as we exist in the world, and it would be quite contradictory here to reverse an implicit position running throughout the book, by judging Rousseau's work as somehow misguided in relation to a life which is itself taken to be normal. Writing autobiography does not change the basic terms of existence; it simply transposes them into a different key. The ongoing, open character of the life becomes the 'logorrhea' of the autobiographer; his relations with other individuals, a dialogue with the reader. Writing perhaps exacerbates certain tendencies in Rousseau, bringing elements of his life to the fore which would not otherwise have been so readily noticeable. But I have shown, in the development from the first to the second half of the thesis, that the basic structures of the autobiography are present already in Rousseau's existence, and that life can be bound up with an imaginative, quasi-linguistic circuit even before a person writes, just as writings can embody and show forth an existence.

My basic hesitation concerns instead the heading of moral truth under which I initially presented the topic of autobiography. In following the development of Rousseau's project, we were to follow his conferring of value and meaning, in an extended sense of these terms. We have observed this process in the autobiographer's activity of producing and lending credence to his texts. But observing this process from a critical perspective, within the finite range offered by the notion of a textual world, has in no way explained the process itself, nor given any justification for it. If this critical fiction has enabled us to understand Rousseau, what it succeeds in making visible is a mechanism for the production of values. The mechanism itself is value-neutral. In the several analyses which come closest to defining it — the analyses of Rousseau's version of *amour,* in Chapter II, of his account of figural naming, in Chapter III, or of his step into autobiography, in Chapter IV — I characterized it as involving a 'mistake', the epistemological error of taking an image for reality.

That the mechanism itself is without fundamental value is perhaps best demonstrated by the mirror-play of values which it produces. Rousseau's assumption of what he takes as natural and good automatically generates its moral counterpart, forcing upon him a consciousness of unnatural monstrosity. When the autobiographer brings his image of unity and happiness into the narrative of *Les Confessions,* the text slowly builds into a counter-image, issuing in the struggle of the *Dialogues.* The alternation could go on indefinitely. The outstanding feature of this analysis of moral truth is its thoroughgoing, unredeeming dualism. In the immanent interaction between life and the text which we have followed, good and evil are balanced in a moral Manichaeism. This subsumes the human exercise of freedom in an aesthetic domain, and the redemptive aspect of the aesthetic conversion of experience into a work, for I have argued that it is primarily in this very process that Rousseau constructs and finds his images and values. And the major implication of the mechanism is a neverending supply of pathos, the side-effect, as it were, of value-production, and equally visible in Rousseau's work. It is not far wrong to state that man suffers from the opportunity to confer meaning on his existence.

In conclusion, there are two unhesitating responses to the dilemma I have sketched here. One is aesthetic and finite, staying within the terms of Rousseau's autobiography and those of my analysis, but turning them on their head. This is irony. As a character trait, it is almost completely lacking in Rousseau. The ironist never claims to understand, and actively refuses to identify with any form of textual world. He remains instead in a virtual position of withdrawal, the better to proclaim fiction as no more than fiction, and to deflate the claim for understanding that anyone so 'mistaken' as an autobiographer might make.

The ironist has a point, quick though he would be to deny it. For all his efforts at identification and understanding, irony afflicts Rousseau in the indirect guise of the 'complot' in the *Dialogues.* The madness to which he succumbs there, viewed ironically, would be a rigorous form of sanity. For the ironist, moral truth does not exist. He remains on the horns of the moral dilemma, sceptical about everything, and most of all about himself. This response aptly characterizes the critical spirit. Some critics, giving close attention to texts, have come to see irony as the limiting rhetorical category, not just as one among several possible character traits. When this position is taken to its logical conclusion, misunderstanding and the impossibility of reading are the norms for the author and the critic. They become trapped in the alluring mirror-play of the textual worlds that they or other writers create.

The second response is ironical in an infinite mode, or in a general sense religious. This is more a beginning than an ending, since it proposes that the autobiographical drama we have followed here is but one scene in divine play, within but not *of* the world of finite texts that men produce and may assume to be real. Can the figures of language (and the pathos they involve) be transfigured? Accepting this grace reveals the providential in every accident. It releases, like Rousseau's awakening in the *Rêveries,* one from texts to the world. Man is an image of what is called God, not God an image of man. We are His fiction, though it goes by the name of Creation. This response changes nothing – one continues to live, texts continue to be written. It gives new eyes to see, to read.

# NOTES

## INTRODUCTION

1. The Subject Index of *Books in Print* provides an indication of the rising interest in autobiography, at least in American publishing. In the 1965 listings, no subheading for autobiography is given; in 1971, a section with more than eighty titles is included. The growing number of titles under the subheading 'Authors – Correspondences, Reminiscences' (where many autobiographies are listed) is also symptomatic of this trend. For one sampling of the numerous recent critical works on the topic, see section 3b of the bibliography.
2. See p. 208 of the *Confessions* for a description of charity as the basis of Augustine's dialogue with the reader. After he has found himself in God, Augustine inevitably seeks human readers to share this knowledge. A similar imperative will inform Rousseau's autobiography.
3. Hereafter referred to as the *Rêveries*.
4. See 'De l'exercitation'.
5. *Les Mots*, p. 145.
6. *Cahiers*, Volume 2, p. 304
7. *Cahiers*, Vol. 2, pp. 280–1.
8. Hereafter referred to as the *Dialogues*.
9. Kierkegaard, with whom Rousseau can be contrasted in fruitful ways, takes the opposite path, chooses impersonality, and produces an anti-autobiography of pseudonymous works which are none the less his most intimate writings. Kierkegaard's choice is consistent with his own inheritance and aims: against a thoroughly Romantic background, he attempts to reinstate a sense of the religious.

## CHAPTER I

1. See *JJR: La Quête de soi et la rêverie*, pp. 159–63.
2. For other instances of a nominal reiteration leading to a syntactic break and 'tout cela', see I: 58 and I: 63–4. I: 58 involves a reverie-like situation and provides support for the *explication* developed above; I: 63–4 does not, and simply shows the extent to which this stylistic construction pervades Rousseau's writing.
3. Other Rousseau critics also distinguish two stages of reverie. Cf. Poulet, 'Expansion et Concentration chez Rousseau'; Gouhier, 'Expansion et Reserrement'; and Munteano, 'La Solitude de Rousseau'.
4. *Critique of Judgment*, Part I, Book I, 2: 'The delight which determines the judgment of taste is independent of all interest'.

5. A very helpful, detailed discussion of the instant (as *present* time) can be found in Augustine's *Confessions*, Book XI, 15. See also Kierkegaard's *Concept of Dread*, pp. 74–5n.

6. The text of *Le Devin du village* is found in Volume II of the Pléiade edition, pp. 1093–1114. I refer to it hereafter as the *Devin*.

7. The significance of this title may become more clear in the light of the discussion in Chapter II.

8. In an analysis of Rousseau's exhibitionism, Starobinski proposes that the episode above also involves an indirect sexual satisfaction. 'Un événement erotique se produit', he writes: 'le bonheur réside dans une communication à distance. Quoique les regards des spectatrices soient tournés vers la scène, Jean-Jaques se sent le maître des cœurs. Ces femmes . . . sont à lui . . . On se passionne pour lui, et par lui, parce qu'il a su se faire infiniment absent, dans une musique qui chante la séduction de l'absence et la bonheur du retour'. See *La Transparence et l'Obstacle*, pp. 270–1.

9. See *Le Cru et le cuit*, p. 25.

10. The question of the priority and relative importance of metaphor and metonymy can be seen as a current, linguistic version of the same debate.

11. See, for instance, the remarks on the importance of an unchanging bass line in *récitatif*: 'la basse, par une marche uniforme et simple guide en quelque sorte celui qui chante et celui qui écoute . . .' The bass has an effect similar to the lapping of lake water, the steady rowing of oarsmen, or the movement of walking legs which accompany Rousseau's reveries (*O.C.* VII: 181).

12. Starobinski introduces the idea of writing as 'rêverie seconde' in *JJR: La Transparence et l'obstacle*, p. 419.

13. I am indebted to François Roustang for this insight into style. A remark by Pater in *Appreciations* (pp. 36–7), in the line of Buffon, seems appropriate here. 'A relegation, you may say — a relegation of style to the subjectivity, the mere caprice of the individual . . . Not so! . . . If the style be the man, in all the colour and intensity of a veritable apprehension, it will be in a real sense "impersonal" '.

14. See I: 114 for Rousseau's comments on his 'worked' style.

## CHAPTER II

1. This chapter is indebted to other examinations of *amour* and *amitié* in Rousseau. Three major sources are: Burgelin, *La Philosophie de l'existence de J.J. Rousseau*, esp. p. 179, and 'La Dialectiquè de l'amour', pp. 383–8; Derrida, *De la grammatologie*, esp. 'le débat actual: l'économie de la Pitié', pp. 243–73; and Grimsley, J. J. Rousseau: *A Study in Self-Awareness*, esp. Chapter III, 'Two Idols: Love and Friendship'.

2. Cf. also p. 121 in the *Essai*.

3. There are several intermediate stages in the movement from pity to *amitié* which I have not included above. First, pity must be abstracted from the individual instances of suffering we have followed, in order to become a general concern for the well-being of humanity as a whole. This frees the pitier from being affected by every instance of suffering which he encounters – a potentially debilitating care. Second, friends are freely chosen from among those whom one meets, on the basis of this generalized sentiment. This sketch completes the genetic account, such as it is presented in Rousseau, but is not indispensable to the exposition above.

4. See 'Notes on Convention', especially p. 63.

5. Cf. the article by A. Pizzorusso, 'La Comédie de *Narcisse*', which makes mention of the connection between the play and the later text of the *Dialogues*.
   *Narcisse* and Rousseau's preface to it are in vol. II of the Pléiade edition, pp. 957–1018.

6. Notice the word 'revêtue', which makes the exchange of clothes a metaphor for the process whereby Rousseau effects the transfer between the imaginary world of the novel and the real woman, Sophie. Notice also the phrase, 'fascina mes yeux'. Strictly speaking, Rousseau sees Sophie through the eyes of Saint-Preux and Saint-Preux's love for Julie. The process is the same as in *Narcisse*, though the outcomes will differ.

7. See *Rousseau par lui-même*, by G. May, p. 149. See also I: 444.

8. Grimsley, p. 91.

9. An exception to this rule would be *amitié* across different sexes. Though we have not made any distinction about heterosexual and homosexual *amitié*, the basic form of the sentiment is a single-sex relationship, whether between men or between women. Heterosexual friendship introduces a discernible element of difference, and with it a sexual, *amour*-like affection.

10. Given the fact that one must look at the relationship with Mme de Warens through the written text, it is not certain whether Rousseau's writing 'replaces' and substitutes for his relation to her, or whether (as in the case of reverie) writing itself helps to create needs which she is then made to fulfill, thereby contributing to the emphasis placed on this part of his past. We can be more certain of another aspect of the imperative to write – it makes the author an active creator of his 'être'. Referring to 'Maman', Rousseau claims to be 'tout à fait son œuvre, tout à fait son enfant'. 'Je lui disois: vous voila dépositaire de tout mon être; faites en sorte qu'il soit heureux' (I: 221). Writing will involve the same notion of a 'dépôt de l'être', but in a work which the author has made.
    In this connection, see 'Remarques sur la Notion du Dépôt' by F. Baker, especially pp. 58, 82, and 93. Baker analyses the place of the 'dépôt' in *La Nouvelle Héloïse*, and states more generally: 'L'autobiographie de Rousseau . . . révèle comment, par un isomorphisme frappant, l'écriture se confond chez lui avec l'amour et

avec le dépôt. Le dépôt englobe tout ce qui reste de la relation interpersonnelle dans la solitude des dernières années. L'écriture assume dans la vie même de Rousseau la forme que la dépôt a eue dans son roman'. The reader thus eventually becomes the destination of the author's 'dépôt de l'etre', an idea developed in Chapter V.

11. Starobinski makes reference to Goethe's criticism in his reading of *Pygmalion* in *La Transparence et l'obstacle*, p. 91. Rousseau, it is argued, does not give autonomy to the work of art, and instead attempts to subsume it within his life, or to reduce it to the natural order. The sculptor in the pantomime is a 'greedy artist'; 'he has doubled himself' in the statue, and wants to transform his creation into a 'lived happiness'. The reading here differs from this criticism by trying to take into account the extent to which Nature is already an aesthetic category for Rousseau, and to see the positive value of the supposed reduction.

   *Pygmalion* is found in Volume II of the Pléiade edition, pp. 1224–32.

## CHAPTER III

1. Starobinski presents Rousseau's career along similar lines, but in terms of 'accuser' and 'accused'. See his article in *Daedalus* (Summer 1978). In Book IX of *Les Confessions*, Rousseau himself encourages this division (at least for the first two time periods, with which we shall be concerned here). He describes his initial literary activity in 1749 as a 'révolution', 'Mon début . . . dans un autre monde intellectuel' (I: 417; 416); and the events following the move to l'Ermitage in 1756 as a 'seconde revolution' (I: 418).

2. See L. Crocker, *The Quest 1712 – 1758*, p. 291.

3. J. Scherer's introduction to Rousseau's dramatic works (II: lxxxvii – lxxxix), outlines the unusual circumstances surrounding the withdrawal of *Narcisse*.

4. See Book IX, I; 404–10, and the third of the *Lettres à Malesherbes*.

5. See H. de Saussure, *J. J. Rousseau et les manuscrits des confessions*, especially pp. 16–19 and p. 26.

6. By the nineteenth century, after autobiography has become a more established form of writing, a reversal of priorities is possible. Although Stendhal is an uncommon example (and linked to Rousseau in numerous other ways), he comes to fiction only after several incomplete but significantly developed autobiographical pieces. In a wider version of the same reversal, is not the nineteenth-century novel also greatly indebted to *Les Confessions* for psychological depth? The ramifications of Rousseau's 1756 fragments and of the relationship novel/autobiography which they pose, are quite far-reaching.

7. *L'Autobiographie en France*, p. 47.

8. See the analysis in Chapter IV of 'les Charmettes', and its place in *Les Confessions*, pp. 26–34.

9. The profound, impersonal level of memory in the reverie by the Pont du Gard goes under the name of *anamnesis*, and would correspond to the first stage of reverie analysed in Chapter I. Its paradoxical character has strong affiliations with writing. For example, when Rousseau tries to remember the details of the 1749 'inspiration', in order to describe it in Book VIII of *Les Confessions*, he hits a blank. The reason? He has already written them down in one of the letters to Malesherbes. 'C'est une des singularités de ma memoire qui méritent d'être dites', Rousseau explains. 'Quand elle me sert ce n'est qu'autant que je me suis reposé sur elle, sitot que j'en confie le dépot au papier elle m'abondonne, et dés qu'une fois j'ai écrit une chose je ne m'en souviens plus du tout' (I: 351). But the forgetfulness which writing engenders is balanced in this quotation by the word 'dépôt', similar in meaning to the 'monument' in the sense given by Littré, 'tout ce qui garde le souvenir' (see I: 130, note 1). The Pont du Gard is one such monument; we shall soon encounter another, in Book I, and in an analysis of writing. If the process of making a textual 'dépôt' causes memory loss, it also acts to preserve memory, in the form of the written work. Rousseau has this in mind when he designates *Les Confessions* 'le seul monument sûr de mon caractére' (I: 3).

10. Extended, the argument here suggests the exercise of a social imagination, in the creation of a shared past as a bond across individuals. This would involve social memory as a means of forging ideological values, the assumption being that ideologies are one form of fiction and constitute themselves as collective identities, along similar lines to the process enacted individually by Rousseau above.

11. The concept of distance, as it is used in this argument, should not be confused with that of mediation. Rousseau consistently rejects pleasures which require an intermediary. See, for example, his remarks on money (I: 38). When conceived as qualitative or imaginative, rather than quantitative or proximate, distance is an essential aspect of the immediacy which Rousseau desires. As we shall note in a moment, the immediacy of meaning increases in direct proportion to the distance he puts between himself and the object of meaning.

12. See, for instance, L. Crocker, *The Prophetic Years 1758–1778*, pp. 67–78; or 'Julie ou la Nouvelle Duplicité', pp. 118–28, for analyses of control as behavioural authoritarianism in Rousseau's work.

13. See R. A. Leigh's comments: *C.C.* XII, p. xxiv.

14. Before recounting the chosen story, the author delays, and slips in a short, prefatory anecdote adduced to fulfil the reader's supposed need of a pleasurable tale. 'Celle du derriére de Mlle Lambercier, qui . . . fut étalé tout en plein devant le Roi de Sardaigne'

introduces an erotic note which Rousseau, telling a story by saying that he won't tell it, quickly disavows and passes on to the reader's account. Lejeune has analysed how this sexual interest carries indirectly into the 'noyer de la terrasse'. See *Le Pacte autobiographique*, pp. 79–80, and pp. 126–7.

15. The 'énonciation/énoncé' distinction, linguistic in origin, concerns two different aspects of the general concept of discourse. *Énoncé* is discourse taken simply as 'une suite de phrases, identifiée sans référence à telle apparition particulière de ces phrases'; *énonciation* is 'l'acte au cours duquel ces phrases s'actualisent assumées par un locuteur particulier, dans les circonstances spatiales et temporelles précises' (Ducrot and Todorov, p. 405). Literary critics have appropriated these terms. In literary discourse (the written text), *énoncé* is generally made to refer to the 'content' of a work, what is being written about; *énonciation* to the author's particular manner of structuring an *énoncé*, to his interventions, comments. In an autobiography, for instance, one could say that the *énoncé* is the life of the author, the *énonciation* his presentation of it in the text. I employ the distinction in this extended sense.

16. In these and subsequent remarks on allegory, I draw from the work of P. de Man, especially his article, 'The Rhetoric of Temporality'.

17. 'Prolonger' is used in connection with both writing and pleasure, as in 'la grande histoire du noyer de la terrasse', and usually when Rousseau attempts to give duration to the passage 'in-between' one state of events and another. The transition from Nature to Culture in the second *Discours*, the belated puberty of Émile, Rousseau's account of his own passage to manhood in *Les Confessions*, are all moments of change which he attempts to prolong. See III: 171; IV: 596, 518; I: 225; *Essai*, p. 136; see also, Saint-Preux's copying of the letters of Julie in *La Nouvelle Héloïse*, Rousseau is trying to give duration to what has no temporal duration whatsoever, namely, to the instant, rather than to any one particular period of life or history. He simply feels the passage of time more acutely in these instances of unavoidable and, to him, undesirable change.

18. Constatively, the function of language is to refer, whether to an object in the world (e.g. 'the cat is on the mat') or an idea in the mind. Performatively, language refers to itself, or creates its referent in the act of utterance (e.g. 'I bet that . . .', 'I promise that . . .'). This distinction is originally Austin's (see bibliography) and has been elaborated in speech act theory. In connection with literary texts, the performative/constative opposition is linked to the *énonciation/énoncé* distinction: in a performative use of language, the *énoncé* is taken up into the *énonciation*; in a constative utterance the *énonciation* tends to disappear into the *énoncé*. Our shift towards the process of *énonciation* in Rousseau's text therefore goes hand-in-hand with the present emphasis on a performative use of language.

19. Letter 11 of Part IV runs from p. 470 to p. 488 in Vol. II of the Pléiade edition of Rousseau's work.

20. See D. Mornet, *Le Sentiment de la nature*, pp. 229–37; and 470, note 1.

21. P. de Man draws attention to this allegorical significance of 'l'Élysée', contrasting it with Rousseau's symbolic diction in the description of Meillerie in Part I of the novel, and mentions *Robinson Crusoe* with the *Roman de la Rose* as a second literary model for the garden. See 'The Rhetoric of Temporality', pp. 184 ff.

22. See *Essai*, pp. 132–8. Rousseau first invokes water as a geographical determinant: 'Dans les pays chauds, les sources et les rivières, inégalement dispersées, sont d'autres points de réunion . . . La facilité des eaux peut retarder la société des habitants dans les lieux bien arrosés. Au contraire, dans les lieux arides il fallut concourir à creuser des puits, à tirer des canaux.' He proceeds to give fulsome praise to the constructive labour and water-control of certain countries. Finally, we are led to a fully imaginative vision of 'cet âge heureux', when people gathered around 'puits et fontaines' and where nothing marked the passing hours, no one was obliged to count them: 'rien ne marquait les heures rien n'obligeait à les compter: le temps n'avait d'autre mesure que l'amusement et l'ennui.' Time is suspended in this fiction of Rousseau's historical anthropology, just as in the 'other world' of the second half of *La Nouvelle Héloïse*.

23. Cf. the article by T. Tanner, 'Julie and "La Maison paternelle": Another Look at Rousseau's *La Nouvelle Héloïse*', especially pp. 27–9.

24. The political undercurrent in the garden constitutes only one of the many channels coursing through it, and it is unwise to draw conclusions in this regard without reference to Rousseau's explicitly political works. The maternal framework of 'l'Élysée' for instance, the fact that it is Julie's garden, seem at odds with the role of the 'législateur' so crucial in the domain of law and politics, and embodied in the paternal Wolmar in *La Nouvelle Héloïse*. If Rousseau's political theory is part of a textual world which itself develops in separation from the father, we must either admit an inconsistency in our interpretation or (as has been suggested) distinguish sharply between the unchanneled paternal force outside the garden and the passionless paternal overseer inside it.

25. This quotation is taken from the 'Manuscrit Favre'. For a more developed version of the same structure, see Book I of *Émile*, IV: 245–6.

26. *L'Eau et les rêves*, p. 14.

27. *Émile et Sophie*, like *Les Confessions*, is an account of the 'sentiments' behind the 'évènements', where the narrator states, 'Je dirai tout, le bien, le mal . . .' (IV: 890, 892). In this text Rousseau gives to Émile a degree of awareness which he will not gain in his

own life until the very end of the autobiography, when he returns to *Émile et Sophie* just before composing the *Rêveries*. Here fiction not only helps Rousseau find the voice of the autobiography, it also reaches a complexity and extremity of pathos which the autobiography does not match until the end of its own extended development.

28. It is not certain when Rousseau in fact wrote the *Essai*, but the work is generally thought to be contemporary with the second *Discours*, and can be considered as an expanded footnote to that work. Critical attention to the *Essai* began in earnest with J. Derrida's *De La grammatologie and* P. de Man's 'Theory of Metaphor in Rousseau's *Second Discourse*', to which my argument here is clearly indebted.

29. In this section, page references to the *Essai* will be abbreviated to, for example (p. 96).

30. De Man cites the example of fear as an error on Rousseau's part in *Blindness and Insight*, p. 139.

31. The saying/showing distinction is properly Wittgenstein's and belongs to the very different context of his *Tractatus*, in connection with his notion of logical form (4.12–4.1212, p. 26). I employ it here in a non-technical manner.


CHAPTER IV

1. See *Beginning, Intention and Method*, especially pp. 76–8. Said distinguishes between a temporal, transitive beginning, and a beginning which is intransitive and involves a 'necessary fiction'. The introduction of *Les Confessions* would be of the second type – it is an act in which 'fiction and reality come together as identity'. Although the fiction/reality dichotomy resurfaces *within* the narrative once the temporal line beginning with 'Je suis né' has been established (the transitive beginning), Rousseau has to bridge the dichotomy to generate the narrative itself.

   Said also distinguishes between beginnings and origins, i.e. between human and divine beginnings, but does not discuss the latter. One could argue, however, that the concept of a 'necessary fiction' in Said's intransitive beginning is formally identical to the concept of God in a divine origin. It is the act of belief, itself a sort of positive forgetting, that makes God a necessary reality, not just a necessary fiction. Rousseau is really interested in origins, not in beginnings, in believing in himself, and in making himself a necessary reality.

2. See I: xxxii–xxx and I: 1854–5 for more extensive remarks on the two versions.

3. One can also discern a related polarity in the important reflection on style in the 'Préambule'. It surfaces there in Rousseau's double intention of being unfailingly objective, working in the photographic 'chambre obscure' of the self, and of inventing a 'nouveau

langage' in order to be adequate to his uniqueness (I:1153—4). The first goal corresponds to a constative, referential ideal; the second to a performative, expressive ideal. In this connection, see Starobinski, *La Transparence et l'obstacle*, pp. 232–9.

4. The 'doublement' of past and present also corresponds to the critical terms *énoncé* and *énonciation*; and these entail further distinctions regarding tense and pronominal structures of the text, which can be used to discern and to calibrate the shifts in the narrative at any point in *Les Confessions*. I have not engaged in this sort of close reading here, but refer the reader to the linguist Benveniste as the primary source for these distinctions (see 'La Nature des pronoms' and 'Les relations de temps dans le verbe français', in *Problèmes de linguistique générale*). For an introduction to how they might be applied to a literary text, see Barthes, 'To Write: Intransitive Verb?', in *The Structuralist Controversy*.

5. See Chapter V, pp. 25–6.

6. These episodes have been conspicuously ignored by some critics, and interpreted from a variety of perspectives by others. The most recent work on the episodes is by P. Lejeune: 'Lecture d'un Aveu de Rousseau', in *Le Pacte autobiographique*; and 'Le Peigne Cassé'. I refer the reader to these articles for a detailed account of past criticism, and for very delicate analyses of the complexities of voice and tone which underlie the apparently seamless narrative of Rousseau. For Lejeune's reading of the relation between the two episodes, see *Le Pacte autobiographique*, pp. 120–5; 154–60.

7. See the *Essai*, p. 158: 'Que celui donc qui vent philosopher sur la force des sensations commence par écarter, des impressions purement sensuelles, les impressions intellectuelles et morales que nous recevons par la voie des sens, mais dont il ne sont que des causes occasionelles.' The term is used consciously by Rousseau, if not in a widespread manner, to distinguish a definite idea – the difference between sensation and sentiment. But it has a long history before it: the notion of the occasional cause begins with the Scholastics, and is used by religious philosophers to designate the limited powers of human causation in contrast with those of the sole efficient cause of the universe, God. Malebranche gave the notion its most significant development. (See *The Philosophy of Malebranche*, by B.K. Rome, especially Chapter IV. 'Occasionalism'.) Rousseau may or may not have been aware of this history; in any event, he almost certainly found the term in Malebranche. (See E. Bréhier, 'Les lectures malebranchistes de J-J Rousseau'.)

8. The passage we are quoting is the second of two versions of the events narrated, the first being a shorter passage in the 'Ébauches'. Changes occur in the second version, and the existence of both provides a good opportunity for analysis of how the elaboration of memory in writing influences the truth of 'facts' in the *énoncé*. If I do not follow this opportunity here, it is because it is peripheral

to the question at hand, and because the analysis has already been performed in a different context. See Lejeune, *Le Pacte autobiographique*, pp. 64–76.

9. In the two articles mentioned earlier, Lejeune untangles many of the feints in the narrative voice adopted by Rousseau in his avowals. De Man, in an article interpreting the different but closely related episode of the 'ruban volé' (see 'The Purloined Ribbon'), argues on the other hand that the problem of disjunction is primarily a linguistic one, and that considerations of voice miss the point. The reading above is indebted to both critics on this issue, and I would suggest here that both emphases are necessary. Someone is speaking in the text; it is not just language, but also the voice of Rousseau. And writing implies a set of constraints and freedoms which are not Rousseau's, but those of language. Yet another problem arises if the critic attempts to establish a definite priority in either direction, for an autonomous narrative voice or for language as an autonomous set of constraints and freedoms. Neither exists without the other.

10. It is, incidentally, at this point in the second *Discours* that the text moves into narrative, and begins to tell a story about and in time. The change from the static Part I is quite noticeable, and probably occurs because time in fact begins at the start of Part II. But Rousseau also cannot begin his narrative until he has already constructed the fiction of a natural state; and he sustains it most movingly in the 'in-between' temporal state which is placed between the non-existent fiction and the actual present. Like Books X–XII of *Les Confessions*, the narrative at the end of the second *Discours* accelerates rapidly and tends to lose its coherence.

11. See Chapter II, pp. 59–60.

12. See also I: 290; 351.

13. Because of the court order issued against him in 1762, Rousseau used a pseudonym ('Renou') after his 1767 return to France from England, and kept it until 1770. He may be referring to this temporary change of name in the passage above.

14. See (I: 837–42), pages which consist almost entirely of the discourse of 'J.J.' which 'Rousseau' conveys by quotation to 'le François'. The embroiled and pathetic aspect of the *Dialogues* is nowhere more evident than in this section (unless one is willing to read it as bizarre comedy).

15. Rousseau made six copies of the *Dialogues*, a glut of manuscripts which exceeds the number of copies produced for any of his other texts.

16. The two sources for these general remarks are *Sacrifice, its Nature and Function*, by Hubert and Mauss, and *La Violence et le sacré*, by R. Girard. The analyses in the latter work include readings of literary texts. Although I have not attempted this above, it seems to me that the *Dialogues* lend themselves to an interpretation in

the light of Girard's theory of sacrifice and the religious.

17. See Chapter V, pp. 215–16.
18. In the 'Histoire du Précédent Ecrit' Rousseau alludes to 'un passage d'*Émile*' (I: 985) in terms which suggest the *Solitaires*. It is not possible to ascertain the reference, but the author definitely thought well of this unfinished work, and returned to it in coversation and live readings at the end of his life.
19. See Starobinski, *La Transparence et l'obstacle*, pp. 285–6
20. 'As You Leave the Room', in *The Palm at the End of the Mind*, pp. 395–6.
21. See the analyses in M. Raymond, pp. 177–85; 214–19; and in Poulet, 'Expansion et concentration chez Rousseau', in connection with the reading here.
22. The letters which Rousseau wrote and received during this forty-five day period in 1765 show him to be more taken up with ongoing concerns than the fifth 'Promenade' suggests. See *C.C.* XXVII, pp. 10–180. But the island sojourn is, on the whole, very calm, an interlude between the expulsion from Môtiers and the journey to England, and not greatly at variance with the autobiographical account. Certainly, the discrepancy between fact and fiction is not so marked as in the case of 'les Charmettes'.
23. See Beaujour's article, 'Autobiographie et autoportrait', for an indication of this distinction.
24. Beaujour, p. 445 and *passim*.
25. See *The Gift, forms and functions of exchange in archaic societies*. See also Emerson's essay, 'The Gift', for an interesting continuation of Rousseau's general line of thought here.
26. Starobinski examines the episode with the apple-seller in 'Sur Rousseau et Baudelaire: le dédommagement et l'irréparable'.

## CHAPTER V

1. *The Rhetoric of Fiction*, pp. 75 ff.; p. 137.
2. *Figures III*, p. 265.
3. *Le Pacte autobiographique*, pp. 15, 22, 23.
4. See the remarks in Chapter III, p. 70.
5. See 'L'Autobiographie considérée comme acte littéraire', *Poétique*, 17, 1974, pp. 14–26, where E. Bruss outlines a thesis developed in *Autobiographical Acts: the Changing Situation of a Literary Genre*.
6. *Le Pacte autobiographique*, p. 26.
7. W. Iser has stated the nature of this identity in his equation of 'the intention of a text' with 'the reader's imagination'. See 'Indeterminacy and the Reader's Response in Prose Fiction'; pp. 43–5.
8. See, for example, I: 21–2, where Rousseau addresses himself, in quick succession, to 'le lecteur', and 'O vous, lecteurs'. In Books II and IV, he employs the more general third person singular, perhaps since he is expressing an expectation which no particular

'vous' would be likely to want to fulfil. For a more complete list of references to the reader, see J. Voisine, 'Le Dialogue avec le lecteur dans *Les Confessions*'.
 9. See W. Booth, p. 137.
10. For background information on this episode, and an interpretation of its significance in *Les Confessions*, see M. D. Ellis, *Rousseau's Venetian Story*, pp. 59–68.
11. For further instances of the two types of sight, see I: 769; 914; 939.
12. The *Dialogues* do not engender the belief which informs this type of open reading, nor the value which comes from it. Rousseau's conception of 'la ligue', described as a series of 'personnes interposées', a relay network of agents acting in concert against 'J. J.', pre-empts and distorts the relation between the work and the reader 'outside' it. The author's efforts to cordon off his text are distinctly visible in this reconstruction of the independent reader.

## CONCLUSION

1. Starobinski describes Rousseau's version of salvation as a 'grâce immanente'. See *La Transparence et l'obstacle*, p. 79.

# BIBLIOGRAPHY

The bibliography is divided into four sections. Section I lists primary sources, works of Rousseau in the editions which have been consulted. Section II lists critical works on Rousseau which I have found helpful. Section III deals with autobiography and cognate material, and is divided into two sub-sections: IIIa lists the autobiographical works mentioned or quoted in the book; IIIb the critical works on autobiography which have been an aid in my research. Section IV is a catch-all, those works which do not fall under the other headings, but which have a general bearing on my reading of Rousseau.

I PRIMARY SOURCES

Rousseau, Jean-Jacques, *Œuvres complètes*, édition publiée sous la direction de B. Gagnebin et M. Raymond (Paris 1959 – Gallimard, Bibliothèque de la Pléiade), Vols. I–IV.
– – *Œuvres complètes* (Paris 1865 – Hachette), Vols. VI and VII (*O.C.*).
– – *Essai sur l'origine des langues*, introduction et notes par A. Kremer-Marietti (Paris 1974 – Aubier).
– – *Lettre à d'Alembert*, édition critique par M. Fuchs (Lille et Genève 1948).
– – *Correspondance générale*, éditée, commentée et annotée par T. Dufour (Paris 1924–34), Vols. I–XX.
– – *Correspondance complète*, edited and annotated by R.A. Leigh (Geneva and Oxford 1965– ), Vols. I–XXXIII (*C.C.*).


II CRITICAL WORKS ON ROUSSEAU

*Annales de la Société Jean-Jacques Rousseau* (Geneva 1905– ), Vols. I–XXXVII.
Baker, Felicity, 'Remarques sur la notion du Dépôt', in *Annales JJR*, XXXVII (1966–8), 57–93.
Blanchot, Maurice, 'Rousseau', in *Le Livre à venir* (Paris 1959), pp. 53–62.
Bréhier, Émile, 'Les lectures malebranchistes de Jean-Jacques Rousseau' in *Revue internationale de Philosophie*, I, No. 1 (1938), 98–120.
Burgelin, Pierre, *La Philosophie de l'existence de Jean-Jacques Rousseau* (Paris 1973 – second edition).
Cassirer, Ernst, *The Question of Jean-Jacques Rousseau*, trans. and ed. P. Gay (New York 1954).
Clément, Pierre-Paul, *Jean-Jacques Rousseau, de l'éros coupable à l'éros glorieux* (Neuchâtel 1976).

Crocker, Lester, *Jean-Jacques Rousseau, The Quest 1712–58, The Prophetic Years 1758–78* (New York 1968 and 1973 – two vols.).
— — 'Julie ou la Nouvelle Duplicité', in *Annales JJR*, Vol. XXXVI (1963–5), 105–52.
de Man, Paul, 'Madame de Staël et Jean-Jacques Rousseau', in *Preuves*, No. 190 (December 1966), 35–40.
— — 'Theory of Metaphor in Rousseau's Second Discourse', in *Romanticism: vistas, instances, continuities*, ed. Thorburn and Hartman (Ithaca, New York 1973), pp. 83–114.
— — 'The Timid God: a reading of Rousseau's *Profession de foi du vicaire savoyard*', *Georgia Review*, XXIX, No. 3 (1975), 533–58.
— — 'The Purloined Ribbon', in *Glyph I* (Baltimore 1977), 28–49.

(The last three articles have become chapters of the recently-published *Allegories of Reading, Figural Language in Rousseau, Nietzsche, Rilke and Proust* (New Haven and London 1979), which includes two additional chapters on Rousseau – 'Self *(Pygmalion)*' and 'Allegory *(Julie)*'.

Dérathé, R., 'La Problématique du sentiment', in *Annales JJR*, XXXVII (1966–8), 7–19.
Didier, Béatrice, 'L'inscription musicale dans l'écriture autobiographique', *Poétique*, X, No. 39 (1979), 91–101.
Eigeldinger, M., *Jean-Jacques Rousseau, univers mythique et cohérence* (Neuchâtel 1978), especially Chapter IV, 'Le Mythe de l'Insularité', pp. 133–52.
Ellis, M.D., *Rousseau's Venetian Story, an essay upon Art and Truth in* Les Confessions (Baltimore, Maryland 1966).
Ellrich, R.J., *Rousseau and his Reader, the rhetorical situation of the major works* (Chapel Hill, N.C. 1969).
Foucault, Michel, 'Introduction' to *Rousseau Juge de Jean-Jacques, Dialogues* (Paris 1962, Colin), pp. VII–XXIV.
Gouhier, H., *Les Méditations Métaphysiques de Jean-Jacques Rousseau* (Paris 1970), especially 'Expansion et Reserrement', pp. 107–17.
Grimsley, Ronald, *Jean-Jacques Rousseau: A Study in Self-Awareness* (Cardiff 1979).
Launay, Michel, 'Signes et forme-sens de l'écriture contractuelle dans *Rousseau Juge de Jean-Jacques – Dialogues*, in *Index de Rousseau Juge de Jean-Jacques, Dialogues*, J. Givel and R. Osmont (Geneva and Paris 1977).
Lecercle, J., *Rousseau et l'Art du roman* (Paris 1962).
Lejeune, Philippe, 'Le Peigne Cassé', *Poétique*, VII, No. 25 (1976), 1–30.

Maccannell, J.F., 'The Postfictional Self/ Authorial Consciousness in three texts by Rousseau', *Modern Language Notes*, 89 (1974), 580–99.

May, Georges, *Rousseau par lui-même* (Paris 1961).

Mornet, Daniel, *Le Sentiment de la nature en France de J–J Rousseau à Bernardin de Saint-Pierre* (Paris 1907).

Muntéano, B., 'La Solitude de Rousseau', *Annales JJR*, XXXI (1964–9), 79–169.

Pizzorusso, A., 'La Comédie de *Narcisse*', *Annales JJR*, XXXV (1959–62), 9–21.

Poulet, Georges, 'Rousseau', in *Études sur le temps humain* (Edinburgh 1949), Chapter X.

— — 'Expansion et concentration chez Rousseau', in *Les Temps modernes*, 26, No. 178 (February 1961), 949–73 (reproduced in *Les Métamorphoses du cercle* – Paris 1961, pp. 102–29).

Raymond, Marcel, *Jean-Jacques Rousseau: La Quête de soi et la rêverie* (Paris 1962).

Saussure, Hermione de, *Rousseau et les manuscrits des Confessions* (Paris 1958).

Simons, M.A., *Amitié et Passion, Rousseau et Sauttersheim* (Geneva 1972).

Starobinski, Jean, *Jean-Jacques Rousseau, la Transparence et l'obstacle*, followed by *Sept essais sur Rousseau* (Paris 1971).

— — *L'Œil vivant* (Paris 1961).

— — *La Relation critique* (Paris 1970).

— — 'The Accuser and the Accused', *Daedalus* (Summer 1978), pp. 41–58.

— — 'Sur Rousseau et Baudelaire: le dédommagement et l'irréparable', in *Le Lieu et la formule, hommage à Marc Eigeldinger* (Neuchâtel 1978), pp. 47–59.

Tanner, Tony, 'Julie and "La Maison Paternelle": Another Look at Rousseau's *La Nouvelle Héloïse*', *Daedalus* (Winter 1976), 23–45.

Voisine, Jacques, 'Le Dialogue avec le Lecteur dans *Les Confessions*', in *Jean-Jacques Rousseau et son Œuvre* (Paris 1964), 23–32.

Weber, S.M., 'The Aesthetics of Rousseau's *Pygmalion*', *Modern Language Notes*, 83 (1968), 900–18.

IIIa AUTOBIOGRAPHICAL WORKS

Augustine, *Confessions,* trans. R.S. Pine-Coffin (Baltimore, Maryland 1969 – Penguin).

Goethe, J.W. von, *Dichtung und Wahrheit*, trans. J. Oxenford (London 1891).

James, Henry, *The Middle Years* (London 1917).

Montaigne, *Essais,* texte établi et annoté par A. Thibaudet (Paris 1950).
Sartre, Jean-Paul, *Les Mots* (Paris 1967).


IIIb CRITICAL WORKS ON AUTOBIOGRAPHY AND COGNATE TOPICS

Beaujour, Michel, 'Autobiographie et Autoportrait', *Poétique,* VIII, No. 32 (1977), 442–58.
Bruss, Elisabeth W., 'L'Autobiographie considérée comme acte littéraire', *Poétique,* V, No. 17 (1974), 14–26.
(I have been unable to consult Bruss's *Autobiographical Acts, the Changing Situation of a Literary Genre* (Baltimore, Maryland 1978).)
Cox, James M., 'Autobiography and America', in *Aspects of Narrative,* ed. J. Hillis Miller (New York and London 1971), pp. 143–72.
de Man, Paul, 'Autobiography as De-facement', *MLN,* 94, No. 5 (December 1979), 919–30.
Gusdorf, Georges, *La Découverte de soi* (Paris 1948).
–– *Mémoire et personne* (Paris 1950).
–– 'Conditions et limites de l'autobiographie', in *Formen der Selbstdarstellung/ Festgabe für Fritz Neubert* (Berlin 1956), pp. 105–23.
Hart, Francis R., 'Notes for an Anatomy of Modern Autobiography', *New Literary History,* I (1970), 485–511.
Lejeune, Philippe, *Autobiographie en France* (Paris 1971).
–– *Le Pacte autobiographique* (Paris 1975).
–– 'Autobiography in the Third Person', *New Literary History,* 9 (1977), 27–50.
Mehlman, J., *A Structural Study of Autobiography: Proust, Leiris, Sartre, Lévi-Strauss* (Ithaca, New York 1974).
Olney, J., *Metaphors of Self, the meaning of autobiography* (Princeton 1972).
Pascal, Roy, *Design and Truth in Autobiography* (Cambridge, Massachusetts 1960).
Starobinski, Jean, 'Le Style de l'Autobiographie', *Poétique,* I, No. 3 (1970), 257–65.
Sayre, R.F., 'Autobiography and Images of Utopia', *Salmagundi,* 19 (1972), 18–37.
Vance, Eugène, 'Le moi comme langage: saint Augustin et l'Autobiographie', *Poétique,* IV, No. 14 (1973), 163–77.


IV GENERAL

Austin, J.L., *Philosophical Papers* (Oxford 1970 – second edition).
–– *How to do things with Words* (Oxford 1962).

Bachelard, Gaston, *Dialectique de la durée* (Paris 1950).

−− *L'Eau et les rêves, Essai sur l'imagination de la matière* (Paris 1947).

Benvéniste, Émile, *Problèmes de linguistique générale* (Paris 1966).

*Books in Print* (New York, Bowker Company 1965− ).

Booth, Wayne, *The Rhetoric of Fiction* (Chicago and London 1961).

Brooks, Peter, *The Novel of Worldliness: Crébillon, Marivaux, Laclos, Stendhal* (Princeton 1969).

Brown, Peter, *Augustine of Hippo, a biography* (London 1967).

Deleuze, Gilles, *Différence et répétition* (Paris 1968).

−− *La Philosophie critique de Kant* (Paris 1963).

de Man, Paul, *Blindness and Insight, essays in the rhetoric of contemporary criticism* (New York and London 1971).

−− 'The Rhetoric of Temporality', in *Interpretation, Theory and Practice* ed. Charles Singleton (Baltimore, Maryland 1969), pp. 173−209.

Derrida, Jacques, *De la grammatologie* (Paris 1967).

Dostoevsky, F., *The Double* (London 1971 − Penguin).

Durcot, D. and T. Todorov, *Dictionnaire encyclopédique des sciences du langage* (Paris 1972).

Dunne, J.S., *A Search for God in Time and Memory* (London 1975).

Eliade, Mircea, *The Myth of the Eternal Return* (London 1955).

Emerson, R.W., *Essays* (New York 1926).

Felman, Shoshana, 'Turning the Screw of Interpretation', *Yale French Studies*, No. 55−6 (1977), 94−207, especially Part IV, 'The Turn of the Story's Frame: a Theory of Narrative', pp. 119−38.

Fletcher, Angus, *Allegory, the Theory of a Symbolic Mode* (Ithaca, New York 1970).

Gadamer, Hans-Georg, *Truth and Method* (London 1975).

Genette, Gérard, *Figures III* (Paris 1972).

Gilbert, K.E. and H. Kuhn, *History of Aesthetics* (London 1956).

Gilson, Étienne, *God and Philosophy* (New Haven, Connecticut 1944).

Girard, René, *La Violence et le sacré* (Paris 1974).

Iser, Wolfgang, 'Indeterminacy and the Reader's Response in Prose Fiction', in *Aspects of Narrative* ed. J. Hillis Miller (New York and London 1971), pp. 1−46.

Kant, I., *Critique of Judgment,* trans. J.C. Meredith (Oxford 1978).

Kierkegaard, S., *The Concept of Irony,* trans. L.M. Capel (London 1966).

−− *Repetition,* trans. W. Lowrie (New York 1964).

−− *Philosophical Fragments,* trans. D.F. Swenson and H.V. Hong (Princeton 1967 − second edition).

−− *Concluding Unscientific Postscript,* trans. D.F. Swenson and W. Lowrie (Princeton 1968).

−− *The Concept of Dread,* trans. W. Lowrie (2nd ed., Princeton 1973).

edition).

Levin, Harry, 'Notes on Convention', in *Perspectives of Criticism* (Cambridge, Massachusetts 1950), pp. 55–83.

Lévi-Strauss, Claude, *Le Cru et le cuit* (Paris 1964).

Locke, John, *An Essay Concerning Human Understanding*, ed. D.H. Nidditch (Oxford 1975).

Lorris, Guillaume de, and Jean de Meun, *Roman de la rose*, ed. and trans. A. Lanly (Paris 1971 – 4 Vols.), Vol. 1.

Macksey, R. and E. Donato (eds.), *The Structuralist Controversy* (Baltimore and London 1972).

Marcel, Gabriel, *Journal métaphysique* (Paris 1935).

Mauss, Marcel and H. Hubert, *Sacrifice, Its Nature and Function*, trans. W.D. Halls (London 1964).

Mauss, M., *The Gift, forms and functions of exchange in archaic societies*, trans. I. Cunnison (London 1954).

Natanson, Maurice, 'Empirical and Transcendental Ego', in *For Roman Ingarden, Nine Essays in Phenomenology* (The Hague 1959), pp. 42–53.

Pater, Walter, *Appreciations* (London 1924), 1st edition 1889.

Preston, J., *The Created Self: the reader's role in eighteenth century fiction* (London 1924).

Robert, Paul, *Dictionnaire alphabétique et analogique de la langue française* (Paris 1966).

Rome, Beatrice K., *The Philosophy of Malebranche* (Chicago 1963).

Said, E.W., *Beginnings, Intention and Method* (New York 1975).

Schiller, Friedrich, *On the Aesthetic Education of Man in a series of letters*, ed. and trans. E.M. Wilkinson and L.A. Willoughby (Oxford 1967, repr. 1982).

Starobinski, Jean, 'Kierkegaard et les Masques', *Nouvelle Revue française*, 25 (1965), 607–22 (part I), 807–25 (part II).

— — 'Histoire du traitement de la mélancholie des origines à 1900', *Acta Psychosomatica*, IV (1960).

Stevens, Wallace, *The Palm at the End of the Mind*, ed. H. Stevens (New York 1972).

Todorov, T., 'Les Hommes-Récits', appendix to *Grammaire du Décameron* (The Hague 1969), pp. 85–97.

Tuve, Rosemond, *Allegorical Imagery, some medieval books and their posterity*, (Princeton 1966).

Valéry, Paul, *Introduction à la méthode de Leonardo da Vinci* (Paris 1919).

— — 'Le Moi et la personnalité, in *Cahiers II*, édition établie, présentée, et annotée par J. Robinson (Paris 1974), pp. 275–333.

von Wartburg, W., *Französisches Etymologisches Wörterbuch* (Basel 1928–61), Vols. I–XIV.

Wittgenstein, L., *Tractatus Logico – Philosophicus,* trans. D.F. Pears
and B.F. McGuiness (London 1961).

# INDEX